AFRICA AND THE AFRICANS IN THE OLD TESTAMENT

David Tuesday Adamo

AFRICA AND THE AFRICANS IN THE OLD TESTAMENT

David Tuesday Adamo

Wipf and Stock Publishers
150 West Broadway • Eugene OR 97401
2001

Africa and the Africans in the Old Testament

By Adamo, David Tuesday
Copyright©1998 by Adamo, David Tuesday
ISBN: 1-57910-658-7

Reprinted by *Wipf and Stock Publishers*
150 West Broadway • Eugene OR 97401

Previously published by Christian Universitites Press, 1998.

Acknowledgements

I will like to acknowledge the invaluable service of Dr. Bruce Cresson, Dr. James Breckenridge, and Mr. Robert Reid. Without their assistance at the time I was writing my dissertation, this book would have been impossible.

My thanks also go to First United Methodist Church, Waco, Texas; St. Philips United Methodist Church, Garland, Texas; First United Methodist Church, Quanah, Texas; First Presbyterian Church of Richardson, Texas; and all other United Methodist Churches in Texas who have supported me both financially and emotionally during my studies. I will forever be grateful to Perkins School of Theology, Southern Methodist University, Dallas,who gave me scholarship to enable me go to the USA. Rev. Richard Freeman of First United Methodist Church, Waco, Texas; Rev. Robert Spencer who was at St. Philip United Methodist Church, Garland, Texas. I would like to acknowledge and appreciate the permission to use my articles from Journal of Religious Thought, USA, Africa Theological Journal, Tanzania, Journal of Religion and Philosophy, Uganda, and African Christian Studies ,Kenya. I also acknowledge the contribution of my former Secretary, Mr. M.S.O. Okotie, who typed the manuscript. I am grateful to Dr. James Cox, the Coordinator of African Christianity Project, Centre for the Study of Christianity in the Non Western World, University of Edinburgh, for the time he took to read this manuscript to encourage me to complete it. Pauline Logan, USA, who did all she could to encourage me during this research.

Finally, I want to express may appreciation to my publisher who has agreed to take the risk of preparing the camera-ready proof of this manuscript with the agreement of deducting the cost from the royalty. Without such action to bear the cost, the publication of this book would probably have been impossible.

David Tuesday Adamo
January 1998

This book is dedicated to my beloved wife,
Grace Ebunlola Adamo,
for her support and patience during the
revision of this work.

Contents

List of Abbreviations

AB:	Ancient Bible
AJBSL:	American Journal of Semitic Languages and Literature
ANET:	Ancient Near Eastern Texts Relating to the Old Testament
ARAB:	Ancient Records of Assyria and Babylonia
ARE:	Ancient Records of Egypt
BASOR:	Bulletin of the American Schools of Oriental Research
BBC:	The Broadman Bible Commentary
BJRL:	Bulletin of John Rylands Library
CAH:	Cambridge Ancient History
HUCA:	Hebrew Union College Annual
IB:	Interpreter's Bible
ICC:	International Critical Commentary
IDB:	Interpreter's Dictionary of the Bible
JBL:	Journal of Biblical Literature
JCS:	Journal of Cuneiform Studies
JEA:	Journal of Egyptian Archaeology
JITC:	Journal of Interdenominational Theological Center
JNES:	Journal of Near Eastern Studies
JPOS:	Journal of Palestine Oriental Studies
JQR:	Jewish Quarterly Review
NCB:	New Century Bible
NICO:	New International Commentary on the Old Testament
TBC:	Torch Bible Commentary
VT:	Vetus Testamentum

Chapter 1
Introduction

Despite the fact that many antiquarians have, and continue to, maintain the view that the ancient black people of antiquity were the earliest of all the civilised people and were the first civilised inhabitants of ancient Egypt, some historians continue to ignore their findings and maintain the opposite view that black Africa has no history before the introduction of western civilization by the Europeans.[1] For instance, at the beginning of the development of science of history in western Europe, the prevailing tendency was the study of what we call "Western Civilization" originating from Greece, Rome and Palestine.[2] As a result of this, very little attention, if any, was given to the other parts of the world which were believed to have contributed far less to the "general progress of mankind."[3] Hegel, in his lectures on the philosophy of history, held the view that Africa "is no historical part of the world: it has no movement or development to exhibit."[4] Professor Hugh Trevor-Roper, Regis Chair of History in Oxford University (1970), observing the African past, advanced the view that `This is...only the unrewarding gyrations of barbarous tribes in picturesque...[5]Professor A. Newton, in his concern for the history of the world into which Europe had expanded, also advanced the view that Africa had no history before her colonization by The Europeans.[6] Still, in these modern times, the assumption prevails that the ancient world in Africa was limited to Egypt and that sub-sahara Africa had no historic past before the Portuguese colonization. The aforementioned assumptions about Africa have affected the attitudes of not only modern man and historians, but also theologians in their examin-ation of the Bible and Africa and Africans, to the extent that they have produced a doctrine of inferiority of black people all over the world.[7] Eurocentric Biblical scholars have made a frantic effort to either "de-Africanize" or reduce Africa and Africans in the Bible to slavery. While some have denied that Africa and Africans have any influence, others deny their total presence at all in the Bible. This denial of African presence and influence is so strong because for the past century the thrust of biblical scholarship has been in the hands of western scholars. An examination of various books on Introduction to the Old Testament, histories of ancient Israel, and Bible atlases reveals very vividly that the field of biblical studies is dominated by American and European scholars and that the de-Aricanization of the Bible is feverishly pursued.[8] Among the maps in Dake's Annotated Reference Bible is a particular map titled "The Egyptian

Empire." This map includes the area so-called Fertile Crescent which Egypt was supposed to have conquered and ruled. But unfortunately, this map does not include the immediate southern or southern-most part of Africa which was part and parcel of the so-called Egyptian Empire.[9]

Several attempts to de-Africanize the Bible can be seen in Speiser's commentary on Genesis. He calls the identification of Kush with Africa a mistaken identity.[10] George Rawlinson and Clau Westermann argued that Kush in Genesis should be located in Mesopotamia instead of Africa.[11] Aalders and Francisco are also examples of western scholars who were out to "de-Africanize" the Bible by their denial of the possibility of African location of Kush.[12]

Others who accepted the presence of Africans in the Bible denied or minimised their influence and worth. Everywhere the presence of Africans is identified in a text, such personality is reduced to nothing but a slave. Thus McKane and Laird identified the Kushite man in King David's army as a Negro slave.[13] Hammershaimb in his commentary on Amos says that the dark-skinned people from Africa were held in contempt by the Israelites.[14] James Luther Mays says that Israel knew Africans as slaves.[15] Details of their Eurocentric type of their exegesis will be discussed later in this book.

Africa has a culture, with its own pre-history, its own language and its own anthropological and artistic development, perhaps as old as her existence, set geographically between the pyramids of Egypt and southern Africa. This area of African civilization has a centre at the confluence of the Blue and White Nile and stands geographically at the edge of the ancient known world. It became a place where the peoples of the Fertile Crescent (Egypt, Mesopotamia, Syria, and Palestine) came into contact with the civilization of sub-sahara Africa. It also became the primary place from which the ancient African civilization spread to the ancient world of the Fertile Crescent.[16] Africa and Africans existed, played an important role and have made their presence felt not only in the ancient known world of Asia, Mesopotamia, Egypt, Greece, and Rome, but also ancient Israel, which is the main area of concern in these studies.[17]

Although the Hebrew Bible is primarily the record of, and a witness to, the vertical and horizontal revelation of God within the history and experience of a particular people (Israel), it cannot but recognize God's involvement with other nations which have contact with these "chosen people." This is because Israel had to struggle for her survival among the African people. She had to fight against the Amorites, Canaanites and several other peoples. Even when she arrived at the Promised Land, the struggle did not end. She came in contact with traders, soldiers, priests and prophets of powerful nations such as the Philistines, the Phoenicians, and Assyrians, the Babylonians, and others. The religions of these nations also became "a never-ending threat to the faith of Israel." As Israel came into contact with these foreign nations, she was forced to acknowledge the reality of their presence, and to redefine her own identity in the light of God's plan. This was because Israel was located in a strategic and exposed position thus subject to outside influences. Although some of these nations sometimes played a secondary role in shaping the political, religious and economic history of ancient Israel, others played a major role. Therefore, in order to understand properly the Old Testament, it is important to understand the life and thought of the peoples who have played major or minor role in Israel's destiny.

While the role of most of these foreign nations (Egypt, Mesopotamia and Syria) has been investigated extensively, the presence, the role and the contribution of Africans, and particularly sub-sahara Africa in the Old Testament have not been adequately researched. Few Biblical scholars who have done some preliminary work on this crucial subject have emphasized the urgent need for further detailed research on the role of Africa and Africans in the Old Testament. Kwensi Dickson in his essay, expressed this need when he says that continuity between the Old Testament and African life and thought should be exposed into the cross-events, which for Christians is a judgment on whatever insights might be gained by looking at the Old Testament and African life and thought together.[18] He continues in another essay, "The Old Testament and African Theology":

> To study this aspect of the matter calls for close study of not only
> the Old Testament, but also of African life and thought; the latter
> has not been given close attention as it deserves....[19]

Other essays on Africa and the Old Testament include "Some African insights and Old Testament" in *Relevant Theology for Africa*;[20] "The Approach to the Old Testament in an African Setting";[21] "Relations Between the Hebrew Bible and Africa" in *Jewish Social Studies*;[22] "Hebrew Installation Rites, a contribution to the study of Ancient Near-Eastern African Cultural Contact"[23] and "Ritual Approach to the Hebrew-African Culture Contact.[24] These essays mentioned above lack some essential documentation in historical and archaeological sources; they are mostly based on ritualistic parallel practices in the Old Testament and Africa. What appears to be the most helpful essay is "Africa and the Biblical Period,"[25] but it is too brief and fragmentary a treatment of such a broad and important subject. *Ethiopia and the Bible* by E. Ullendorff,[26] has only eight pages relevant to this study. Its emphasis is on the modern traditions of Ethiopia and the translation from the Hebrew to Ethiopic language. Other relevant materials include *Egypt and the Bible* by P. Montet,[27] and a doctoral dissertation, "The Interaction of Israel, Judah and Egypt: From Solomon to Josiah,"[28] by R. J. Randles. Although there are a few reference to Ethiopia, his main emphasis is Egypt.

Another interesting and useful book is *The Black Man in the Old Testament and Its World* written by Alfred G. Dunston, the Bishop of the African Methodist Episcopal Zion Church. It is commendable that the Bishop's work attempts to do what "should have been done at least four hundred years ago," that is, to portray the presence of the black man in Old Testament times. However, without denying that his book will be useful, this work is inadequate. It is mostly based on the English Version (King James Version). His facts to which he calls the attention of his readers are things shared in his sermons, lectures, seminars and conferences, thus lacking standard scholarly documentation. The chapters on Egypt and Cush (or Mush) were dealt with in "a cursory manner." The Bishop, admitting the inadequacy of his work on the subject, expresses further need for more competent scholars who will one day do better research in the original biblical languages. The following are his exact words:

> We must continue to await the day when truly capable scholars will delve into the original languages of the Bible and bring forth additional light upon the subject that is dealt with within the following pages. There is no dearth of biblical scholars. Fortunately for the church, there are many men and women within the Christian community who are very capable of searching their way through all the various translations of the ages. If they will do so, these people have the talent and education that are needed to unearth myriads of historic truths that bear directly upon the subject of black man's participation in the Old Testament world. So far the writers have barely `scratched the surface,' but it is known that great treasuries of facts are locked away in places wherein only the most highly trained scholars can enter and probe and weigh and interpret. This book does not attempt to be the last word on the subject. It is our hope that this is only the beginning of a procession of books on the subject.[29]

Another publication on this subject is the book, *Stony the Road We Trod*, edited by Cain Hope Felder.[30] Three articles written by eminent African-American biblical scholars, Charles Copher, "The Black Presence in the Old Testament," Randall C. Bailey, "Beyond Identification: The Use of Africans in Old Testament Poetry and Narratives," and Cain Hope Felder, "Race, Racism and the Biblical Narrative," are directly relevant. While Professor Copher identifies and maintains the actual presence of Africans in the Bible without detailed commentary, Professor Bailey went beyond this identification and maintains that Africans were used as valuation and relied upon by ancient Israel. Professor Felder described how Eurocentric Biblical scholars have tried to secularise and sacralize the Bible. He emphatically affirmed the fact that the Biblical world was without prejudice against the Africans.

Another recent relevant book on this subject is *Troubling Biblical Waters*.[31] However, only Chapters one, two and three are great contribution to this subject. These chapters argue convincingly the presence of Africans in the Bible. In my book, I have tried not only to argue for the presence of Africans in the Old Testament, but to highlight their substantial contribution to the culture, religion, civilization, economic, military and political life of ancient Israel.

Thus, the significance and the purpose of this book, Africa and Africans in the Old Testament and Its Environment, is the critical and objective investigation of the presence, the role and the contribution of Africa and Africans in the political, religious and economic history of ancient Israel in the period of the Old Testament.

The degree of negligence of linking the history of Africans with African diaspora is serious. As a result of this negligence and bias against African people, no nation's achievements have been given to other nations like that of Africa. In this book I try to extend the boundaries of African history to include the history of African diaspora in ancient Israel. That is the reason why I called the blacks, Africans or the people of African descent. Using historical, comparative, descriptive and exegetical methods, this investigation examines some references to Africa and Africans in the Old Testament and its environment. Although the examination of these references will center on the word "Cush," it will not be limited to this single term. Although this study intends to examine the place of Africa and Africans in the Old Testament and its environment, it does not intend to deal in detail with every country in the continent of Africa. This is because during the ancient time, what we call Africa today was not broken up to pieces as the colonial powers have divided it. Whenever the word Africa is mentioned, I refer to the entire continent inhabited by African peoples including Egypt.[32]

I think that it is important to state that this book is not an attempt to glorify the past of African achievement, but an attempt to put the fact of the history and achievement of Africans during the biblical period in its right perspective. Since the past of Africans in the biblical period has been distorted, it has to be straightened by African biblical scholars. I consider this to be absolutely important because history is not a glorification of the past. Without the past, there can be no present and future. The past affects the present and the future.

Finally, it is important for my readers to relax whatever is their past and present conception about Africa and Africans, and be ready to listen to a radical new ideas different from the mainline Eurocentric conception of the black people. I believe that this will help them to enjoy reading this book, regardless of whether they agree with my Afrocentric reconstruction of the history of ancient Israel or not. I will congratulate myself if only this book helps trouble someone's mind or to put it in Cain Felders words, "troubles biblical waters," because of its new and Afrocentric perspective.[33] I hope that this book will stimulate other Afrocentric scholars to research farther on Africa and Africans in the biblical period.

Endotes

1.   John G. Jackson, *Introduction to African Civilizations* (Secaucus: The Citadel Press, 1970), 11, 60-92. C. F. Volney, *The Ruins of Empires* (New York:Peter Eckler, 1890). A. H. L. Heeren, *Historical Researches into the Politics, Intercourse and Trade of the Carthaginians, Ethiopians and Egyptians* (New York: Negro University Press, 1969), reprint of 1832. Charles Seignobos, *History of Ancient Civilization* (London: T. Fisher Unwin, 1910).
2.   F.D. Fage, ed., *Africa Discovers Her Past* (London: Oxford University Press, 1970), p.
3.   Ibid. One of the most prestigious works, which was a landmark in study of world history (Cambridge Modern History) at the beginning of this century, has no treatment of Africa in its first edition.
4.   Ivor Wilks, "Africa Historiographical Traditions, Old and New," in *Africa Discovers Her Past*, 7.
5.   Ibid., 7, Cited by Ivor Wilks.
6.   F.D. Fage, *Africa Discovers Her Past,* 1.
7.   Robert Bennett, Jr., "Africa and the Biblical Period," *Harvard Theological Review* 64 (1971): 484-85.

8. This process of de-Africanization was also discussed in Bailey's article "Beyond Identification: The Use of Africans in the Old Testament Poetry and Narratives," in *Story the Road We Trod*, Can H. Felder ed., (Minneapolis: Fortress Press, 1991), 165-168.

9. Finis Jennings Dake, *Dake's Annotated Reference Bible*, (Lawrencerville: Dake Bible Sales Inc., 1961) Map No. 3. For example, the land of *Kush, Wawat, Punt* and the Medja were not even included as part of the Egyptian Empire. These were the people who eventually conquered Egypt during the so-called Kushite Dynasty.

10. Speiser Genesis: *The Anchor Bible*, 3rd ed. (Garden City N.Y. Doubleday an Co. 1979 , 14-20.

11. G. Rawlinson, *Origin of Nations* (New York: Charles Scribners' Son, 1894) Westernmann, *Genesis 1 - 11* Trans. J.J. Sculling, S.J. (Minneapolis: Augsburg Publ. House), 208 -220.

12. G. Ch. Aalders, *Genesis*, Vol. I, Translated by W. Heynen, Grand Rapids: Zondervan Publishing House, 1981), C.T. Francisco, *Broadman Bible Commentary* Vol.I revised ed. Clifton J. Allen (Nashville Broadman Press, 1973), 127.

13. 13 W. McKane, I 4 *II Samuel* (London: SCM Press, 1963) Z67. Laird, *Interpreter's Bib le* (IB) ed. G.A. Buttrick Vol. II, Nashville, Abingdon Press 1952), 1143.

14. See also Erling Hammershaimb, *The Book of Amos: A Commentary*, trans. John Sturdy (New York: Shockin Books 1970), 134.

15. Such is the Eurocentric biblical exegesis mainly to humiliate Africans. James Luther Mays, A*mos* (Philadelphia: Westminster Press, 1969), 157. Edward Ullendorf and W.R. Harper said that Israel saw Africans as uncivilized, despised Ullendorf, *Ethiopia and the Bible*, (Oxford the Schweleh Lectures, Oxford Univ. Press 1968: Harper, *Critical and Exegetical Commentary on Amos and Hosea* ICC (New York: Charles Scribner's Sons, 1915), 192. The majority of Western Eurocentric scholars are holding these dehumanizing and unbiblical theories. There will be more elaboration on them in the text of this book.

16. Frank Snowden, Jr. *Before Color Prejudice: Ancient View of the Blacks* (Cambridge, Harvard Univ. Press, 1983). See also Y. Adams, *Blacks in Antiquity: The Art of Ancient Nubia and Sudan* , Vol. I (New York : The Brooklyn Museum Division of Publications and Marketing Services, 1978), 9-10.

17. See also Ladiclas Bugner, *The Image of the Black in Arts* (New York: William Morrow and Company, Inc. 1976.).

18. Bennett, Jr., *Harvard Theological Review 64* (1971), 501-24.

19. Kwensi Dickson, "Continuity and Discontinuity Between the Old Testament and African Life and Thoughts," in *African Theology En Route*, ed. Koffi Appiah-Kubi and S. Torres (Maryknoll: Orbis Books, 1979), 109. K.

Dickson, "The Old Testament and African Theology," *Ghana Bulletin of Theology*, vol. 4, no. 4 June 1973): 0- 1.

20. H. G. Becken, *Relevant Theology for Africa* (Duban: Lutheran Publishing House,1972).

21. P. E. S. Thompson , *Ghana Bulletin of Theology*, vol. 2, no. 2 (Dec. 1962): 1-11.

22. E. Isaacs, *Jewish Social Studies*, vol. 26, No. 2, (April 1964): 87-98.

23. Raphael Patai, *Hebrew Union College Annual*, 20 (1947): 143-225.

24. Raphael Patai, *Jewish Social. Studies* 24 (April 1962): 86-96.

25. Ibid.

26. Ibid.

27. P. Montet, *Egypt and the Bible*, trans. by Leslie R. Keyiar (Philadelphia: Fortress Press, 1968).

28. R. J. Randles, "The Interaction of Israel, Judah, and Egypt: From Solomon to Josiah" (Unpublished Ph.D. dissertation, Southern Baptist Theological Seminary1980).

29. Alfred G. Dunston, *The Black Man in the Old Testament and Its World* (Philadelphia: Dorrance R Company, 1974),' Vl 1.-Vl I I.

30. Cain Hope Felder, *Stony the Road We Trod* (Minneapolis: Fortress Press, 1991)

31. Cain Hope Felder, *Troubling Biblical Waters* (Maryknoll, New York: Orbis Books,1989).

32. Several scholars believe that the history of ancient Africa is as unthinkable without Egypt as the history of Egypt is without Africa. See Basil Davidson, *The African Past* (New York: Grosset and Dunlap), 43. The exclusion of special studies on Egypt does not imply that I accept the view that Egypt is an extension of Europe or that it is not a negro country and therefore has no connection with Black Africa south of the Sahara. Collins, *Problems in Africa History*, ed.,Cliffs, New Jersey, 1968); John G. Jackson, *Introduction to African Civilizations* (Secaucus, New Jersey, The Citadel Press, 1974); Rudolph R. Windsor, *From Babylon to Timbuktu: A History of the Ancient Black Races Including Black Hebrews*(Smithtown: Exposition Press, 1969); Ladislas Bugner, *The Image of the Black in Western Art*, gen. ed.; J. D. Fage, *Africa Discovers Her Past*; and Chancellor Williams, *The Destruction of Black Civilization* (Chicago: Third World Press, 1974).

33. Cain Felders, *Troubling the Biblical Waters*, xiv

Chapter 2
Identification of
Various Terms Used for Africa
and Africans in the Ancient Near East

Although there has not been a unanimous agreement among eminent scholars (anthropologists, Egyptologists and Africanists) concerning the exact racial classifications of the people of Africa, the fact that African[1] is the cradle of one of the earliest and most spectacular civilizations of antiquity has been generally accepted.[2] Upon the basis of archaeological and historical records discovered in Egypt, Mesopotamia and the Greco-Roman World, Africans have shared this civilization, either through military or trade interactions, with other nations of antiquity. Through these interactions, the people of the ancient world have come to know Africa and Africans and have coined some terms by which they referred to Africa and Africans. Unfortunately, some of these ancient terminologies are too general and vague, sometimes referring to particular districts or sections of Africa.

The task of this chapter therefore is to examine the main terminologies, their various meanings and the approximate geographical locations in Africa. Since it is impossible to deal with all the insignificant terms used to refer to Africa and Africans in antiquity within the scope of this research, this examination shall be limited to the following important terms: *Wawat, Kush, Punt, Nehesi* (Egyptian), *Magan* and *Meluhha* and Ethiopian (Greece). This examination will include lists of some of the Egyptian African, Sumero-Akkadian inscriptions, and the classical writings of the Greco-Roman world in which these terms were significantly used to refer to Africa and Africans.[3]

WAWAT

Since Africans themselves (the Egyptians) were the first people to put into writing and leave with us the record of their experience with the other African people of antiquity, the Egyptian hieroglyphic inscriptions are the best sources for the examination of the term "Wawat." Another reason for turning to the Egyptians' inscriptions for the consideration of the term is because *Wawat* is an Egyptian term.

According to Professor E.A. Wallis Budge, the distinguished antiquarian, in his hieroglyphic dictionary,[4] *Uwuat* could mean "fire" or "flame" a "measuring line" or "cord of palm fibre" or "a part of a head."[5] "*Uauaiu*" means "a tribe or people."[6] It is likely that from the above meaning the term "*Wawat*" originally meant "fire" and a cord of palm fibre used to measure things, thus having double meaning during the earliest use. Later this term probably came to be used to refer to a tribe immediately south of Egypt since there were many palm trees in the southern countries along the Nile Valley.[7] According to Sir Alan Gardiner, *Wawat* was first applied to a limited area, but later extended to all of the land between the first and Second Cataracts.[8] Gaston Maspero sees *Wawat* as the district on the right side of the Nile which spread toward the Red Sea from the district around Ombos to the area of Korosoko.[9] However, by the Twelfth Dynasty, scholars were not sure of the southern limit of Wawat.

Scholars generally believe that the inhabitants of the area of *Wawat* are the people whom the Egyptians called "*Medjay*." These people later become the desert police who guarded the boundary stelae for the Egyptians as police men.[10] In fact, J. A. Wilson maintains that this word "*Medjay*" could be translated "police."[11]

There are several references to *Wawat* in the Egyptian inscriptions. The earliest is found in the inscription of Una during the time of Pepi I of the Sixth Dynasty. Because of disturbances in the eastern desert he enlisted the Negroes of Tcham, Amam, Wawat, Kaam and Tathem.[12] Una also gave account of his journey to the southern countries to dig canals. He made the Negroes of *Arthet, Wawat, Amam,* and *Metcha* to bring wood.[13] King Mernenre also recorded his visit to the First Cataract to receive gifts or homage of the *Medjay*, Irtje and *Wawat*.[14] inscription on the rock at the entrance to the valley of Girgani at Korosoko states that Amenemhat I smote the inhabitants of *Wawat*.[15] In the teaching of Amenemhat I, the King himself says: "I seized the people of *Wawat* and captured the people of *Medjay*."[16] During the reign of Rameses VI, one "Pennut" was the Antennu or Viceroy of Wawat and Akita.[17] He bore the title "King's Son of Kush" which Sir Alan Gardiner believes refers to the governor of *Wawat*.[18] In the "Tradition of Seven Lean Years in Egypt" which was carved In the rock on the Island of Sheheil near First Cataract *Wawat* was mentioned.[19] Although some scholars are fairly sure that Africa, south of Egypt, was divided into two administrative districts (*Wawat* and *Kush*), it is difficult to be certain as to the exact southern boundary of *Wawat*.[20] This is because these inscriptions which refer to *Wawat* are very vague concerning the geographical limits of *Wawat*. Since archaeological evidence is wanting, scholars will probably have to wait for future discoveries which might yield definite geographical limits and the exact locations of these cities or districts.

KUSH

Kush is used more frequently in the Bible than any other term to be examined in this book. Its importance can be seen not only in that fact that it is the most widely used by the people of antiquity to refer to Africa and Africans, but also it is the term on which this research centers its investigation of the Old Testament references to Africa and Africans. Unlike *Nehesi, Wawat* and *Punt* (they are all used only by Egyptians), the term "*Kush*" is used by the ancient Egyptians (*Kush, Kash,* or *Kesh*), Assyrians (*Kusu, Kusi*) and the Hebrews (Cush) to refer to Africa and Africans.

It appears that the first people to use the word "*Kush*" were the ancient Egyptians. The various spellings of the word "*Kush*" in the Egyptian monuments are probably for two main reasons: (1) one letter in Egyptian writing may be pronounced in different ways and the original pronunciation may have been "*Kaushu*" which later became "*Kushu, Kush.*[21] The term "*Kush,*" like the term "Africa,"[22] was originally used by the ancient Egyptians to refer to a very limited area of land or tribe beyond Semna and Kerma, and was later extended to embrace all the lands further south.[23]

Lepsius says that the Kushites who live in the land south of *Wawat* originally came from Asia between the time of Pepi I (2000 B.C.E.) and Amenemhat I (1700 B.C.E.), and drove back the Africans who occupied the place.[24] D. Baldwin maintains that the Kushites originated from Arabia and built settlement throughout Africa, down to the eastern coast, nearly to the Cape of Good Hope.[25] Lepsius' idea has been rejected by several eminent scholars because a comparative study of the names which appear in the inscription of Una with the names which appear in the later monuments indicates that there has been no change in the population of this area.[26] Baldwin's theory of the origin of the Cushite people appears unlikely in the light of the fact that the oldest human skeletal remain was found in Africa (Kenya) and none that approaches it has been found in Arabia. A skeletal remain of a boy (Homo erecthus) dating to 1.6 million years ago was discovered in Kenya by Alan Walker of Richard Leakey's group. During a discussion with Dr. Arthur Murphy, a professor of anthropology at Baylor University, he said that the question as to whether Africa is the place of origin of man is settled. Furthermore, the ancient records of the Egyptians, although sometimes vague, always point to the south of Egypt when referring to *Kush*. Although there is yet no certainty as to the exact geographical limit of the Kingdom of *Kush*, Barry J. Kemp, of the Faculty of Oriental studies, University of Cambridge, says that "the brick castle and the great tumult" uncovered during the excavation at Kerme on the east bank above the Third Cataract, is an evidence that "the seat of the Kings of *Kush*" was there and became the place from where the whole "Kingdom of *Kush*" was ruled at least from the seventeenth and early sixteenth centuries B.C.E.[27] However, it is possible that from Kerma, the Cushite Kingdom, with its administrative center in Kerma or Meroe, extended to part of Arabia. Scholars are also aware that, although the use of the term "Kush" ceased during the fall of Meroe and the decline of the "Kingdom of *Kush*," the people of Kordofan and Darfur in the west of the Nile river still retained the name *Kush* (*Kash* or *Kaj*) up to the Christian era.[28]

Although Egyptian inscriptions maintain the fact that the Egyptian people had expeditions to the south (probably as far as the land of *Kush*) as early as the sixth Dynasty, under Pepi II, the earliest reference to the term "*Kush*" in the known Egyptian monuments is in the inscription of Ameni.[29] This inscription, written during the reign of Sesostris I, tells us that the King travelled south, overthrew his enemies, the "Abominable *Kash*," obtained tributes and passed the boundary of *Kush*, to the end of the earth.[30] Sesostris II and III also recorded their expeditions to Kush.[31] By the time of the second intermediate period, Egypt recognized the growth of the power of the Kushites. Ahmose, who reigned just before the Eighteenth Dynasty, says in the Carnarvon Tablet I:

> Let me understand what this strength of mine is for! (One) prince is in Avaris, another is in Ethiopia (Kus),[32] and (here) I sit associated with an Asiatic and a Negro (Nehesi)! Each man has his slice of this Egypt, dividing up the land with me. I cannot pass by him as far as Memphis.[33]

He also mentioned his expedition to Hent-hen-nefer to overthrow the Kushites.[34] Menhotep I mentioned in his inscription that he sailed up the Nile to "*Kesh*."[35] The annals of Thutmose III inscribed on the walls of the corridor of the Temple of Amon at Karnak say that *Wawat* and *Kush* brought tributes. In the forty-seventh year of his reign Thutmose III also recorded on his stela set up at Barkal that his southern boundary reached the "Horns of the earth."[36] He also had three lists of the Kushite cities under his domain on his pylons at Karnak. These contain seventeen, fifteen, and four hundred names respectively.[37] Unfortunately, no scholar has been able to locate these cities. During the fifth year of the reign of Thutmose IV, he recorded in his stelae that the "Abominable Chief of Kesh" rebelled and declared himself independent and this led to the defeat of the Chief of Kesh.[38]

On the wall of the desert temple of Redesiay, Seti I is seen slaughtering the "chiefs of Kesh, the Abominable,"[39] and on the Kubban Stela, he boasted that he was a mighty bull against "Kash the Abominable" and a raging monster that trampled down the Nehesi.[40]

During the reign of Rameses II, on a "rock-hewn temple" built in honor of the goddess of Hathor and his wife Nefertari, was the stela of Ani, the "Prince of Kash."[41] By the time of the twenty-fifth Dynasty, commonly called the "Kushite" Daynasty, the Kushite Kingdom extended to Egypt. Piankhy was referred to as "King's Son of Kush."

One of the stelae of Aezanas recorded the campaign in which the King led his army to the heart of Kush and Meroe:

> By might of the Lord of all, I made war upon Noba, for the peoples had rebelled and had made a boast... And I came to *Kasu* and I fought a battle and made prisoners of its people at the junction of rivers (Nile) and (Atbara),.[42]

Assyrian records relating to Africa and Africans are mainly of military encounters. In such annals they used the term "*Kusi*" and "*Kusu*." It is very likely that the Assyrians borrowed this term *Kusu* or *Kusi* from the Egyptians. Below are some important Assyrian texts using *Kusu* or *Kusi* to refer to Africa and Africans especially from the eighth to the sixth centuries B.C.E.

The annalistic texts of Esarhaddon in which he records events of his tenth campaign say:

> In my tenth campaign, I directed my march (against I ordered ...) towards the country...which is called in the language of the people of Nubia (*Kusu*) and Egypt (*Musur*)...I called up the numerous army of Ashur which was stationed in...in the month of Nisaru, the first month (of the year), I departed from my city Ashur...In the course of my campaign, I threw up earthwork (for a siege) against Ba'lu, King of Tyre who had put his trust upon his friend Tirhakah (*Targu*), King of Nubia (*Kusu*), and (therefore) had thrown off the yoke of Ashur my lord, answering (my admonitions with) insolence.[43]

In the Dog River Stele which commemorates Esarhaddon's victory of his enemy, he also says:

> I entered Memphis (Me-im-pi), his royal residence amidst (general) jubilation and rejoicing...(u)pon the *Sadalum* which was plated with gold, I sa(t down) in happiness...weapons, (...) Kurnanati of gold, silver, plateaus of)...Afterwards...(I en)tered and his personal property (ht: palace), the gods and goddesses of Tirhakah (*Targu*), King of Nubia (*Kusu*), together with their possessions.[44]

Other monuments of Esarhaddon which used the word *Kusu* or *Kusi* include the inscription of the brick and vases which record his building activities,[45] the Senjirli Stele which records his victory over Syria, and the Alabaster Tablets[46] from Assur which give a summary of Esarhaddon's building activities in Assur and Babylon Ashurbanipal also had to struggle with the Kushites in his days. The Rasam Cylinder of Ashurbanipal found in the ruins of Kuyunjik says:

> In my first campaign, I marched against Egypt (*Magan*) and Ethiopia (*Meluhha*). Tirhakah (*Targu*), King of Egypt (*Musur*) and Hubia (*Kusu*), whom Esarhaddon, King of Assyria, my father, had defeated and in whose country he (Esarhaddon) had ruled, this (same) Tirhakah forgot the might of Ashur, Ishtar and the (other) great gods, my lords, and put his trust upon his own power.[47]

Other texts of Ashurbanipal include the Cylinder B.[48] C,[49] and E[50] inscriptions and Ashurbanipal historical tablets commemorating the rebuilding of the temple of Sin at Harran.[51]

Perhaps, one would be right to say that the term "*Kush*" passed from Egypt to the Assyrians and to the Hebrews.[52] This term is used very frequently and extensively. It is used in the Old Testament to cover a wide area corresponding to Ethiopias[53] of the classical period. The term "*Kush*" with its gentilic appears about fifty-seven times in the Old Testament.[54] Only a brief summary of its use in the Old Testament will be given here. A fuller critical and exegetical work will be done later in the coming chapters.

In the Old Testament, *Kush* and Kushites are used to refer to Africa and Africans in terms of a particular geographical location, and as names of persons who came from Africa or whose ancestors are of African origin. In terms of a geographical location, it is described as the extreme part of the world (Ezekiel 29:10, of Isaiah 45:14, Job 28:19). The inhabitants of Kush were described as tall and smooth-skinned people. Their blackness becomes proverbial (Isaiah 18:2, Jer. 13:23). Moses' wife was from *Kush* (Num. 12:15). A Kushite man was a messenger who reported the death of Absalom to David (2 Sam. 18:21, 31-33) Ebed-Melech, the Kushite in the palace of King Zedekiah, rescued prophet Jeremiah from death (Jer. 38:6-14, 39:16-18). Their power was comparable only to the power of the Assyrians. Judah depended on them and the Egyptians for deliverance from the hand of the terrible Assyrians (2 Chron. l2:3-9, Isa. 18:2, I Kings 18:19-21, 2 Chron. 32:9-15, 3:8). However, despite the mighty power of the Kushites, they experienced defeat during Zerah and Asa's encounter (2 Chron. 14:9-15) and the encounter with the Assyrians (2 Kings 18:21).

Kush, like any other nation, was also subjected to God's judgment (Ezekiel 30:4). The prophet Zephaniah prophesied the conversion of the Kushites who would bring tribute to Yahweh (Zeph. 3:10). They would stretch their hands to God (Psalm 68:31). They will be one of the nations who will acknowledge Zion as their spiritual home (Psalm 87:4-5)

PUNT

Generally speaking, Egyptologists agree as to the proper transliteration of the word Punt, except Professor Alan Gardiner who thinks that it should be transliterated differently—Pwene.[55] It is Punt in most Egyptological books, and general agreement has been reached by most scholars that it refers to the African coast south of Egypt. Professor Gaston Maspero agrees that "Punt" lies between the Nile Valley and the Red Sea and is very rich in "ivory, ebony, gold, metals, gums and sweet-smelling resins."[56] E. A. Wallis Budge does not hesitate to agree with Maspero. He goes further to emphasize that Punt was the original home of the Egyptian ancestors and that it was the place where the Egyptians got their minerals, woods, incense and even their hieroglyphic writings. Budge also was emphatic that the Egyptians themselves saw themselves as connected with the land of Punt because they belong to the same race and that the relationship between them was very cordial.[57] Budge continues:

> Many facts go to show the persistence of the Negro influence on the beliefs, and manners, and customs of the Dynastic Egyptians, and the most important thing of all in connection with this is the tradition which makes them to come from the land of Punt. We

may accept without any misgiving the opinion of Professor
Maspero and of Professor Naville, both of whom believe that it
was situated in Africa, at a considerable distance to the
south-east, and south of Egypt...The products of the country as
enumerated in the inscriptions of the great Queen Hatshepsut
suggest that Africa was their source, and that the particular
region whence they came was in some part south-eastern Sudan
or a neighboring country.

There is no reason for assuming that the Egyptians knew of
two countries of Punt, or that the Punt of the XVIIIth was
different from that of the IVth Dynasty; we must therefore think
that the "spice-land" of Punt was the home of one of the peoples
who were the ancestors of the Dynastic Egyptians. The influence
of their Punt ancestors shows itself in many ways, especially in
the matter of their long, plaited beards, and the animals' tails
which hung down behind from their girdles, and their
head-dresses. Some think that the men of Punt were Semites, but
the evidence for this view seems unsatisfactory, and is, in many
cases, insufficient.. It is, of course, possible that a number of
Semites entered Egypt by way of Punt, but, if this were so, we
should have found traces of their Semitic speech in the early
hieroglyphic inscriptions. All things considered, it seems
tolerably certain that the men of Punt, who influenced the
manners, customs, and beliefs of the people in the Nile Valley
were of African original.[58]

Professor George Rawlinson also agrees with Maspero and Budge. He
says that Punt is to be sought, not on the Arabian but on the African side of
the gulf where the present Somali land is located.[59] According to him, many
Egyptian products and principal gods came from Punt.[60] According to
Professor David O'Connor of the University Museum, University of
Pennsylvania, Punt lies in the coastal plain and the hilly country between
latitudes 17° and 12° N. He describes the Puntites as follows:

Typically, the men have dark reddish skins and fine features;
characteristic negroid types...and the Egyptians have always
visited Punt from the time immemorial . The relationship has
been of trade rather than political or subordination.[61]

Despite this agreement among scholars, Arkell still thinks that the location of Punt is debatable. However, he agrees that the location probably includes the Somali coast.[62] Unfortunately, no Egyptian map of Africa has survived. All that are available are references to peoples and places in Egyptian texts which are mostly political military and religious achievement.[63] Some of these texts, written on temple walls, columns, stelae and statuary are problematic because they contain vague references to places in the south without any geographical limit. Scholars are therefore left to interpret this term which refers to Punt.

The earliest of such records is in the Palermo stone which mentions the bringing of produce from Punt.[64] Under the reign of Mentuhotep III during the Eleventh Dynasty, an expedition was made to Punt under command of Henu to search for precious stones and balsam.[65] Amenemhat II also made an expedition to Punt to bring the products of Ta-kenset.[66] During the reign of Queen Hatshepsut several expeditions were sent to *Punt*. According to her inscriptions, they went as far as Cape Guardefui where the Queen's gifts were presented to the governor of Punt called Pa-hehu. Five ships were sent and they brought back ebony, ivory, green gold, incense, myrrh and precious stones.[67] As stated earlier, this important inscription of Hatshepsut sees the Puntites as ancestors. The inscriptions at the Temple of Karnak give the account of Thutmose III's expedition to *Punt* and list the names of places conquered: *Kash*—23, *Wawat*—24, *Punt*—195. Ramses III also made an expedition to Punt for the exchange of Egyptian produce for myrrh according to Papyrus Harris.[68] Some scholars maintain that the word "Punt" was also used in the Bible. In this case, the Hebrew word *Kush* was said to refer to the Egyptian *Punt* instead of Libya as other scholars have maintained.[69] More shall be said concerning this in the subsequent chapters.

NEHESI

While many scholars agree that the term "*Nehesi*" is one of the most prominent Egyptian terms which refer to Africa and Africans, others still wrestle with the exact transliteration of the word. While Sir Alan Gardiner[70] prefers the transliteration "*Hehasyu*," George Steindorff and Keith Seele[71] prefer "*Nehsi*." A. J. Arkell,[72] E. A. Wallis Budge,[73] James H. Breasted[74] and Hermann Junker[75] transliterate it "*Nehesi*." This writer will use the latter throughout this work. The reason for this variation is said to be because the Egyptian hieroglyphic inscriptions adapted different spellings of this same word. However, these variations have the same basic meaning. E. A. Budge in his dictionary, *An Egyptian Hieroglyphic* Dictionary,[76] listed the variations of this word "*Nehesi*" with their meaning "*Nehsi*" according to him means "he of the Sudan,"[77] "Sudani" or Negro. "*Nehesu* means "he of the Sudan," "Sudani" or "negro." *Nehesiu*[78] hetepu means "friendlies in the Sudan" or "Sudani police," and "*Nehesitt*" means "negress" or "Sudani slave woman."[79] *Nehimu* refers to "a Sudani country" and "*Nehestt*" means "the land of the "negro."[80] From the meanings given above, it seems clear that Budge translates the meaning of "*Nehesi*" to be "a black man or negro." In his book, *Egyptian Sudan*, he clearly states that the phrase *Ta-Nehesu* which appears in the inscription of Seti I means, "the Land of the Blacks.[81] He goes on to say,

> Toward the close of the XIIth Dynaty there reigned in the Delta a king who styled himself, "King of the South and North, Ra-Nehsi or Nehsi-Ra." Now the word "Nehsi" means "Black," or "Negro"; therefore this King's name inscription at Tanis, "the royal son *Nehsi*, " it is probably that he was in reality a black man.[82]

James H. Breasted agrees with Budge's translation of the word "*Nehesi*" as meaning "black" or "negro."[83]

Several scholars refuse to accept Budge's translation of the word "*Nehesi*" as "black" or "negro." The term "*Nehesi*," they say, has a geographical rather than ethnic meaning. One of the foremost advocates of this view is Hermann Junker.[84] After rejecting the idea that dark color of the skin is the `chief distinct character' or characteristic of a negro (even though the word negro means black and describes the color of the body), he accuses anthropologists for not emphasizing what he calls the "real characteristics" of a negro.[85] Professor Junker calls the following the "real characteristics" of a negro: long and narrow skull, woolly hair, thick lips, the buttocks and thighs appear to be pushed backward.[86] He demonstrastes that the term "Nehesi" never possesses the meaning "black" or "negro" "but rather designates at all times the inhabitants of the south and sourtheast and only later referred to the Negroes, and only through the inclusion of these among the southern peoples."[87] Below are his reasons in his exact words:

(a) The archaeological evidence is clear contrary to the view that Negroes inhabited Nubia in the periods of the Old and Middle Kingdoms; thus *nhsyw (nehesyu)*[88] which is applied to the Nubians, cannot mean "negroes."

(b) We possess three Old Kingdom reliefs of persons expressly stated to
     be *nhsyw*; all these exhibit a type related to the Egyptian not only in
     physical conformation but in dress and treatment of hair and beard,
     and show no trace of negroid characteristics. The Old Kingdom
     hieroglyphic determining *nhsyw* points the same way.

(c) Even in the New Kingdom the Puntites, who are demonstrably not
     negroes, are more than once referred to as *nhsyw*.

(d) The Nubians are called indifferently *iwntyw* and *nhsyw* in the Middle
     and New Kingdoms, and t e term *iwntyw*, "Troglodytes" or the like,
     cannot refer to pure Negroes. Moreover, these old terms were applied
     to the inhabitants of Nubia after the population of that country had
     completely changed, in race, if not in appearance.

(e) Although Negroes may have predominated much later in several
     provinces they were not called *nbsyw* because they were Negroes, but
     so to speak, in spite of the fact, the term being, as previously,
     geographical and not ethnic.[89]

     After this "epoch-making" article in which Professor Junker set out to
demonstrate that there was no direct contact with the African blacks by the
Pharaohs until the Eighteenth Dynasty (about 1450 B.C.) and that the word
"Nehesi" does not mean Black or Negro, several Egyptologists did not only
accept his criteria or the so-called real characteristics of the Negroes, but it
seems they also swallowed his views uncritically.[90] The direct result of this
is that they stopped translating the term "*Nehesi*" as "Negro" or "Black."
They also conclude that the contact that the Egyptians had with the *Nehesu*
in the South before the Eighteenth Dynasty was not with pure Negroes, but
with the so-called Hamites.[91] Sir Alan Gardiner accepts Junker's views with
some variations. He maintains that the word "*Nehesyu*" refers to the people
of *Wawat*, *Kush* and Punt because they spoke a language which required an
interpreter (dragoman).[92] Further, he said that in some contexts, this term
may refer to the southerners who live along the river, in contrast to the
"desert-dwellers" called "Medjay" who later became policemen for the
Egyptians.[93] A. J. Arkell,[94], Steindorff and Seele[95] Snowden[96] and Jean
Vercoutter[97] did not hesitate to accept Junker's view that "*Nehesi*" refers to
the southerners. In fact, Vercoutter goes further to suggest that the term
"*Nehesyu*" would seem to be derived from a place name, but what place, he
refuses to tell.

A close examination of Junker's essay, which so much revolutionized the thinking of several modern scholars, reveals that his ideas that "*Nehesi*" cannot mean "Black" or "Negro" were based on the judgment that there were no Negroes in the Nile Valley during the Old and Middle Kingdom because there was no representation of any pure negro in the archaeological findings. Junker's conclusion of the absence of the Negroes in the Nile Valley was based on his criterion of who is a Negro. According to him, dark color plays no important role. To Junker and his followers, the inhabitant of the Nile may be black or dark, yet they are not Negroes but Hamites. It may be difficult to recognize indisputably Negro representations in the Nile Valley. This is because the question of whether those representations are whites (Hamites) or blacks, depends on one's criteria of who is a black or a white person. To several anthropologists and most people who consider dark or black color (so also many dictionaries) as the most important criterion, those representations would be blacks or Negroes. Concerning this W. Y. Adams, speaking about the people of the Nile Valley, observes:

> I do not mean their skin color and facial features have changed significantly in the historic period; I believe in fact that they have remained pretty much the same since the earliest times. But race is largely in the eye of the beholder; it is more a matter of social ascription than of biology...To be technically accurate the Nubians are mostly of a chocolate-brown colour; one could, and can, see them either as "black" or as "white" according to the prejudices of one's time and termperament.[98]

What Professor Junker calls the criteria or the "chief characteristics" of a negro which exclude dark color as an important characteristic may be due to the "prejudices and temperament" of his time.[99] There could also be the possibility that other scholars who accept his views may have done so because it fit the taste of their prejudices and temperament of their time. I think that scholars should guard against hasty conclusions and wait for further archaeological evidence wherever facts are as controversial as those representations which Junker examines. Jean Vercoutter may be right when he says:

> Yet on one hand we must keep in mind the stylization of the art of the Old Kingdom: a given head, which looks to us like the classic representation of an Egyptian, may just as well belong to a genuine black.[100]

Since the division of the African people into two difference races (the so-called "Hamitic" and "Negro" races) has been considered arbitrary because it has no historical or biological basis,[101] and the representations of the Nile Valley people are still controversial (based on the prejudices and temperament of the time), it seems premature for scholars to accept Junker's view without reservation. What seems to be the possible meaning of the term *"Nehesi,"* therefore, is the southern blacks or the southern Negroes, thus carrying both the ethnic and geographical meaning. This term "southern Negroes" was probably used by the Egyptians to distinguish the southern Negroes from themselves who may also be Negroes but living in the north. This meaning seems more plausible when one sees that the Arabic term, "Sudan" which means "black" was used to refer to that portion of the land of *"Nehesi."* One cannot help but think that the term "Sudan" may be the translation of the Egyptian term.[102] Professor D. O'Connor suggests that *"Nehesi"* was a generic term for *"Phinehasi."* This then becomes the name of a Kushite from Aniba in *Kush* who bears the title "King's Son of *Kush*" and the Viceroy of *Kush*.

Having discussed the meaning of the Egyptian term *"Nehesi,"* it is important to consider the approximate geographical location and some important references to the term in the hieroglyphic texts. The earliest references to *"Nehesi"* in the Egyptian texts are in the Palermo stone during the Third Dynasty.[103] In this stone, King Snefru, the father of the builder of great Pyramid at Giza was said to have destroyed *Ta-Nehesi*, the Land of the southern negro and captured 7,000 prisoners and 200,000 cattle and sheep. The next appearance of this term is in the "longest narrative inscription and the most important historical document from the Old Kingdom," the Inscription of Una at Abydos.[104] During the Sixth Dynasty, under the reign of Pepi I, Una, the "governor of the South" recorded that when he led the army against the Asiatics, his soldiers contained the southern blacks (*Nehesi*) from *Medjay, Yam, Wawat* and *Kaam*. Still in the Sixth Dynasty, probably under Pepi II, in the "Admonition of Egyptian Sage,"[105] the southern blacks (Nehesi), the "*Medjay*" and *the Temehu* were said to be dangers to Egypt. A. J. Arkell maintains that Amenemhat I, the first ruler of the Twelfth Dynasty, was the son of a Nehesi woman.[106] Toward the close of the Thirteenth Dynasty, a king set himself up in the Delta. He called himself "King of the South and North, *Ra-Nehsi* or *Nebsi Ra*." Written also in the inscription at Tanis, as already mentioned, was "the Royal son of *Nehsi*."

In the reign of Set-Usert III, he set up two boundary stelae at Semneh on the Second Cataract.[107] The main purpose of these stelae was to prevent the southern blacks (Nehesu) or their lords from passing by the boundary either by land or by sea, to the northern part of Egypt, except for trading. On the wall of Taharqa's temule at Kawa, Napata, was described as the whole land of the southern blacks (*Nehesu*).[108]

The major problem is that most of these places mentioned in these inscriptions have not yet been located with exactness. Although scholars are certain and also unanimous that the inhabitants of the land south of Egypt, namely *Wawat*, *Kush* and *Punt* are called "*Nehesi*," the extent of this southern land is difficult to know. What appears reasonably possible is that the term "*Nehesi*" refers to all the Negroes inhabiting the southern land, perhaps as far as the Cape of Good Hope.

MAGAN AND MELUHHA

The problem of the location of *Magan* and *Meluhba* which appears so frequently in the cuneiform inscriptions has been a subject of debate among Assyriologists for several years. Professor C. J. Gadd says that these terms have "provided one of the enigmas of ancient geography.[109] "Professor Gaston Maspero lists *Magan* and *Melabha* as parts of the vague and unknown regions.[110] The main problem with the location of *Magan* and *Melahba* is their identification during their earliest appearance in the time of Naram-Sin and Gudea (3000-2000 B.C.E.). Despite the fact that the Assyrians and the Babylonian inscriptions clearly identified Magan with Egypt and *Meluhha* with Ethiopia in Africa at the latter period[111] (second to first millennium B.C.E.) some scholars maintain that their identification in the earlier period was either uncertain or located somewhere other than Egypt and Ethiopia.

While some scholars locate Meluhha as far as Wadi Arish and the Mediterranean, and Magan in the Sinaitic Peninsula, others maintain that *Magan* and *Meluhha* are synonymous with Sumer and Akkad.[112] In other words, *Magan* and *Meluhha* are two great divisions of Babylon. A. Leo Oppenheim, C. J. Gadd, Robert R. Stieglitz, Henry Rawlinson, and John Bright find the possible location of *Magan* and *Meluhha* of the Agade Dynasty in India and Arabia. Although R. R. Stieglitz[113] accepts the possibility of Egyptian and Mesopotamian domination of seafaring traffic as early as the third millenium B.C.E., he is dogmatic that *Magan* and *Meluhha* cannot be anywhere in Africa in the third millenium B.C.E.[114] While A. L. Oppenheim[115] is also dogmatic that the location cannot be anywhere in Africa, John Bright[116] and Morris Jastrow[117] still allow the probability of identifying Magan and Meluhha with Egypt and Ethiopia respectively. Most of these scholars who advocate a non-African location of *Magan* and

Meluhha seem not to give any concrete reason for their locations somewhere else. The only reason John Bright gives for the location of *Magan* in Oman and *Meluhha* in the Indus Valley is that he believes there is evidence of trade between the Indus Valley and the Mesopotamian peoples in the period of Agade.[118] Although C.J. Gadd agrees that Africa south of Egypt (Nubia) was the general gold-mine of the ancient world and the main source of its riches, according to ancient testimony and modern survey, he refuses the location of *Magan* and *Meluhha* in Africa because it appears unimaginable that Sumer's army would have been able to penetrate so far a country at that early period.[119] R. R. Stieglitz, who admits the maritime links between Mesopotamia and Egypt (through Marl, Yarmuti, and Ebla) from the "very early" time, gives no reason for locating *Magan* and *Meluhha* outside Africa except that there were other seafaring people trading with Mesopotamia other than the Egyptians.[120] Professor Oppenheim's reasons appear more extensive, but seem far-fetched. His reasons are as follows:[121]

(1)   There are evidences of unmistakable trade contacts via shipping lines between southern Mesopotamia and the regions to the east (namely, Persian Gulf—Bahrein and Oman);

(2)   raw materials, copper ore, ivory and precious stones came by boat from coastlands that cannot be properly identified may be Oman;

(3)   when an unknown event interrupted their trade link to the east, *Magan* and *Meluhha* became "a mytho-geographical term" (about 2nd millenium B.C.E.) to refer to Egypt and Ethiopia and probably beyond; and

(4)   in the early period these terms referred to the outmost eastern fringe of the known world (Arabia and India).

There is no unanimous agreement concerning the origins of the Sumerian and Egyptian civilizations. Orientalists have formed two major schools of thought concerning the world's earliest civilization. "Panbabylonians" claim priority for Mesopotamia, the "Panegyptians" make a similar claim for the Nile valley. Several Sumerologists and Assyriologists maintain that the Sumerians were the originators of their civilization and culture and later introduced it to Egypt and other parts of the ancient world.[122] But several Egyptologists and Africanists, on the other hand, maintain that the Egyptians were the originators of ancient civilizations and culture and later introduced it to the Sumerians who eventually perfected them.[123] Although some scholars deny that the Egyptians and the Sumerians originated their civilization independently of one another, without influencing one another, several Africanists argue vehemently that according to the Greek, Persian and Sumerian traditions, the ancient civilization of Egypt and Sumer originated from Africa, south of Egypt (Ethiopia).[124] Since the main concern of this study is not finding the solution to the origin of either Egyptian or Sumerian civilizations (which is beyond the scope of this work), it suffices therefore merely to recognize these diverse scholarly opinions. More attention will now be given to the overwhelming evidences supporting the early contact between the early Sumerians and Africans which makes it unlikely for the Sumerians to confuse the location of *Magan* and *Melahha* in Africa with that of Bahrein and Oman even if there is unknown topographic shift. Although it is difficult to be overly dogmatic, the overwhelming body of evidence available makes the location of *Magan* and *Meluhha* in Egypt and Ethiopia more reasonable. These evidences concern the relationship and the contact between Africans and the Sumerians. Maritime trade contact in the Agade period have not been denied by eminent scholars mentioned previously.[125]

According to inscriptions of Sargon of Agade and those of Gudea of Lagash, the main articles of trade between *Magan-Meluhha* and Sumer are "gold in dust form," stones, logs, ivory, pearls and carnelian.[126] Several evidences are supportive of the location of *Magan* and *Melahha* in Africa. Africa has been regarded as the general gold-mine of the ancient world and the main source of its riches,[127] both according to ancient testimony and in modern survey. It is therefore more appropriate to locate *Magan* and *Melahha* in Africa from where these resources might have come via sea route through Marl, Yarmuti and Ebla to Sumer. No other country has attained such popularity because of her resources in this early time. If Professor Maspero is correct when he maintains that "Egyptians no doubt carried their products to the Market of Ur," *Magan* and *Meluhha* will appear more reasonable in Africa. According to Henri Frankfort, the Mesopotamian objects (the three cylinder seals and the objects depicted in the Egyptian monuments) and the temporary adaptation of Mesopotamian usages found in Egypt show Mesopotamian influence in the Pre- and protodynastic Egypt.[128] The simlilarities between the Egyptian and early Sumerian religion, writing and language is a strong evidence for early contact. Because of these similarities between the Egyptian and Sumerian religion, writing and the dark color of their skins, several authorities have also emphasized that the early Sumerians and their civilization originated from Africa. Among these authorities is one of the most qualified scholars, known as the "Father of Assyriology," Sir Henry Rawlinson, who says:

> Without pretending to trace up these early Babylonians to their original ethnic source, there are certainly strong reasons for supposing them to have passed from Ethiopia to the Valley of the Euphrates shortly before the opening of the historic period: (1) The system of writing which they brought with them has the closest affinity with that of Egypt—in many cases indeed, there is an absolute identity between the two alphabets; (2) In the Biblical genealogies, Cush (Ethiopia) and Mizraim (Egypt) are brothers, while from the former sprang Nimrod (Babylonians); (3) In regard to the language of the primitive Babylonians, the vocabulary is undoubtedly Cushite or Ethiopian; (4) All the tradition of Babylonia and Assyria point to a connection in very early times between Ethiopia, Southern Arabia and the cities on the lower Euphrates; (5) In further proof of the connection between Ethiopia and Chaldea, we must remember the Greek traditions both of Cepheus and Memnon, which sometimes applied to Africa, and sometimes to the countries at the mouth of the Euphrates; and we must also consider the geographical names of *Cush* and *Phut*, which, although of African origin, are applied to races bordering on Chaldea, both in the Bible and in the Inscriptions of Dairus.[129]

Professor George Rawlinson, an equally distinguished scholar, whose research reinforces the opinion of his brother Henry Rawlinson, did not hesitate to emphasize that "the uniform voice of primitive antiquity," supports the view that all Ethiopians, both in Africa, India and the Euphrates valley are of the same race.[130] He continues:

> Recent linguistic discovery tends to show that a Cushite or Ethiopian race did in the earliest times extend itself along the shores of the Southern Ocean from Abyssinia to India. The whole peninsula of India was peopled by a race of this character before the influx of the Aryans. It extended from Indus along the sea coast through the modern Baluchistan and Kerman which was the proper country of the Asiatic Ethiopians; the cities on the northern shores of the Persian Gulf are shown by the brick inscriptions found among their ruins to have belonged to this

race; it was dominant in Susiana and Babylonia, until overpowered in the one country by Aryan, in the other by Semitic intrusion; it can be traced both by dialect and tradition throughout the whole south coast of the Arabian peninsula.[131]

Richard Lepsius, one of the finest German Egyptologists of great reputation agrees with Professor Rawlinson by saying that the early Sumerians imported their civilization from the Nile Valley:

> In the oldest times within the memory of men we know of only one literary development, viz, those of Egypt, and we know of only one contemporary people which could have had knowledge of this culture, appropriated its results, and convey them to other nations, this was the Kushites, the masters of the Eurythraean Sea to its furthest limits. It was by them that Babylonia was colonized and fertilized with Egyptian culture. And it is thus only that the thorough-going correspondence between Babylonian knowledge and institutions and the Egyptian ones becomes intelligible. The pictorial writing forming the basis of the cuneiform characters is unmistakably only a species of the hieroglyphics; the astronomy of Babylon is only a development of that of Egypt; its unit of measure, that is, the royal architectural ell of 0.525m, is completely identical with that of Egypt its architecture, that is to say, its temples as well as its pyramids and obelisks, is an imperfect imitation of Egyptian originals and so with the other arts. At every step we meet in Babylonia with the traces of Egyptian models.[132]

In Sumer, all the gods and goddesses are children of "Anu," the king of the Sumerian gods, and Professor Flinders Petrie applies this term "Anu" or "Annu" to an original race of pre-dynastic Egypt.[133] The great British anthropologist from the University of London, Dr. W. J. Perry, points out that the Sumerians seem to have been in touch with Africa from their earliest times and the mention of Magan and Meluhha were archaic names for Egypt and Ethiopia.[134] When Smith examines the similarity between Sumerian and African civilization, he concludes it is very certain that the civilization of Sumer must have been planted and grown by someone acquainted with Africa.[135] On the basis of the above facts, the American Orientalist, John D. Baldwin, also concludes:

> If every competent investigator would allow himself to see and comprehend the country which the ancients designated as Ethiopia and the land of *Cush*... there would be a more intelligent appreciation of the large amount of ancient tradition which brings the Cushites into that part of Asia, and sometimes describes it as a part of Ethiopia. It was Ethiopia in race, language and civilization, and constituted a portion of the widespread territory occupied by the Cushites.[136]

Considering all the above factors, concerning the relationship and the origin of the Sumerian people, it is very improbable that any "unknown" and unrecorded catastrophe would have happened that would make the Sumerians confuse Babylon, India or Arabia with Egypt and Ethiopia, as Professor Oppenheim has suggested. Even though many of those who advocate a location of *Magan* and *Melahha* outside Africa agree to the possible early relationship between Egypt, Ethiopia and Sumer, they fail to suggest what the Sumerians called Egypt and Ethiopia during that early period of exchange. In the light of the relationship and origin of the early Sumerians in Africa, and the absence of any known and recorded catastrophe in Asia, I have a very considerable difficulty in accepting those suggested locations of Magan and Meluhha outside Africa (India, Babylon and Arabia). Until the evidence of such catastrophic events which Oppenheim suggested, and other names which the early Sumerians used to refer to Egypt and Ethiopia can be uncovered, the most probably location is Africa.[137] Concerning the location in Africa, "an uncontestable authority on the civilization of Sumer," Professor Samuel Noah Kramer,[138] is probably right when he says:

> In brief span of time Agade became the most prosperous and resplendent of the cities of the ancient world; to it gifts and tributes were brought from the four corners of Sargon's realm, and at its guaya ships docked from far-off Dilmun, Yiagan, and *Meluhha* (that is, perhaps, India, Egypt and Ethiopia.[139]

Professor Kramer continues:

> In fact, most cuneiformists agree that by the first millenium B.C. *Magan* and *Meluhha* did correspond roughly with Egypt and Ethiopia. It is for the early period for days of Sargon the Great, Gudea, and the Third Dynasty of Ur, for example—that this

identification has been generally thought to be most unlikely,
since it would involve the seemingly incredible assumption that
the peoples of those early days had seagoing ships that could
reach the East Coast of Africa. This has led to the hypothesis
that over the millennium there was a shift in toponymy, that is,
that in the third and second millenniums B.C. the names *Magan*
and *Meluhha* corresponded to the lands bordering the east and
southeast Arabia but that for one reason or another these names
were later transferred to Egypt and Ethiopia. Now metho-
dologically speaking, the verification of a hypothesis involving
a name shift in the cuneiform documents for countries of such
recognized importance as those referred to by the names *Magan*
and *Meluhha* should be based on evidence that is reasonably
assured and decisive. But as of today, there does not seem to be
that kind of evidence; there is still a strong possibility, as will
become evident from what follows, that there was no toponymic
shift and that *Magan* and *Meluhha* correspond more or less to
Egypt and Ethiopia in the third millennium B.C. as well as in the
first millennium.[140]

ETHIOPIA

Having exmined the terms *Wawat, Bush, Punt, Magan* and *Meluhha*, the
next important term to examine is Ethiopia. Although this term is nowhere
used in either Egyptian texts or the Mesopotamian texts to refer to Africa
and Africans during the biblical period, it is nevertheless one of the most
important terms used to refer to Africa and Africans in antiquity by some
segments of people during the biblical periods. This chapter which examines
various terms used to refer to Africa in antiquity will not be complete
without the inclusion of Ethiopia. The importance of this term "Ethiopia"
can be seen in the fact that the translators of the King James Version and the
Revised Standard Version translated the Hebrew word *"Cush"* and
"Cushites" into Ethiopia and Ethiopians respectively, and the passages where
this term appears are the main focus for this study. This section therefore
proposes to examine the origin of the word Ethiopia and how it was used by
various classical writers. Its appropriateness in the texts to be exegeted in the
following chapters will be examined. Moreover, the need for the alternative
shall be suggested. In the examination of this term, I will not examine all the
Greek and Roman writers, but mainly those who have some significant
discussions on Ethiopia.

To the ancient Greek writers, scholars owe the origin and the development of the term "Ethiopia." Contrary to the prevailing view that the earliest appearance of this term was in the Homeric poem (*Iliad* and *Odyssey*) dating back to the ninth century B.C.E,[141] there is evidence that the first appearance dated back to the second half of the thirteenth century B.C.E. This earliest appearance is in the fragmentary tablets uncovered in the Palace of Nestor at Pylos. Accompanied by frescoes depicting blacks, the word *ai-ti-jo-go* (which was translated to mean aithiops) appeared several times.[142]

During the post-Homeric era, the term Ethiopia became a common expression for the Greco-Roman poets,[143] historians,[144] geographers,[145] and naturalists.[146] Professor Hansberry says that except for Hellas and Hellas' own heroes, no country and its peoples are more repeatedly mentioned throughout the long and brilliant course of classical literature.[147] This pride of place given to Ethiopia and Ethiopians by the Greco-Roman geographers, historians and romanticists shows that these writers were definitely "Ethiopic conscious."[148]

Many theories concerning the etymology of the term "Ethiopia" have been put forward. One of the classical writers says that *Aethiops* which means "glowing" or "black" was the original name of Zeus as he was worshipped in the Island of Chios.[149] But Pliny, the Elder says that the term "Ethiopia" derived from *Aethiops*, the son of Vulcan, who was the god of metal working and fire and the Greek counterpart of the Ethiopian god of Bes.[150] Professor Edward Glaser maintains that the name *Etiopyawan* (Ethiopia) derived from the word "incense," the frankincense so highly prized in the ancient time.[151] However, the scholars' consensus is that the word "Ethiopia" originated from the Greeks to designate African people both at home and abroad in terms of the color of their skins. This term which the Greek geographers generally used to refer to any member of the black people, derived from the words (burnt) and (face[152]). Ethiopia, therefore, literally means "burnt-faced person" of Africa and African diaspora. This term was probably chosen by the Greeks to describe the Africans according to their "environmental theory" that the dark color of their skins and the wooly or coiled hair of their heads were as a result of the intense heat of the southern sun."[153]

According to the Homeric testimony, the land of Ethiopia is at the remotest border of the world beside the steam of the ocean. It was the place where the "blameless race called Ethiopians lived and made sacrifices pleasing to the gods, including Zeus.[154] Two Ethiopias exist, the Ethiopia of the rising and the setting sun.[155] The exact meaning of the Ethiopians of the rising and setting suns has been the subject of debate even among the Homeric scholars. While some scholars say that the two divisions of Ethiopia mean that one Ethiopia is Africa and the other Asia, other scholars interpret it to mean that Ethiopia south of Egypt was divided by River Nile.[156] Hesiod lists Ethiopians with the Ligurians and Scythians as quoted by Strabo.[157] In the Theogony, Memnon, the son of Eos is the King of Ethiopia.[158] In the *Work and Days* Hesiod referred to the Ethiopians for the first time as black men.[159]

Aeschylus is the first Greek writer to place Ethiopians definitely in Africa when he refers to the dark race as Ethiopians who dwell near Ethiopian river (Nile) the spring of the sun where Ethiopian river (Nile) is located.[160] Hanno's voyage is described as one of the "most picturesque incidents in the history of ancient geography."[161] Unfortunately, the name Hanno was so common in Carthage and that makes it difficult to identify which Hanno. However, generally, scholars date it between sixth and fifth centuries B.C.E.[162] Although scholars doubt the southern limit of Hanno's voyage, because the places mentioned have not been located, Hanno seems to have been the first to describe his voyage to the most southern part of Africa for the purpose of colonization. Hanno sailed as far as river Lixus, where the natives told him about the high mountains and the hostile Ethiopians who were cave-dwellers in inner Africa.[163] They sailed beyond Cerne into a great lake where wild people threw stones at them, thus preventing them from landing. The report said that they sailed to a large river full of "crocodiles and hippopotami" (this river is generally identified with Senegal.[164] They went further to a bay, generally identified with Gambia in West Africa. Beyond this bay, was the great gulf called Western Horn. Sailing beyond the Western Horn, they arrived at a bay called the Southern Horn where they saw an island full of people covered with hair and called "gorillas." This was the southern limit of their expedition.[165]

A man who earned himself the title of the "Father of History" (given by Cicero), and "the first artist of Greek prose" is Herodotus. His travels to Persia, Palestine, Europe and Egypt for inspection of ruins in ancient fallen civilization in order to determine differences among nations resulted in his book *Histories*. Of interest to scholars is the signature of Herodotus that was uncovered at Asmara, Northern Ethiopia.[166] However, some scholars consider this signature a spurious one. Despite the fact that the Ancient Greek geographer, Strabo, called him the "compiler of lies," and some modern scholars distrusted his work, archaeological discoveries appear to authenticate his records, especially concerning Africa (Book II and III). Herodotus, like Homer, made mention of two types of Ethiopians in the army of Xerxes which invaded Greece in 480 B.C.E (Western and Eastern Ethiopians).[167] Budge interprets Herodotus as follows:

> It seems certain that classical historians and geographers called the whole region from India to Egypt, both countries inclusive, by name of Ethiopia, and in consequence they regarded all the dark-skinned and black peoples who inhabited it as Ethiopians. Mention is made of Eastern and Western Ethiopians, and it is probable that the Easterners were Asiatics and the Westerners Africans .. During the preparation I have been driven to the conclusion that the Ethiopians whose manner and customs have been so fully described by Herodotus, Diodorus, Strabo, Pliny and others were not Abyssinians at all, but the natives of Upper Nubia and the Island of Meroe, and the Negroes and Negroid peoples who inhabited the hot, moist lands, which extend from Southern Abyssinia to the Equator.[168]

The Father of History did not just generalize about the Western and the Eastern Ethiopians without making some valuable distinctions. According to him, both were black, but the hair of the Western Ethiopians was coiled and woolly while the hair of the Eastern Ethiopians was straighter and there was a difference in the languages they spoke.[169] Herodotus, who spent about two years in Egypt for his research, regarded the Egyptians and the Colchians as black people. He says: "There can be no doubt that Colchains are an Egyptian race. Before I heard any mention of the fact from others, I had remarked it myself. My own conjectures were founded first on the fact that they are black skinned and have wooly hair."[170]

The Ethiopians in the army of Xerxes wore leopard and lion skins, and were armed with spears, bows and arrows.[171] In order to prove that the ocean surrounded Africa he reports what took place during the reign of Pharaoh Necho. The Phoenicians, he says, circumnavigated Africa in the period of three years and returned through the Pillar of Hercules.[172] He believes this incident but rejects the idea that the sun was on their right hand during the expedition. He also relates another abortive attempt to circumnavigate Africa by the Persian noble man, Sataspes, who was sentenced to death unless he circumnavigated Africa (Ethiopia).[173] He failed and was executed. E. H. Brunbury agrees that the above incident cannot be disproved or pronounced impossible.[174] Other statements about Ethiopia and Ethiopians which are of historical value are: Shabaka's invasion of Egyptian,[175] Psammetichus' employment of the Greek mercenaries against his southern neighbours,[176] Cambyses' plan to attack them and his failure,[177] their longevity[178] and their heights and good looks ("the tallest and handsomest men in the whole world").[179] According to Herodotus, gold and copper were in abundance to the extent that they bound their prisoners with gold chain.[180]

Additional interesting material which is of major importance concerning the Ethiopians was given by Eudoxus of Cyzicus and was preserved by Strabo.[181] Eudoxus was sent on a honorary mission to sail around Ethiopia. During his voyage he saw the Ethiopians (West) who spoke the same language as those of the Eastern Ethiopians and there he learned that their territory adjoined that of Brocchus, King of Mauretania.[182] He went beyond his Mauretania and then reported that Ethiopia was surrounded by the ocean.[183]

Another interesting account about Ethiopia was given by an unknown author in his work *Periplus of the Erythrean*. He was regarded as the first person to show a definite knowledge of the southern extension of Africa among the Greek writers. Some of the places mentioned are identifiable with reasonable certainty.[184] He sailed south of Aromata as far as Zanzibar, Rhapta, and further to about 1,500 miles south of Cape Guardafui.[185]

Diodorus Sicilus (59-30 B.C.E.), the Greek-born writer, set out to write the general history of mankind. Although charged with lack of methodology of his plan, and deficiency in his critical judgment as to his selection and use of materials, modern scholars believe that his work is one of the most trustworthy and valuable, especially the section which deals with Ethiopia.[186] Although he says that some Ethiopians were primitive,[187] he is not blind to the achievement of the Ethiopians. To him the Ethiopians were people of great wisdom and religious zeal. These are the inhabitants of the Island of Meroe, according to his sources, were the first of all men; they were pioneers in the worship of God; they originated many Egyptian customs; they were the people who sent the Egyptians out as colonists; they originated the Egyptian burial practices, the role of priests, the shape of statues and their forms of writing.[188] According to Diodorus, the stories about Osiris of Egypt and Dionysus of the Greeks were nothing but the "glorified editions of events and exploits which were originally performed by the prince belong to the old royal family of inner Ethiopia.[189] Diodorus mentioned the king of Ethiopia, Sabach, who invaded Egypt, as noted for kindness and zeal more than his predecessors.[190] To him the reason why the people beyond Egypt are different in life, manners and bodies is because of the intense heat of that region. Strabo, who is one of the most remarkable scholars of antiquity, earned himself the appellation "the Father of Geography," mainly because of his monumental work, *Geography*. Although his first efforts in the field of "productive scholarship" were in history, his book on geography is by far the most important geographical work ever produced by the Greco-Roman writers that has come down from antiquity.[191] Agreeing with Alexander van Hamboldt's statement on Strabo's geography that this work surpassed all other geographical labors of antiquity by the grandeur of its composition and diversity of its subjects, W. L. Hansberry says that this is not an over-statement:

> For in no other volume that has come down from ancient times is one likely to find so varied an assortment of geographical and historical matter so systematically and artistically presented as in the seventeenth book.[192]

Unfortunately, this seventeenth book which is said to be the most "complete and satisfactory portion of Strabo's entire work," is the one that deals with Ethiopia.[193] Strabo, like Diodorus, mentioned the power of the priests to punish even the king of the country and one king who abolished this type of power accorded to the priests in Ethiopia. In their religion, says strabo,[194] the Ethiopians honored one being as God who is regarded as immortal and caused the existence of all things.[195] In addition to the people of Meroe, Strabo mentioned the Egyptian fugitives who deserted their king Psameticus and dwelled beyond Meroe. He called this people "Sembutae." According to him the Nubae (probably the Nubia) lived at the left bank of the Nile. Other groups include Megari and Blemmyes.[196] The natural products of inland Africa were copper, iron, gold, various kinds of precious stones, ebony trees, palm, the Persea and carob trees which were introduced to Egypt from Ethiopia.[197] Some of the historical events about the Roman invasion of Meroe when the Ethiopians seized the statues of Caesar were said to have been authenticated by archaeological discoveries. Such a statue was reported to have been uncovered in 1914 by the Liverpool Expedition who, when they excavated Meroe, uncovered a bronze head which appeared to be a portrait of Caesar.[198] G. A. Reisner of the Harvard-Boston Expedition who excavated the ruins of the great Temple of Ethiopia, near Nepata, claimed to have uncovered what he regards as evidence of the damages done by the Romans.[199]

The work of Pliny the Elder is very important because his work is one of the most important of the Latin writers. Among his contemporaries, he was regarded as one of the "most learned," most diligent and most voluminous writers of the ancient times.[200] Of all the books he wrote, only the *Natural History* survived. This work contains the most numerous references to Ethiopia. This might be because he had the privilege of consulting most of the works of other classicial writers before him.[201] According to Pliny, the region designated Ethiopia in ancient times has different names. The earliest of these names is Aetherea, then, Altantia, and last Aethiopia, which he said derived from Aethiops, the son of Vulcan, the Latin name of the god of the metal working and fire.[202] Pliny was more detailed and more specific about the cities of Ethiopia.[203] Pliny says that the Egyptians who deserted Psammetichus settled in the cities five days journey beyond Meroe. Another eight days journey further south is another city called Nubae. Beyond Nubae, says Pliny, are scattered towns like Asara, Araba, and Summara. The people called Cisori, Misyti, who are remarkable for the unerring aim of their arrows, settled beyond these towns mentioned above. Further south are still many other towns—Longompoli, Oecalices, Usibalei, Isbeli, Pemsii and Cespil. Finally, imaginary people inhabited the southern land beyond.[204] Pliny was the first ancient writer to mention the river Niger which he calls river Nigries.[205] This river Nigries, he says, has the same characteristics as the river Nile. It produces reeds, papyrus which becomes swollen at the same time.[206] The question of identification of the river Nigris of Pliny to the River Niger in West Africa is still debatable. However, Professor Bunbury says that in the absence of any river in the north of the great desert which fits the description of river Nigris, it must refer to the inner African river known in the modern time as river Niger.[207]

Although these cities have not been identified with certainly, the fact that these ancient writers mentioned them is remarkable and gives some indication that the nation called Ethiopia is not confined to the area of Meroe and probably includes all the modern territory of the continent of Africa. This appears very probable when one examines the reports of Herodotus and Eudoxus of Cynicus. Herodotus reported that the Phoenicians circumnavigated Ethiopia. Euxodus went beyond Mauretania and reported that Ethiopia was surrounded by the ocean.[208] From the above discussion of the term Ethiopia during the classical period, it appears that it is reasonably certain that these classical writers were well-acquainted with and well informed about Ethiopia and Ethiopians. It also appears reasonably certain that the term "Ethiopia" and "Ethiopians" were first used in a more general sense (especially in the time of Homer, Hesiod and Herodotus) to refer to all dark-skinned people and all the land which they inhabited. (Egypt, Sudan, Arabia, Palestine, Western Asia and India),[209] but more frequently to African people and the land. The use of Ethiopia in this way probably roughly corresponds to *Cush, Punt,* and *Nehesi* of the Egyptians, Assyrians and Hebrews.

When the King James Version of the Bible was translated, the word *"Kush"* was translated as "Ethiopia," thus transliterating the Septuagint (LXX). In 1901, the revision done by the "American divines," *The American Standard Version,* retains the term "Ethiopian." The same term is used in the *Revised Standard Version* of 1952 which set out to make the Bible clearer to the public reader by changing some of the archaic words. *The New American Standard Version* of 1960 used this same term in some of its passages. *The Jerusalem Bible* and *The New International Version* used the transliteration of the Hebrew word (*Kush*). *The Good News Bible,* which translates *Kush* as "Sudan," seems to have a better translation even though it is equally an unsatisfactory translation like others mentioned above. Before suggesting what should be the most appropriate translation, it is important to discuss some relevant principles of translation according to authorities.

Dr. E. A. Nida, a distinguished authority in translation, a linguist, anthropologist, and biblical scholar, who has assisted in translating the Bible into about 200 languages, states that there are several principles of translation. Four are especially crucial to this work:

(1)   a translator must reproduce the meaning of the passage as understood by the writer;[210]

(2)   the translator must choose the closest or most natural equivalent meaning; [211]

(3)   meaningless words or vocabularies must be avoided in the text,[212]

(4)   priority must be given to the need of the audience or readers over the forms of the written language.[213]

The translator should not be concerned merely with "the possibility of his readers understanding it correctly, but with overwhelming likelihood of it. "Professor Nida continues:

> In other words we are not content merely to translate so that the average receptor is likely to understand the message; rather we aim to make certain that such a person is very unlikely to misunderstand it.[214]

To William L. Wonderly, the purpose of the translator is not to educate, but to communicate the Bible message in a form that is intelligible and comprehensible to their readers.[215] One of the tests of intelligibility and comprehensibility is primarily concerned with "the discovery and the elimination of expressions that are likely to be misunderstood."[216]

In the light of the above principles, the questions to be rightly asked are as follows:

(1)   Is it likely that the words "Ethiopia," "Cush," and "Sudan" will be misunderstood by the common Bible readers?

(2)   Are these words the closest equivalent meanings of the biblical *Kush* in the light of modern usage of these words?

The answer to the first question is certainly affirmative because most of the Bible readers think that Ethiopia in the Bible refers to the modern Ethiopia excluding the rest of black Africa. Bishop Alfred Dunston regretfully expressed how the translation of the Hebrew word *Kush* to "Ethiopia" has misled the Christian world when he laments:

> This term "Ethiopia" in the English Bible has misled the Christian world for the past three-hundred-sixty odd years, and it is highly conceivable that a more proper or an English term identification of the Cushite might have changed the whole European attitude towards chattel slavery for black people. The myths of savagery, cannibalism, and general debasement would have been re-examined had the Bible reflected the fact that the people under the myths were then being called "Negroes" in the Western world. The color and geography of the Cushites would have contributed to a better appreciation all around, and the most ignorant, rabid racist would not have pretended to doubt the existence of a soul in any man about whom he had read in the pages of the Holy Bible.[217]

Although the word "Sudan" means "black," yet it is deficient because it still excludes some parts of Africa represented by the biblical *Kush*. On this account, the Bishop laments again that the translation of the term *Kush* as "Ethiopia" is "a definite disservice to the Christian Church in general, and to the black African and his descendants in particular," because the translation of this term as Ethiopia obscures the role the black people have played in the Bible. This obscurity of the role of blacks in the Bible might have contributed in some ways to the "continuing scourge of slavery that mars the pages of Western history, because the Western conscience might possibly have reacted differently had the biblical Ethiopians been more closely identified.[218] In other words, the subsequent generation might have been protected from the "color disease" if a different translation which reflects black people had been employed.[219]

In the light of the principle of translation discussed above (that the translator must avoid meaningless words which could not be readily understood by the common readers), the transliteration of the Hebrew word Kush to "*Kush*" by the Jerusalem Bible and the *New International Version* is equally deficient. The word "*Kush*" is an archaic word borrowed by Mesopotamian people and the Hebrews to refer to the black people and their land. This is no longer in use except in the modern Hebrew language.[220] It is not understood by the common readers of the English Bible as meaning black or black land. Therefore it does not fulfill the objective of translation, that is, to communicate to the common readers. The "*Kush*" is meaning-less to the common English readers. During the time of ancient Egyptian, Assyrian and the Classical writers, and even the time of King James, *Kush*, Ethiopia and Sudan would have been appropriate words.

What this writer thinks should be the most appropriate translation of *Cush* according to the principle of translation discussed above is "Africa."[221] This term "Africa" is the most natural equivalent of the biblical term today. This term will not only convey the black identity of the people referred to as *Kush*, but it is also likely not to be misunderstood by the common English readers. For this reason, in the following chapters, the word "*Kush*," shall be translated "Africa" and "Kushites," or "Africans."

Endnotes

1.   The division of mankind into races began by F. Bernier in the seventeenth century of our era when he divided mankind into four or five races. This division was followed by another four varieties of Homo (Mongolian, Ethiopian, American and Malayan) according to skin colors by C. Linneans in 1735. Professor J. E. Blumenbach in 1775 had five divisions not only according to the color or the skins but also skull forms by adding Caucasian to C. Linneans' divisions. According to J.F. Blumenbach, the Cucasians are the inhabitants of Western Asia, Europe and North Africa. The word Caucasian was chosen to refer to the above people because he thought they were the most beautiful race of people. Professor G. Cuvier was the first person to derive his anthropological terms from the biblical story. He derived mankind from the Biblical sons of Noah. He sees Japhet as the parent of the

Caucasian, Shem, the Mongolian, and Ham, the African peoples, thus originating another classification called "Hamitic." But when asked to explain the difference among the brothers who have the same parent, he could not explain, except attributing the blackness of Ham to the curse of Noah on Canaan who was the son of Ham (Gen. 9:25). During the eighteenth century, the anthropological divisions of mankind into races were as numerous as sixteen. During the nineteenth century, division of mankind into races according to the quality of hair was presented by Prunner Bey, Bory de Saint Vincent. Isidore Geoffrey Saint Hillaire's classification came back to the color of the skins. C. H. Stratz's classification was according to the proportion of the body and he divides humankind into three races. F. Boas' classification was according to oceans (Indian and Pacific oceans). According to Professor J. D. Baldwin, the American Orientalist (in *Pre-Historic Nations* (New York: Harper and Brothers Publishers, 1969, 309) Reed said that, since Africans were exceptional people, they cannot be classified into any distinct race. This is also because those who originally inhabited what we call Africa today were people of the "red-skinned" race who later became so degenerated in body and mind, thus changing their types so that in the course of generations their fine forms became "ugly, their long curly black hair" became "short, crisp and woolly, their fine, olive- colored complexion turned to a coal black." Professor Ripley vehemently disagreed with the above classification, because he thinks they have not led to the classification of any ideas in the complex problem of European ethnology. Professor A. C. Haddon, who was the Professor of Ethnology at Cambridge University, England, having tried to make sense of these numerous diverse classifications and could not, regards them as arbitrary. Some scholars even avoid using anthropological classification completely, especially for African people simply because of the arbitrariness of the classification and the confusion these anthropological terms have created. For full treatment of the history of anthropological divisions of mankind into races, see *History of Anthropology* by Alfred C. Haddon (London: Watts 5 Co., 1934), 70-79.

2.   B. G. Trigger et al., *Ancient Egypt: A Social History* (Cambridge: Cambridge University Press, 1983), 1. Professor E. Pittard, a professor of anthropology at the University of Geneva, after a careful study of this subject concludes that "such a thing as a pure race is non-existent today" and "practically every nation was already an ethnic complex" at the beginning of the historical time. J. J. Williams, *Hebrewism of West Africa*, 145. Professor R. B. Dixon, of Harvard University, also says: "By migration and conquest the original racial factors, whatever they were, have been so interwoven and blended that the vast majority of all living men must have a complex racial ancestry, and such a thing as a pure race can hardly be expected to live."

3.   Ibid. 145. The racial and tribal divisions and sub- divisions in Africa are so complicated for archaeologists, anthropologists and others that America with

its complex race problem, "have long since disregarded any scientific distinctions between African types." The popular usage here defines Negro in terms of color of the skin. G. H. Beardsley, *The Negro in Greek and Roman civilization* (New York: Arno Press, 1979), XI - XII.

4.   E.A.W. Budge, *An Egyptian Hieroglyphic Dictionary* (New York: Dover Publications, reprinted in 1978) from the original edition, 1920, 146.

5.   Ibid.

6.   Ibid.

7.   *The Geography of Strabo*, trans. Horace Leonard Jones, Vol. 8 Cambridge: Harvard University Press, 1949), 66 Book 7, 317 (henceforth Strabo). Strabo mentioned that there were many palm trees and these trees were among many trees and precious stones introduced to Egypt by the Ethiopians. William Leo Hansberry, *Africa and Africans As Seen by Classical Writers* (Washington, D.C. Harvard University Press, 1977), op. cit., 133. (Henceforth Africa and Africans).

8.   Sir Alan Gardiner, *Egypt of the Pharoah* (Oxford: Oxford University Press, (1961), 34.

9.   Gaston Maspero, *The Dawn of Civilization*, 2 vols., trans. M. L. McClure (New York: Frederick Ungar Publica-tion Co., reprinted in 1968 from 1894 edition), vol. 1,194.

10. J. A. Wilson, *The Culture of Ancient Egypt* (Chicago: University of Chicago Press, 1951), 137, *JEA* XXXI (1945), 3ff. See also J. H. Breasted, *Ancient Records of Egypt*, 5 vols. (Chicago: University of Chicago Press, 1920), vol. 1, 3-11.

11. Wilson, *The Culture of Ancient Egypt*, 137-38.

12. G. Maspero, *Dawn of Civilization*, vol. 1, 419. Budge, *Egyptian Sudan*, vol. 1, 516-17, J. H. Breasted, *Ancient Records of Egypt*, vol. 1, 140-44. The inscription of Uni was found in the Mastaba tomb in Abydos by Mariette. It is now in Cairo. It is also the longest narrative inscription and the most important historical document from the Old Kingdom.

13. E. A. Wallis Budge, *Egyptian Sudan* (New York: AMS Press, 1976), vol. 1, 518-19; Gaston Maspero, *The Dawn of Civilization*, vol. 1, 419. J. Pritchad (ed) *Ancient Near Eastern Texts Relating to the Old Testament* (Princeton, Princeton University Press, 1969), 228 (*ANET*).

14. Inscription of Una, J. H. Breasted, *Ancient Records of Egypt*, vol. 1, 146-50.

15. Budge, Egyptian Sudan, vol. 1, 534; A. J. Arkell, *A History of the Sudan* (Westport: Greenwood Press, 1955), 59. *ANET.*, 419. 67.

16. The Teaching of Amenemhat found on the rock at the entrance of the valley road leading from Korosoko to Abu Hamed by Dr. Luttge. Breasted, *Ancient Records of Egypt*, vol. 1, 232. ONE, 419.

17. The tomb inscription at Biban el-Moluk. See E.A. Wallis Budge, *Egyptian Sudan*, vol. 1, 643. See also Alan Gardiner, *Egypt of the Pharaohs* (Oxford: Oxford University Press, 1961), p.298

18.   *Egypt of the Pharaohs*, 298.

19.   *ANET.*,31

20.   Ibid. See also Maspero, *The Dawn of Civilization*, vol. 394-95.

21.   Maspero, *The Dawn of Civilization*, vol. 1, 488.

22.   The term Africa was first applied to a limited area of the northern continent (north-eastern extremity, but later about 104 B.C.E. the term was extended to the entire continent by the Romans.

23.   Maspero, *The Dawn of Civilization*, vol. 1, 488.

24.   ibid.

25.   J. D. Baldwin, *Pre-Historic Nations or Concerning Some of the Great Peoples and Civilizations Antiquity and Their Probable Relation to a Still Older Civilization of Ethiopians or Cushites of Arabia* (New York: Harper an Bros., Publishers, n.), 345. Hence- forth referred to as *Pre-Historic Nations*.

26.   Maspero, *The Dawn of Civilization*, vol. 1, 488.

27   Barry J. Kemp, "Old Kingdom, Middle Kingdom, and Second Intermediate Period 2686-1522," in *Ancient Egypt. A Social History* edited by B.G. Trigger, B. J. Kemp, D. O'Connor and A. B. Lloyd (Cambridge: Cambridge University Press, 1983), 71-174. 68.

28.   Arkell, *A History of the Sudan*, 174.

29.   Breasted, *Ancient Records of Egypt* (Henceforth referred to as ~ARE, vol. 1, 251.

30.   Ibid., vol. 1, 251; Budge, *Egyptian Sudan*, 534-35.

31.   Breasted, *ARE*, vol. 1, 317-18. See also "The Middle Kingdom in Egypt: The Internal History from the Heracleopolitans to the Death of Ammenemes III," *Cambridge Ancient History* (henceforth *CAH*), edited I.E.S. Edwards et. al. (Cambridge: Cambridge University Press, Paperback edition, 1980), vol. 1, parts 2A, 507.

32.   The word "Kush" is mine to give the word which was translated to Ethiopia.

33.   The Carnarvon Tablet I, James Pritchard, ea., *Ancient Near Eastern Text Relation to the Old Testament ANET* Princeton: Princeton University Press, 1969), 232; Arkell, *History of the Sudan*, 80.

34.   Inscriptions of Kames discovered in 1954 at Karnak by Labib Habachi. *ANET*, 555; Arkell, *A History of the Sudan*, 80.

35.   Budge, *Egyptian Sudan*, vol. 1, 564.

36.   Arkell, *A History of the Sudan*, 88, *ANET.*, 238.

37.   Ibid., 89, *ANET.*, 238.

38.   Budge, *Egyptian Sudan*, vol. 1, 605.

39.   Ibid., 536.

40.   Ibid., 631.

41.   Ibid., 637.

42.   Aezanas was the King of Axam. E.A. Wallis Budge, 69 *A History of Ethiopia, Nubia, and Abyssinia*, 2 vols. (London: Methuen an Co., l928),

252-58. See also Y. Adams, *Nubia: Corridor to Africa* (Princeton: Princeton University Press, 1977), 386-87. The date of King Aezanas is not certain but was generally dated 380 A.D. There is also no certainty whether "*Kasu*" (*Kush*) refers to Meroe City or generally to the territory of the ancient Kingdom of Kush. Y. Adams, Nubia, 247. However, the probability is that it refers to the continent which the black people inhabit.

43.   *ANET*, 292.

44.   Ibid., 293. See also Daniel David Luckenbill, *Ancient Records of Assyrians and Babylon* (New York: Greenwood Press, 1968), vol. 2, 228.

45.   D. D. Luckenbill, *Ancient Records of Assyria and Babylonia*, vol. 2, 285.

46.   Ibid., 224, 273-74.

47.   *ANET.*, 294. See also Luckenbill, *Ancient Records of Assyria and Babylon*, vol. 2, 292.

48.   Luckenbill, *Ancient Records of Assyria and Babylonia*, vol. 2, 325.

49.   Ibid., 340. 50 Ibid., 346.

51.   Ibid., 348.

52.   An inscription discovered in Ethiopia in 1914 has the word "Qevs" or "*Kesh*" on it. From this, some scholars conclude that the word *Kush* or *Cush* originated from Ethiopia rather than from Egypt or Israel. Although this may be possible, such conclusion based on one reference in one inscription which could not be dated with certainty yet could be too hasty. Perhaps, scholars would do better to wait for further archaeological discoveries in the present Ethiopia before any dogmatic conclusion could be made. For the above opinion, see *Egypt Revisited*, edited by Ivan Van Sertima (New Brunswick: Transaction Periodical Consortium, 1982), 139, 70.

53.   Ethiopia as used by the classical writers will be discussed in the following section.

54.   J. N. Oswalt, *"Kush,"* in *Theological Wordbook of the Old Testament*, vol. 2 Chicago: Moody Press, 1980 ,edited by R.L Harris, G.L. Archer, Jr. and Bruce K. Waltke, 435.

55.   Sir Alan Gardiner, *Egypt of the Pharaohs*, 59.

56.   Maspero, *The Dawn of Civilization*, vol. 1, 396.

57.   E.A. Wallis Budge, *The Egyptian Sudan*, vol. I, 512-513.

58.   Ibid., vol. 2, 415-16.

59.   George Rawlinson, *History of Ancient Egypt*, vol. 22 (Chicago: Clarke 4 Co., Publishers, n.d.), 72.

60.   Some of the listed products are ebony, woods, incense, balsam, precious metals, costly stones, rich beasts, camelopards, panthers and apes. The Egyptian gods which came from Egypt include Athor, Ammon, and Bes. Ibid., 73.

61.   David O'Connor, "Egypt, 1552-664 B.C.," *Cambridge History of Africa*, edited by J. D. Cleric (Cambridge: Cambridge University Press, 1982), 917-18.

62. A. J. Arkell, *A History of the Sudan*, 87.
63. *Cambridge History of Africa*, 928.
64. W. S. Smith, "The Old Kingdom in Egypt and the Beginning of the First Intermediate Period," *Cambridge Ancient History* (Cambridge: Cambridge University Press, 1980), 3rd edition, vol. 1, parts 2A, 183.
65. Hammamat Inscription of Hennu, found on the rock of Wadi Hammamat. Breasted, *ARE*, vol. 1, 208-10. Budge, *Egyptian Sudan*, vol. 2, 538. 71.
66. Ibid, vol. 1, 538.
67. Budge, *Egyptian Sudan*, vol. 1, 571.
68. Ibid., vol. 1, 573; Breasted, *ARE*, vol. 2, 267-72.
69. R. O. Faulkner, "Egypt from Inception of the Nineteenth Dynasty to the Death of Ramses III," *CAH*, VOL. "PART" A, 244-45. Breasted, *ARE*, vol. 4,~05.
70. *Egypt of the Pharaohs*, 34.
71. *When Egypt Ruled the East* (Chicago: University of Chicago Press, 19 2)
72. *A History of the Sudan.*
73. *Egyptian Sudan.*
74. *ARE.*
75. "The First Appearance of the Negroes in History," *Journal of Egyptian Archaeology* (1921):121-32.
76. *An Egyptian Hieroglyphic Dictionary* (New York: Dover Publications, 1978), reprinted from 1920 edition, vol. 1, 386.
77. Ibid. The word "Sudan" means "black" in Arabic.
78. Could mean the same with "*Nehesyu*" and plural of "*Nehesi*" or "*Nehsi.*"
79. Budge, *An Egyptian Hieroglyphic Dictionary*, p.386.
80. Ibid., 386. 72.
81. E. A. Wallis Budge, *The Egyptian Sudan*, vol. 1, p. 505. Egyptians divided the world into four quarters: Ta-Nehesu ("the Land of the Blacks"), Ta-Thehem ("the Land of the Libyans"), Ta-Aamu ("the Land of the Asiatics"), and Ta-Men ("the Land of the Egyptians"). The Heavens are also divided into four quarters and the Egyptians, the Asiatics, the Blacks and the Libyans would live in separate groups. Ibid., vol. 1, 500.
82. Budge, *Egyptian Sudan*, vol. 1, 559-60.
83. James Henry Breasted, *A History of Egypt* (New York: Charles Scribner's Sons, 1912), 212.
84. Junker, "The First Appearance of the Negroes in History," *JEA*, (1921), 121-32.
85. Ibid., 122-25.
86. Ibid., 122.
87. Ibid., 124-25.
88. The word in brackets is mine for the purpose of smooth pronunciation of the hieroglyphic word.

89. Junker, "The First Appearance of the Negroes in History," *JEA* (1921):124-25.
90. One of these Egyptologists is Jean Varcoutter, "The Iconography of the Black in Ancient Egypt from the Beginnings to the Twenty-fifth Dynasty," in *Images of the Black in Western Art*, (ed.) Jehan Desanges et. al., (New York: William Morrow and Co., 1976), 33-34.
91. Ibid., 134. The so-called "hamitic" has previously been discussed as arbitrary and of having neither biological nor historical basis by several anthropologists, Egyptologists, and others. The originator (Cuvier) used it probably because of his lack of proper understanding of the nature of Biblical materials especially the genealogical tables of Genesis. 73.
92. Sir Alan Gardiner, *Egypt of the Pharaoh*, 33-34.
93. Ibid, 33.
94. *A History of the Sudan*, 41. He translates Ta-Nehesi to mean The Land of the Southerners" instead of "The Land of the Blacks" of Budge.
95. *When Egypt Ruled the East*, 94.
96. *Before Color Prejudice*, 5.
97. *Image of the Black in the Western Art*, 34.
98. W. Y. Adams, *Nubia, Corridor to Africa* (Princeton: Princeton University Press, 1977), 8. Professor Budge also disagrees that there was any change in race for the Puntites.
99. In fact, several African scholars after an examination of several Egyptians and Nile Valley representations, have held very strongly that the Egyptians and the people of the Nile Valley are of one race—Negroes or Blacks. They emphasize that the so-called Hamitic race which some anthropologists and Egyptologists created from the Bible myth of Genesis 9:25, was an attempt to support their prejudices and myths that the Black has not made any contribution to the world and cannot be responsible for such a massive ancient civilization of Egypt and the Nile Valley. To them, it was a conspiracy to uproot Egypt and its civilization from Africa and then give the credit to the Asians. In other words, the idea of "Black-White" (that is, a person black in color and yet called a white person) is untenable. For adherents of this view, see J. G. Jackson, *Introduction to Civilization*, J. A. Rogers, *The Real Facts About Ethiopia* (Baltimore: Black Classic Press, 1982), J. G. Jackson, *Origin of Civilization* (Baltimore: Black Classic Press, 1939), Cheikh Anta Diop, *African Origin of Civilization: Myth or Reality?*, translated by Mercer Cook (Westport: Lawrence Hill & Co., 1974). See also *The Problems in African History*, edited by Robert O. Collins. Professor Charles B. Gopher aptly described the way this type of prejudice has dominated Egyptologists from the beginning. It is better to quote him:

A few years after Count Volney's trip came Napoleon's invasion of Egypt, 1798, and the opening up of Egypt for archaeological discovery.

The New Hamite Hypothesis, from the beginnings based upon theories about race which placed the Negro at the very bottom, could not permit a possibility that Negroes had developed the civilization of the Nile Valley. And by 1810 Blumenbach, pioneer in racial classification, was in Egypt studying human remains from those days until the present Egyptology has continued with one underlying motive being still to prove that the ancient Egyptians-African Cushites were not Negroes.

But modern Egyptology has been related to the Negro in still another way. It got under way at the very time that justifications for enslavement of Negroes were feverishly being sought;...in America there arose what has been called a "school of anthropologists" bent on debasing the Negro, and using Egyptology in such a way that one member of the school referred to his work as "Niggerology."And so on into the present, with Egyptologists either ignoring altogether a Negro presence or, at best, admitting of only a slight Negro element in the Cushite population. But now to a consideration of the archaeological evidence.

Charles R. Copher, "The Black Man in the Biblical World," *The Journal of the Interdonominational Theological Center*, vol. 1, no. 2, 1974. A personal interview with Professor Gopher during the Nile Valley Conference which took place in Atlanta on 26th-30th of September, 1984, is illuminating. He reminded me of another example of such modern scientific falsification based on prejudice. Dr. William Sharkly of Philadelphia claimed to have found evidence that black people are genetically inferior. Dr. Arthur Murphy of Baylor University denounced such scientific falsification based on prejudice as having no basis. However, one must avoid another type of counter prejudice by African or black scholars who maintain that all the people of the Near East, Africa, and Greece were originally black and that white people came from the black people, but became white as a result of a curse on Gehazi (2 Kings 5: 1-27). More shall be said about this later. Such scholars commit the same academic sin as their counterparts above. For this view, see Robert O. Collins, *Problems in African History*, 75 Sterling M. Means, *Black Egypt and Her Negro Pharaohs* (Baltimore: Black Classic Press, 1945). See most especially, Rudolph R. Windsor, *From Babylon to Timbuktu: A History of Ancient Black Races including the Black Hebrews* (Smithtown, N.Y.: Exposition Press, 1979), 25, for this theory.

100. *Image of the Blacks*, vol. 1, 34. Bruce G. Trigger, "*Nubia*,. Negro, Black, Nilotic?" in *Africa in Antiquity*, vol. 2, 27. See also A. C. Haddon, *History of Anthropology*, 76. Professor Haddon calls the term Caucasoid coined by Blumenbach "an unfortunate title," 72.

102. Budge, *Egyptian Sudan*, vol. 1, 507.

103. Breasted, *ARE*, VOL. 1, 66 and 147. See also Arkell, *A History of the Sudan*, 41.

104. Breasted, *ARE*, VOL. 1, 142. Pritchard, ed., *ANET*, 227-228.

105. J. A. Wilson in *ANET*, 443, translates *Nehesi* "Nubians." This text may be written during the Nineteenth or Twentieth Dynasty, but Wilson suggests it probably refers to the Sixth Dynasty. *ANET*, 442.

106. Arkell, *A History of the Sudan*, 59.

107. Wilson, *The Culture of Ancient Egypt*, 136-37.

108. Ibid., 163.

109. C. J. Gadd, "The Dynasty of Agade and the Gutian Invasion," *CAH*, VOL. 1, PART " A, 453-54.

110. Maspero, *The Dawn of Civilization*, vol. 2, 564.

111. Inscriptions of the Display of Sagon XIV, Sennacherib Historical texts, The Building Annals of Esarhaddon, and the Cylinder Texts of Assurbanipal (705-633 B.C.E.). See Luckenbill, *Ancient Records of Assyria and Babylonia*, vol. 1 and 2, 76.

112. Maspero, *The Down of Civilization*, vol. 2, op. cit., 564.

113. Robert R. Stieglitz, "Long-distance Seafaring in the Ancient Near East," *Biblical Archaeologist*, vol. 47, No. 3, Sept. 1984, 134-42.

114. Ibid., 138.

115. A. L. Oppenheim, *Ancient Mesopotamia* (Chicago: University of Chicago Press, 196), 63-64.

116. John Bright, *A History of Israel* (Philadelphia: Westminster Press, 1975), 2nd ea., 37.

117. Morris Jastrow, *The Civlization of Babylon and Assyria* (Philadelphia: J.B. Lippincott Co., 1915), 136.

118. Bright, *A History of Israel*, 37.

119. Gadd, *CAH*, vol. 1, part 2A, 453-54.

120. Stieglitz, *"Long-Distance Seafaring,"* 138-39.

121. Ancient Mesopotamia, 63-64 and 398.

122. Samuel Noah Kralner, *The Sumerians: Their History, Culture, and Character* (Chicago: University of Chicago Press, 1963), 269-303. See also Henry Frankfurt, *The Birth of Civilization in the Near East* (New York: Barnes and Noble, 195), 100-111; Michael Cheilik, *Ancient History* (New York: Barnes and Noble, 1969), p. 11; and C. L. Woolfey, *The Sumerians* (New York: W. W. Norton and Co., 1965), 189-90.

123. Grafton E. Smith, *The Ancient Egyptians and the Origin of Civilization* (Freeport: Books for Libraries Press, 1970), 86-87. Some Assyriologists also accepted the primary of Egyptian civilization. See Sir Henry Rawlinson, *History of Herodotus*, Book I, Translated by George Rawlinson, with Essay VI in its appendix, Book I. 77.

124. Runoko Rashidi, "The African Presence in Ancient Sumer and Elam," *Egypt Revisited*, edited by I. V. Sertima (New Brunswick: Journal of African

Civilization, 1982), 140. Also George O. Coat says that the Kushites colonized Mesopotamia around 2800 B.C.E. and introduced Babylonian or Sumerian civilization. *African Empires and Civilizations* (New York: African Heritage Studies, 197), 106. See also more discussion on this in Choikh Anta Diop, "Origin of the Ancient Egyptians," in General History of Africa, vol. 2, G. Mokhtar, UNESCO International Scientific Committee for Drafting a General History of Africa, 1981, 32.

125. Namely Professor Maspero, R. R. Stieglitz, Henry Rawlinson and others.

126. *ANET*, 268-69' Stieglitz, "Long Distance Seafaring," 138. Magan and Meluhha are mentioned as early as the period of Sargon of Agade. He mentioned that the boat of Magan, Meluhha and Dilmun anchored in his capital, Agade. Naram- sin said that he captured the King of *Magan* and obtained booty from *Magan*. Gudea mentioned trading with *Magan* and *Meluhha* where he obtained wood and gold for his temple. UrNammu spoke about returning the *Magan*-boats of Nanna. The Economic document of Naram-Sin also mentioned trade between Sumer and Magan and Melahha during the time of the Third Dynasty of Ur. Post-Sumerian documents (Assyrian records) linked specifically *Magan* with Egypt and Meluhha with Ethiopia in Africa.

127. Gadd, *CAH*, 132. There has been no known ancient record as early as the Third Millenium which mentions India or Arabia's popularity in supplying the ancient world such articles. On the other hand, Africa, namely, Egypt and Ethiopia, has been regarded as the main source of gold, wood, iron, resin and precious stones. The Egyptian Inscription of Una, Diodorus, Pliny and Strabo are clearly in support of this claim. Moreover, no country has been credited in the ancient time with such magnificent stone sculptured buildings, gold objects, and temples like Egypt.

128. Henri Frankfurt, *The Birth of Civilization in the Near East* (New York: Barnes and Noble, Fifth impression, 1968), 109. Those objects depicted in Egyptian monuments are costumes at Gebel et Arak, a scalloped battle Axe on the late predynastic stone vase and a ship. 78.

129. John J. Jackson, *Ethiopia and the Origin of Civilization* (Baltimore: Black Classic Press, 1939), 11-13; Sir Henry Rawlinson, *History of Herodotus*, Book I, translated by Professor George Rawlinson, with Essay VI in its Appendix, Book I.

130. Ibid., 12.

131. Ibid., 12-13.

132. Rashidi, "The African Presence," op. cit., 140. Also George O. Coats says that the Kushites colonized Mesopotamia around 2800 B.C.E. and introduced Babylonian or Sumerian civilization. *African Empires and Civilizations*, 106.

133. Flinders Petrie, *The Making of Egypt* (London: Sheldon Press, 1939), pp. 68-69. See also more discussion on this in Diop, *Origin of the Ancient Egyptians*, 32.

134. W. J. Perry, *The Growth of Civilization*, 2nd ed. (Harmondsworth: Penguin Books, 1937), 60-61.

135. Grafton E. Smith, *The Ancient Egyptians and the Origin of Civilization* (Freeport: Books for Libraries Press, new and revised edition and reprinted in 1970), 86-87.

136. There is a possibility that the word Meluhha refers, like the word Ethiopia, to the entire land of Africa south of Egypt. The place of gold may include the West African country of Ghana originally called "Gold Coast." *Meluhhans* are called the place of black men. *The Sumerians* (Chicago: University of Chicago Press, 1963), 277.

137. The Library Journal calls Professor Kramer "an uncontestable authority." See back cover of Kramer's book, *The Sumerians.*

138. Samuel Noah Kramer, *The Sumerians* (Chicago: University of Chicago Press, 1970), 61. 139 Ibid., 276-84. 79.

140. Hansberry, *Africa and Africans*, 5. The distinguished Egyptologist, E. A. Wallis Budge is therefore probably right when he maintains that it is unlikely that the word "Ethiopia" was invented by Homer. Ibid., 5.

141. Snowden, *The Image of the Black*, vol. 1, 138. According to Snowden, in the early Minoan period, the populations of the southern Crete probably included African peoples. Ibid., 136. A fragmentary fresco discovered at Thera in 1968 (dated between 1350-1500 B.C.E.) shows a black man with a thick lip. After S. Marinatos' examination of this fresco, he concludes that the characteristic seems to indicate an African. Ibid., 138. Another fresco depicting blacks dating to about the thirteenth century B.C.E. was found in the Palace of Nestor at Pylos. Ibid., 138. Sir Arthur Evans called the "coal-black" spearmen who appear in another fragment of a fresco, and belonging to Minoan II, "the captain of the blacks." Ibid., 138. The presence of these black men so early shows that the Greek writers are familiar with the African people and further authenticates their testimony concerning African men called Ethiopians. This section on Ethiopia was originally published in the African Christian Studies, vol. 8, no. 2, (1992) :51-54.

142. Some of the poets are Hesiod, Aeschylus, Apollonius, Quintus, Arctinus of Miletus. See Hansberry, *Africa and Africans*, 5.

143. The historians included Herodotus and Diodorus. Ibid., 5.

144. The geographers include Hecateaus, Ephorus, Eratosthenes, Agatharchides, and Strabo. Ibid., 5.

145. The naturalists include Pliny, Callisthenes and Heliodorus. Ibid., 5. In the examination of these Greco-Roman writers only a few representatives of major importance to our treatment of Ethiopia will be examined.

146. Ibid.

147. Ibid., 20.

148. Hansberry, *Africa and Africans*, 5.

149. Pliny, vi:187. 80.

150. Sylvia Pankhurst, *Ethiopia: A Cultural History* (Essex: House, 1959), 0.
151. Beardsley, *The Negro in Greek and Roman Civilization, xii.*
152. Snowden, *Before Color Prejudice*, 7. See also Pliny, *Natural History*, 2.80, Herodotus, 2.22 for the Greek ideas of the result of great heat.
153. Homer, *Illiad*, 1.423-24, 23.205-7.
154. *Odyssey*, 1.22-24; 4.84, 5.282; Hansberry, *Africa and Africans*, 74-75.
155. Hansberry, *Africa and Africans*, 102.
156. *Strabo*, 317.
157. *Hesiod, Theogony*, 984-85.
158. Hesiod, *Work and Days*, 527.
159. Beardsley, *The Negro in Greek and Roman Civilization*, 4. Prometheus, 808-9.
160. Ibid.
161. Harry E. Burton, *The Discovery of the Ancient World* (Cambridge: Harvard University Press, 1932),.
162. Ibid., 29.
163. Ibid., 31.
164. Ibid., 32.
165. Ibid. 81.
166. Haddon, *History of Anthropology*, 100-101. Professor Haddon says, "The writings of Herodotus (C. 480-425 B.C.) are a veritable storehouse of information from the highest civilizations down to the veriest savagery, and his work has lost none of its freshness or value through lapse of time. As a matter of fact, modern investigations, carried out in the areas treated by him, more frequently confirm and amplify rather than refute his statements."
167. Herodotus, VII, 70.
168. Budge, *A History of Ethiopia*, vol. 1, pp. vii-viii. Herodotus is probably justified in calling the black inhabitants of Asia Ethiopians not only because of their black color, but also because their various traditions, culture and religious practices link their origin to Africa. Some of these cultures have been discussed previously quoting Professor Henry Rawlinson's assertions. More of these traditions are written in Jackson, *Ethiopia and the Origin of Civilization*, 16-19; and "African Presence in Ancient Sumer and Elam," in *Egypt*, edited by Ivan Van Sertina, 137-47. Ephorus expressly stated that Ethiopians occupied both Asia and Africa. Egypt, 139. George O. Coats says that Kushites colonized Mesopotamia about 2800 B.C. The discovery of the Sumerian King of Gudea whose sculpture and physical characteristics have been regarded as black supports Herodotus' view. See *The Ancient Near East in Pictures Relating to the Old Testament*, 2nd edition with Supplement (Princeton, Princeton University Press, 1969), 150, figs. 430, 431.
169. *Herodotus*, VII, 70.
170. Ibid.,Book II, 114-15.
171. Ibid., VII, 69.

172. Ibid., IV, 42.
173. Ibid., 43.
174. E. H. Bunbury, *A History of Ancient Geography*, vol. 1, (New York: Dover Publication, 1959), p. 296. 82.
175. *Herodotus*, II, 2:137-40; 2:152-54.
176. Names of these Greek mercenaries who participated in the punitive expedition of Nubia appear in the inscriptions discovered in Abu Simbel. See *Image of the Black*, 139.
177. Herodotus, III, 17-20.
178. Ibid., III, 23; III, 114.
179. Ibid., III, 114; III, 20.
180. Ibid., III, 114; III, 23.
181. *Strabo*, II, 3.
182. Bunbury, *A History of Ancient Geography*, vol. 2, 74-77.
183. Ibid, 78.
184. Burton, *The Discovery of the Ancient World*, 91.
185. Ibid., 91.
186. Hansberry, *Africa and Africans*, 115. This attitude of trustworthiness toward Diodorus is probably due to his sources which he himself acknowledged—Agathar-chides, Artemidus, the Egyptians who were well-informed about Ethiopians and the Ethiopians themselves.
187. Diodorus, 3.8.5., 3.15.2., and 3.9.2.
188. Diodorus, 3.11, 3.2-3.7. Cf. Inscription of Hatshepsut.
189. Hansberry, 118.
190. Ibid., 120. 83.
191. Hansberry, p. 123. His first work on history that is now lost is *Historical Memoirs*. However, this work was mentioned by Plutarch, Josephus, and Strabo himself in his Geography.
192. Ibid., 124.
193. Ibid.
194. Strabo, 17.3.
195. Ibid., 17.2,3.
196. Strabo, 17.2; 17.53.
197. Ibid., 17.2-3.
198. Hansberry, *Africa and Africans*, 133. The members of the expedition suggested that it may be the portrait of Caesar which was referred to by Strabo. Strabo, 17.54.
199. Hansberry, 133; Strabo, 17.54.
200. Ibid., 180.
201. His sources include Herodotus, then Eratosthenes, Artemidorus, Dahon, Aristocreon, Basiles, Bion, Simonides the Yunger and Juba II, King of Numidia who wrote the history and geography of Ethiopia, Ibid., 137-39.
202. Ibid., 139-40.

203. Pliny, 5.8.46, 6.35.188.
204. Ibid., 6.3.194, 195.
206. Pliny, V.8. 84.
207. Bunbury, *A History of Ancient Geography*, vol. 2, 436.
208. Herodotus, IV.42. See also previous discussion on page 68. See also Bunbury, *A History of Ancient Geography* vol. 2, 74-77. Lady Lugard, the wife of the former governor of Nigeria commenting on the massive stone discovery in West Africa, suggested the possibility that the country of Chad and Nigeria were brought "under the same influence of civilization which spread from Ethiopia to ancient Egypt and thence to Europe and North Africa." *A Tropical Dependency: An Outline of the Ancient History of the Western Sudan with an Account of the Modern Settlement of Northern Nigeria* (New York: Barnes and Noble, 1965), 255-26.
209. Jackson, *Introduction to African Civilization*, 66.
210. Eugene A. Nida and Charles R. Taber, *The Theory and Practice of Translation* (Leiden: United Bible Societies, 1982), 8.
211. Ibid., 13.
212. Ibid., 30.
213. Ibid., 3.
214. Ibid., 1.
215. William L. Wonderly, *Bible Translations for Popular Use* (London: United Bible Societies, 1968), 7.
216. Nida and Taber, *Theory and Practice of Translation*, 2.
217. Bishop Alfred G. Dunston, Jr., *The Black Man in the Old Testament and Its World*, 20-21. R. L. Johnstone, *Religion and Society in Interaction* (Englewood Cliffs: Prentice-Hall, 1975). Johnstone says, "Early in colonial American history, the question arose concerning what to do about the religion of black slaves. One mandate said: Convert them to Christianity. but others said: You shouldn't hold a fellow Christian as a slave. Therefore what to do?...Some Southerners resolved by defining blacks as less than human. We don's convert dogs, Kudus, or zebras; therefore we don't need to convert blacks: as a lower animal form, they lack soul to be saved." Ibid., 218.
218. Dunston, *The Black Man in the Old Testament and Its World*, 18.
219. Ibid., 214.
220. It still means black In modern Hebrew language.
221. Africa has been used as a name of a person (Afficanus).

Chapter 3
Africa and Africans in the Torah

THE PRIMEVAL HISTORY

In chapter two, it has already been stated that "*Kush*" is the most frequently and the most extensively used word to refer to Africa and Africans in the Old Testament. The possibility that this word "*Kush*" was borrowed from the Egyptians has also been expressed. Out of the fifty-seven times in which the word "*Kush*" was used in the entire Old Testament, it appears five times in the Torah. It appears four times in the Primeval History (Gen. 2:10-14, 10:6-9), and only once during the wilderness period (Numbers 12:1). In the Torah, the term "*Kush*" is used only once as a geographical location (Gen. 2:10-14), and four times as names of persons. Although the exegesis of this section will center around the term "*Kush*," other terms (*Phut*, Ham, Mizraim and Nimrod) will also be discussed very briefly.

The materials in the Primeval History concern the origin of the world, of man, of sin, of nations, and traditions which tell about some events which took place in Africa.

African and the Garden of Eden (Gen. 2:10-14)[1]

Literary Analysis

Scholars have laboured unceasingly not only to analyse Genesis 2:10-14, but also to identify the rivers, in order to know the locality of the Garden of Eden. In their process of analyses many refuse to see any unity in the entire passage of Genesis 2-3.

Copen in his examination of Genesis 2-3 believes that nothing but ignorance of Hebrew and a total lack of critical judgement would permit one to see any kind of unity in this text.[2] Several scholars consider Genesis 2:10-14 as an original independent element which was later attached to the story in chapters 2-3 without complete assimilation into the text.[3] According to Claus Westermann, Genesis 2:10-14 is independent of the rest of the story in chapter 2—3 and that this passage was inserted with the purpose not to determine the location of the paradise, but "to point out" by way of parenthesis, that the "life-arteries" of all lands of the earth have their source in the river that water paradise.[4] He therefore, concludes that chapter 2:10-14 represents a great age of tradition and that the author of this text[5] does not mean to describe any geographical area.

However, other scholars see Genesis 2: 10-14 not as a secondary material inserted, but as an integral part of Genesis 2-3. Among these scholars who see a unity in 2-3 are Aalders.[6] Aalders, rejecting what he calls, "the source-splitting theory," says that the names of the rivers are not given for the purpose of identification and are "mentioned here only to indicate that these four streams had their source from that one great river that flowed through paradise.[7] Coats argues extensively to support the unity of Genesis 2-3. According to him, the structure of the story in the text does not support that chapter 2:10-14 is an independent narrative.[8] It will always be difficult to see any unity if one holds too strictly to the source analysis theory. The texts becomes fragmentary. However, when one considers the presence of reoccuring motifs (e.g. tree of life) and the dialectic parallel (paradise gained and paradise lost) in the narrative of chapters 2-3, one cannot but sees a unity.[9] Even though there is a shift in the style of the narrative in 2:10-14 from narrative to list, that does not make the passage secondary or independent. What appears to be responsible for that is probably the fact that the author of the narrative of Genesis 2-3 gathered his materials from diverse sources which he later assimilated. However, he fused them together in such a way to achieve unity in the material.[10] Therefore, Genesis 2:10-14 is an integral part of 2-3.

I shall not be able to go deeper further on the literary analysis of this paper since my major purpose is to discuss the possible source of the story in Genesis 2:10-14, the possible location of the rivers with various scholarly opinion put forward, and then, examine whether a more realistic conclusion can be reached in the light of the available discovery and tradition.

Source of the Story

Many scholars do not hesitate to suggest the source of the entire paradise story in Genesis 2-3 as Mesopotamia. According to E. A. Speiser, the fact that the terms `flow' and `Eden' have their equivalent in Akkadian and Sumerian Languages (2-6 flow- Akkadian, `edinu.' Sumerian, Eden) shows that the ultimate source of the story is in the ancient tradition belonging to the "Oldest cultural stratum of Mesopotamia.[11] George W. Coats, discussing the forms of the story considers the entire story in Genesis 2-3 as a tale whose early stages could be found in the tradition of Mesopotamian mythology with its derivation from the royal court and with the intention to "explore the limitation in human experience.[12] Morris Jastrow on the basis of similarity between the biblical Paradise and the "Myth of Adapa, Gilgamesh Epic and Enki Ninhursag, says that the biblical paradise must have a Mesopotamia source.[13] According to him the implied quest for immorality which actually ended in failure in the biblical story of paradise is a common feature of the "myth of Adapa and Gilgamesh Epic.[14] The common motif of enjoyment or pleasure abounds in both the biblical paradise and "Enki and Nihursag."[15] When one considers the linguistic similarity put forward by Speiser, the common motif of enjoyment and failure in both the Mesopotamian and biblical stories, it is difficult to deny the possibility that the Hebrews had a clear knowledge of the Mesopotamian stories mentioned above. However, I will hesitate to conclude that the ultimate source of the story is Mesopotamian. This hesitation is because of the strong possibility that the Hebrews had contact with other similar stories of other nations during their pre-Palestinian settlement. One of these nations is Africa. Africans have aboundance of oral tradition of the creation of man, God's provision, and eventual fall of mankind similar to both the Babylonian and the biblical stories. The following few examples of many versions of the stories of creation in Africa are below:

(1)   According to myths of Chagga[16] people of Tanzania, after God had liberated the first human beings by forcing open a mysterious vessel in which they were locked, he used to visit them every morning and evening to greet them and ask of their health. He commanded them to eat all the bananas and potatoes in the banana grove except the yam called *Ula* or *Ukaho* for if they eat it, their bones would break and they would die. A stranger came and deceived them to eat the forbidden yam. When sickness broke out as a result, the el Der prayed to God for mercy. God intervened but told him that when he grows old he would become young again by casting his skin like a snake. However, the process of casting this skin should be done in total secrecy. But when the man grew old and has to cast his skin, he sent away his grand-daughter for water in order to avoid her seeing the process of removing his skin. In the process of removing this skin in secrecy, the grand daughter arrived and saw him and the process ended immediately. Then the gift of rejuvenation was lost. The old man then mourned in sorrow:

So be it, I have died All of you will die, I have died All of you shall die For you grand-daughter Entered while I cast my skin

Woe is me, woe is you![17]

So the old man died.

(2)   The Bambuti people of Congo also had another fascinating tradition about God creating the world. God created the first person (*Baatsi*) by kneading a clay covered him with skin, poured blood into his body and whispered into his ears to bear children. Then the first man breathed and lived in the forest. He commanded him and his children, `From all the trees of the forest you may eat, except the *tahu* tree.[18] The man taught his children the commandment before he returned to heaven. But one day a pregnant woman who developed an irresistible desire demanded of her husband the fruit of the *tahu* tree. Her husband who refused at first later yielded, secretly plucked and gave her the forbidden fruit. Despite the fact that the peel was hidden very carefully, so that no one would know, the Moon reported the disobedience to God. God was angry and sent death as punishment

(3)   The Meru people of Kenya[19] believe that God made a boy first and when he complained to God that he had nobody to play with, God created a girl for him. Then he gave them food, but forbade them to eat the fruit of a tree. "A crawling creature (*Mugambi*) deceived them and the woman ate it and gave it to her husband. The result was that the man had "a throat apple."

(4)   The Shilluk of Sudan[20] told a story that people created by God originally lived with God in his land. Later they ate fruit which made them sick. Consequently, God sent them away.

Although there is no story of the river and the garden, there are different versions of the paradise which carry the same motif with the biblical and the Mesopotamian stories. According to the Yoruba myths,[21] the Supreme Being (*Olodumare*) gave his deputy (*Orisa-nla*) a primeval palm tree (*igi ope*) and other trees. The seed was to provide juice and kernels for drink and food respectively. Another version says there was "a Garden of Eden period when the heaven was very close to the earth but when a greedy person took too much food from heaven or that when the unsoiled face of the heaven was dirtied by a woman with her dirty hand, extensive gap occurred between the earth and the heaven.

The creation stories narrated above are just few examples from Africa. Different versions of these creation stories (we cannot narrate all here) scattered throughout Africa. These stories represent a floating oral traditions in Africa, passed from generations to generations probably with a pre-historic background. Throughout Africa, these stories, though told in different versions, have common motif of God's creation of the first person, his provision and enjoyment and failure of mankind as the biblical and Babylonian stories of creation.

From the above, this writer does not hesitate to conclude that the ultimate source of the story in Genesis 2-3 is probably Africa. The floating tradition was first circulated throughout Africa in the form of oral tradition and the Hebrews came in contact with this ancient African tradition in one or two of the three ways. The first probability is found in the biblical account (Ex. 12:40). According to the Bible record, the children of Israel lived in Egypt for about 430 years. It was probably this period that they came in contact with this ancient African floating tradition and mastered it. This is likely possible because before that and up to that period, the Kushite or *Wawat* or the *Medjay* were numerous in Egypt. They were the army and the police force defending the Egyptians.[22] By the time they reached Canaan, the story became handy to be used for the defence of their faith.

The second possibility is that the Mesopotamians heard about this tradition during their contact with the Africans as early as the Third millenium B.C.E.[23]

According to the inscriptions of Sargon of Agade and those of Gudea of Lagash the main article of trade between the Africans (called Magan Egypt and Meluhha Ethiopia) were "gold in dust form," stones, logs, ivory and others.[24] The similarity in their system of writing, the biblical tradition that Kush, Mizraim and Nimrod are brothers also support the early contact between Africans and Mesopotamians. The Mesopotamians perfected this ancient African tradition and by the time it got to Mesopotamia it took a new shape or different version by their localizing it and applying it to their gods. The children of Israel probably came in contact with this tradition when they reached the land of Canaan. They were also forced to express their experience and faith in form of this tradition. They did it perfectly well by polemicising and Yahwesizing the tradition.

The third possibility is that Israel were already aware of this tradition from the Africans when they were in Egypt but did not take it seriously until they came to Canaan where they came in contact with the Babylonian versions of the African tradition which threatened their faith in Yahweh.

Although this ancient African tradition of creation was expressed in different versions among the Babylonians, Israel and even among the Africans themselves, the essential motif and teaching as Africans understood it in the original version, remained undiluted.

In all these, some important facts should be recognized. The Paradise story has been fashioned into a unified narrative by the author of the biblical story to the extent that any foreign material that he used is difficult to trace. In the light of this, all that this writer can say is the "possibility" of the Paradise story having its ultimate source in African tradition rather than Mesopotamian.

The Location and the Identification of the River in the Garden of Eden

Having discussed the problem of the source of the story of Eden, the next problem which is of major importance to this section is the location and the identification of the garden. According to the narrative, it is evident that the location of the garden depends on the proper identification of the four rivers.

A close examination of the narrative reveals that certain words are repeated at least three times at the end of the word "river." The words *gan* (garden), *nahar* (river) *etz* (tree), *shem* (name), are repeated. The repetition seems to emphasize the importance of these words.

Although there is an agreement among some scholars concerning the identification of the third (Tigris) and the fourth (Euphrates) rivers,[25] the proper identification of the first (Pishon) and second (gihon) has been problematic.

Pishon has been associated with canals such as Pallakopas in Mesopotamia, Phasis or Araxes, Wady Dowasir in Arabia, Indus and Ganges rivers in India.[26] Gihon has been associated with Oxus, Shatt en Nil, Khosper in Mesopotamia, Waddy Rum in Arabia and the Nile river in Africa.[27]

In order to determine the appropriate location of these two problematic rivers, it is important to examine the biblical description of these rivers. Pishon flows around the whole land of Havilah. Havilah is considered as a land of gold, bdellim and onyx stone.[28] The name Havilah occurs also in Genesis 10:7, I Chronicles 1:9 as a son of *Kush,* and in Genesis 10:29, I Chronicle 1:23 as the son of Joktan. Another occurrence is in Genesis 25:18 as the territory where the Ishmaelites lived. In I Samuel 15:7, Saul pursued the Amalekites from Havilah to Shur. Although Havilah has been variously located, some scholars locate it somewhere in the West Coast of Arabia where existed a region called Haulah according to a Sabean inscription.[29]

When one examines the description of the product of the land of Havilah (gold, bdellium and onyx stone) which the river Pishon surrounds, it appears as if such a description should aid scholars in the identification of this land in Genesis 2:11. The question which is important to determine the location of Havilah is, which country or land is regarded as most famous for gold and precious stones in antiquity?[30]

It is clear that according to the Sumero-Akkadian document, the Egyptian hieroglyphics and the Greek records, Africa South of Egypt (*Kush, Punt* or Ethiopia) has been the most famous place for these products of Havilah. Then if this conclusion according to the ancient documents is accepted and Havilah is referred to as the "son of *Kush*" in the biblical record, the most likely location of the land of Havilah is somewhere in Africa, south of Egypt.[31] It is possible then that the Pishon River is located somewhere in Africa south of Egypt. Gihon flows around the land of *Kush*. It appears that the identification of the Gihon river rests exclusively on the identification of the land of Kush. The debate concerning the location of Kush is still going on. Scholars hold the opinion that this "*Kush*" in Genesis 2:13 cannot be Africa but the Asiatic *Kush*.[32] This automatically takes any attempt to identify Gihon with the Nile river.

Aalders and Francisco give some reasons why they think that river Gihon could not be the river Nile and *Kush* could not be Africa. Since the river Nile was well known to the ancient Hebrews, its common name (Nile) would have been used if it was the Nile river. If the river Gihon had been the river Nile, the Hebrews would have said that it flows through Egypt instead of *Kush*.[33] These two reasons are not valid reasons. Probably Aalders, Francisco and Westermann have not noticed the fact that the names of these two rivers, Pishon and Gihon are Hebrew descriptive or translation names of these rivers and that they may not be the names of the rivers as used in their respective home countries.[34] Several facts show that it is highly probably that *Kush* of Genesis 2:13 refers to Africa.

According to the ancient Egyptian records (where this term originates), the term "*Kush,*" "*Bash*" or "*Kesh*" refers exclusively to Africa south of Egypt.[35] In the ancient Assyrian records (especially from 8th Century B.C.E.), the word "*Kush*" or "*Kusu*" unquestionably refers to Africa.[36] Virtually every place where the Biblical record makes the identification of the term "*Kush*" unquestionably clear, it refers to Africa and has not in any place unquestionably referred to Asia. Admittedly, the present geographical knowledge of either Africa and Asia, has not yielded any suitable identifiable location which absolutely fits the rivers as described in Genesis.[36] Since no one river which flows through the land of Assyria,

Africa, Arabia and India, some scholars have concluded that the rivers are not locatable. C.T. Francisco has a summary of those conclusions:

(1)   The writer, who is no student of geography, is saying that all the rivers of the earth came from the primeval source (von Rad).

(2)   The passage is taking a mariner's view of the rivers, the river source being the Persian Gulf and the four river mouths issuing from it (Kidner).

(3)   The four rivers reflect traditions about the great civilizations of the ancient world. Far East (Indus), Egypt (Nile), and Mesopotamia (Tigris and Euphrates). These civilizations had their source in one original culture the ideal Garden of Eden.[37]

In the light of what appears to be an unsolved problem which led eminent authorities to conclude that no place exists on earth as described in the text, one is tempted to go along with the majority opinion. However, scholars must not ignore the possibility that Genesis 2:10-14 represent an ancient tradition which has a historical foundation, and retold to teach certain truths. Although it is not a scientific history in the sense of modern historiography, this ancient tradition which has a foundation in history may be recited by the author to reveal a theological truth with a foundation in history.[38] If this locality (the garden and the rivers) exists, it may be in Africa *Kush*, the possible ultimate source of the story as disclosed earlier) rather than Mesopotamia. Several reasons could be responsible for the confusion in the description of the rivers.

Since tales repeatedly told and diffused in different places loose their original proper names and local color, it is possible that the original tradition from Africa has lost some of its original proper names and color, but still retaining at least one name (*Kush*). The mentioning of other rivers (Tigris and Eupharates are a well known rivers in Mesopotamia) was an attempt to localise the floating ancient African tradition in Mesopotamia.

It appears that the conclusion that the source of the story and the possible locality for the garden of Eden could be in Africa is supported not only by Africa and biblical traditions, and ancient historians, but also by modern science in their discoveries which demand a reassessment of scholars view that such a place never existed. In 1984, the American Suttle (NASA), through its powerful microscope was able to penetrate beyond the earth land surface while in the space. The result was a startling discovery of "an old river system complete with valley and channel and gravel and sand bar that had been covered with sand sheet" in the southern portion of Egypt.[39] This system, according to the Sir-A-images, was as " large and as complex as the present Nile river.[40] In cooperation with the Geological Survey of Egypt and U.S. Agency for international development, Cairo, and U.S.G.S. Scientists have visited the location of the ancient river and have dug test pits in the ancient river and stream beds for verification of the sir-A data. Along the radar detected river were hand axes and ash layers which are the evidence of the presence of pre-historic people who "migrated to Europe by following the river path" because similar stone age was found in Europe.[41] Further tests show that the area has changed from savanah to desert over the years.

In a recent scientific study by Allan Wilson of the University of California, Berkeley, humanity's family tree was traced to an ancient African Mom.[42] Using genetic engineering techniques in order to highlight normal variations in the genes ("Restriction fragment length polymorphisms"), it was concluded that every human being originated from "one woman who live in Africa.[43] In the Dallas Times Herald, it was reported:

Everyone on earth descended from a woman who lived in Africa about 200,000 years ago... studies of the genes of 147 people from around the world allowed him to reconstruct a family tree relating the individuals to one another. The family tree springs from one woman who lived in Africa between 140,000 and 280,000 years ago, Wilson reported.[44]

The biblical tradition derived the civilization of Asshur from Nimrod who was the son of *Kush*.[45] The ancient Greeks believed that the Africans (Ethiopians) were the first of all men, they originated worship of gods, and sent out colonies.[46] If Africans were the first of all men, and, a locality for the garden of Eden existed, it should be in Africa.

Although this is far from solving the problem of location entirely, the American Shuttle discovery, the result of other scientific researches, the testimonies of ancient Greek Scholars, some section of the biblical narrative referring to river Kush and the biblical tradition of deriving the civilization of Asshur from Nimrod, the source of Kush river point to Africa as the most likely location of the garden of Eden. The above should serve as a caution for most scholars who hastily denounce the possibility of locating the garden of Eden. Further scientific discovery may yield further evidence supporting Africa as the appropriate location of the garden of Eden in Mesopotamia.

Africa and the Table of Nations
(Gen. 10:6-10 and I Chron. 1:-25)[47]

A close examination of the Table of Nations shows that three different formulas exist. Verses 2-4, 6-7, 22-23 use the formula *Benei*. Verses 8, 13-18, 24, 26-29 use *yalad*. Verses 21 and 25 use *Yalad*. This chapter of the Table of Nations also displays a tripartite division: the sons of Japhet (verses 2-5) the sons of Ham (verses 6-20) and the son of Shem (verses 21-31). Since the time of Wellhausen, on the basis of the above formula and divisions, scholars have sought to assign this passage to different sources. Skinner, Gunkel, von Rad and others believe that this text achieves its form by a combination of Priestly and Yahwistic Table of Nations.[48] Robert H. Pfeiffer maintains that part of Genesis chapter 10 (10:9, 14) was written or revised by R (the redactor who inserted S and S materials into the Pentateuch).[49] Simons, who denies the existence of two sources, used this formula to identify what he calls the original nucleus.[50] Grau considers verses 2-4, 6-7, 13-18a, 21-29a, the "discernible nucleus."[51] Although chapter ten appears composite in nature, the variation may be an attempt to avoid too much redundancy, and to achieve artistic literary beauty by the final editor.[52] A close examination of this chapter shows that there is one basic theme and message. Even though some existing sources might be used, Chapter ten appears to be one genealogy, by one author, and one editor.

C. T. Francisco[53] sees some definite schematic arrangement in the list of the nations. Seven and twelve are the prominent numbers used for this scheme. The sons and grandsons of Japhet are seven. The total sons and grandsons of Kush are seven. So also are the sons of Egypt and his descendants seven. The sons of Shem up to Peleg are twelve. Canaan are twelve. Such formula, according to Francisco,[54] is a mnemonic device.[55]

Date

While von Rad dates this material in Chapter ten between the seventh and sixth centuries B.C.E., Cassuto, Francisco and Herman Gunkel date this material earlier.[56] Although it is difficult to hold any dogmatic date for this material, it is highly probable that these materials, and especially the names, represent a tradition dating to the prehistoric period which has been preserved orally. The fact that Israel is absent from the picture shows the antiquity of the tradition. The absence of Israel in the list is not because Israel never became a great nation (except in the time of David and Solomon) but because the tradition is probably earlier than the formation of the Hebrew people. The antiquity of the material may also be the reason why Moab and Edom are absent from the list. However, one must admit the possibility that the compilation and the editorial work which resembles that of P may be late. Ham has four sons, *Kush*, Egypt, Put and Canaan. Ham is the second son of Noah (Gen. 5:32; 6:10; 7:13; 9:18; and I Chr. 1:4). Egypt was originally called Kham or Ham. ("the black land,"). Ham does signify "black"; the name probably refers to the early inhabitants of Egypt who are Black people as represented by the Hebrew Hams.[57] Kam in Egyptian language could also mean "to create." Therefore it could mean the created land.[58]

Kush, Put and Nimrod

The term *Kush* originated from Egypt to refer to their southern neighbors. The Assyrians and the Hebrews borrowed this word to refer to the people of black skin in Africa and their land. The idea of Speiser, Rawlinson, and Driver that Kish in Genesis 2:13 and Chapter 10 cannot refer to African *Kush*, but to the Kassites is rejected by this writer.[59] Professor Driver thinks that *Kush* in Genesis 2:13 and chapter 10 cannot refer to African *Kush* because it is strange that Ethiopia should be mentioned as the home of Nimrod; it is also strange that through him the Babylonian and Assyrian civilization began.[60] Perhaps these scholars are either not aware of or refused to accept the various traditions and scientific discoveries which support the idea that Africa is the origin of civilizations and the origin of human race and not Babylonia.[61] Therefore there is no reason why it should be considered strange.

The word Mizrim is translated "Egypt." The Assyrians called Egypt *Muzr*, probably relating to *Muzau* which means "source" or "an issue of valuer, a gathering or collecting."[62] This word Misrim derived from the Egyptian word Mesh, which means the "product of the river and the cake." The Samaritan Pentateuch (Gen. 26:2) renders *Misrim* as *Nashim* which means "a birthplace," [63] with a sense of issuing forth. In Aramaic, it means "to go out," but in Egyptian it is the equivalent of "*nefika*" indicating "inner land of breath, expulsion" or "going out."[64] Put is named as the son of Ham. Put is mentioned in several places in the Bible.[65] In all these passages where Put was mentioned, it appears that there is no clear answer to the proper identification of Put. The majority of scholars, however, identified Put with Libya for the following reasons.[66]

(1)   In inscriptions of Darius at Maqsh-i-Rustam and of Xerxes at Parsepolis, a region called Putaya is mentioned in association with Ethiopia, and Carians as a province of the Persian Empire.

(2)   The Septuagint translated Put of the Masoretic text as "Libyan.

(3)   In the inscription of Nebuchadnezzar which refers to the Egyptian campaign, a reference to a city called Pu-tu- ja-a-man (Putn of Yawan) is said to favor the location of Put at Cyrene.

The argument supporting the location of Put in Libya is unconvincing. Sometimes, the word "*Kush*" is used to mean the area of Meroe and another time to include the entire land south of Egypt. The Septuagint sometimes changes the actual meaning of some words to suit the need of the Alexandrian reader. In the biblical rendering, the words Ludim and Lehabim would fit more appropriately to mean Libya. It is more probable then to associate Put with Punt of the Egyptian. In this case, it means that the Hebrew writers probably dropped the Egyptian "n" and called it Put. Punt is in close association with Ethiopia. There is also a possibility that Put means a tribe in the southern part of Meroe. At this point all that can be said is possibility since there has been no clear-cut evidence for the location of Put. What appears certain is that it is located somewhere in Africa. Time shall not be wasted on the location of Canaan, since it is universally known that it refers to the people and the land of Palestine, part of Jordan and Syria during the pre-Israelite times.

The sons of *Kush* are Sebe, Havilah, Sabtah, Ra'amah and Saptecs. The sons of Ra'amah are Sheba and Dedan. Much uncertainty still remains concerning the exact location of three names. Some scholars assigned them to the Arabian tribes. But those names probably belong to some African tribes as evident from the fact that they all derived from *Kush*.

The Nimrod passage is of special importance to this discussion because Nimrod is the only person about whom some substantial information about the early civilization is recorded in this chapter (Gen. 10:6-12). Simpson attributes the statement that he was the first on earth to be a mighty man to J and the statement "The beginning of his kingdom was Babel to J." [67] The Nimrod passage has been considered by some to be out of place or an example of textual corruption.[68] Skinner accepts the fact that all names mentioned in chapter ten are names of real cities, tribes or persons except Nimrod.[69] Grau considers verses 1-11 secondary materials.[70] Francisco believes that it is quite possible that the compilers did not understand some of the names in the table of Nations.[71]

Scholars who believe that Nimrod is a historical person have to identify him with several figures in history. Amenhotep III (1411-1375) was suggested by Sether.[72] This is because he was mentioned in Armana Letters as "Nimmuris" and he boasted that he extended his Kingdom as far as to Euphrates. He said that he hunted for lions and wild beasts.[73] Although this is a very attractive suggestion because it still puts Nimrod in the context of Africa (Egypt), yet it appears unlikely because Amemhotep III did not originate any civilization. Nimrod was also associated with Nazi-Maruttas (1350 B.C.E.) of the Kassite Dynasty.[74] This is very unsatisfactory, because he was not considered a successful ruler of the Kassite Dynasty. Other scholars have identified Nimrod with King Lugalanda of the second Babylonian Dynasty after the flood because his name was also read "Nin-Maradda."[75] King Narasin of Akkad (2700 B.C.E.)[76] and Tukulti-Ninurta I of Assyria were also suggested.[77] Nimrod has also been identified with Marduk,[78] Gilgamesh and the Sumarian god Ninurta.[79] The exact identification of Nimrod admits no satisfactory solutions, and will probably remain a strange puzzle until further light can be shed through some spectacular archaeological discovery.

Source

While Cornfeld and Freedman suggest that the Table of Nations derived from Mesopotamian sources,[80] Hermann Gunkel considers it a legend which wandered from race to race, and probably reached Canaan as early as the second Millenium B.C.E.[81] This legend was then "adopted by Israel just as it was assimilating the civilization of Canaan." [82] Meyer thinks that it originated from Libya where a name nmrt/nrro is common.[83]

The majority of scholars see the Table of Nations as Israel's political world view. Von Rad considers it a comprehensive survey of international relations which the author used to tell of the fulfilment of God's command to "multiply," "replenish" and "fill the earth."[84] Brueggemann sees it as "a verbal map of the world," probably reflecting a political world of Solomon's periods.[85] Rawlinson considers the Table of Nations as an earliest ethnographical essay, "written by a Jew and for the Jews," which contains the names of the countries in which the Jews at the date of its composition had some acquaintances.[86]

However, a very careful examination of Genesis chapter ten reveals that the names of places, persons and tribes mentioned are real. It is noteworthy that when the majority of the names occur somewhere else in the Scripture, they occur as real names of people, places and tribes also. It is clear that the content of the Table of Nations deals with a certain time in antiquity, to be more specific, a prehistoric period, when mankind began to migrate and also began to build civilization. To accept the idea that the writer was using the political realities of the Solomonic period (Brueggemann), or of the seventh to sixth centuries (von Rad), is unlikely.[87] This will amount to saying that Genesis 10 was a backward projection of Israel's present political situation. What appears to have taken place is that the writer made use of a floating ancient tradition which originated from a foreign land. This ancient tradition which has its foundation in pre-history,[88] originated somewhere in Africa south of Egypt. From there it was transmitted orally to Egypt where the Hebrews probably first heard of it. From Egypt, it went to the outside world Mesopotamia, Greece, Persia, and others. It is difficult to determine the exact place in Africa south of Egypt, but it is unlikely that it would be Libya. A heroic figure whose name resembles that of Nimrod exists among the Yoruba people of Nigeria. The name is "*Lamurudu*" or *Namurudu*. Samuel Johnson and Modupe Oduyoye considered *Lamurudu* or *Namurudu* as "a dialectic modifica-tion of the name Nimrod. This could be possible when one considers the fact that the consonants "L" and "N" can be used interchangeably and that "Nimrod" and Namurudu have the same consonants (NMRD).[89]

This ancient African tradition is well known in the Greek tradition and history. Memnon, king of Ethiopia, in *Homer's Iliad*, led an army of Elamites and Ethiopians for the assistance of King Priam in the Trojan War. He started the expedition from African Ethiopia, passed through Egypt, then to troy. According to Herodotus, this Ethiopian king founded Susa which is the chief city of the Elamites.[90]

American ancient tradition also appears to be in accord with the Greek's. It says that the name "*Kush*" also applied to Persia, Media, Elam and Aria or the whole region between the Indus and Tigris rivers. Moses of Kherene, an American historian, identified king Belus of Babylon with Nimrod, and that Nimrod was the grandson of *Kush* (Ethiopia) and a son of *Mizraim* (Egypt).[91]

The fact that the result of craniological research, linguistic studies, comparative religious and philosophical beliefs show that the similarities between the ancient Mesopotamian and the Africans far exceed what may be regarded as a coincidence or chance; it is irrefutable evidence for African origin of Sumerian civilization or Kingdom as the book of Genesis seems to suggest. To this, Henry Field testifies:

> The earliest historical crania (hyperdollchocephalic) are from Jemdet Nasr 18 miles northeast of Kish and those from Y trench at Kish... The forehead is retreating, the browrid are always prominent, and the cheekbones rather wide. The nose is broad, in some cases inclining to extremely platyrhine, although the face has seldom survived. This is the type described by Sergi Giuffrida Ruggeri and Fleure and named Eurafrican type.[92]

Professor Charles H. Hapgood, of the University of New Hampshire, having made a special study of the ancient map, published his findings in *Maps of the Ancient Sea Kings*. In chapter eight of his work which he entitled "A Civilization That Vanished," he made the following remark: "The evidence presented by the ancient maps appears to suggest the existence in remote, before the rise of any of the known cultures, of a true civilization, of a comparatively advanced sort, which either was localized in one area but had worldwide commerce, or was, in a real sense, a world-wide culture. This culture, at least in some respects, may well have been more advanced than the civilization of Egypt, Babylonia, Greece, and Rome. In astronomy, nautical science, map making and possibly ship-building, it was perhaps more advanced than any state of culture before the 18th century of the Christian era.[93]

Although Professor Hapgood did not name either the people or the part of the world...this ancient culture might have originated, a German historian of good reputation has no hesitation of locating it among African Ethiopians. A. H. Herren says:

> In Nubia and Ethiopia, stupendous, numerous, and primeval monuments proclaim so loudly a civilization contemporary to, age, earlier than that of Egypt, that it may be conjectured with the greatest confidence that the arts, sciences, and religion descended from Nubia to the lower country of Mizraim.[94]

The French orientalist, Count Constance Volney, after visiting Africa, was very emphatic about the origin of civilization:

> There a people, now forgotten, discovered, while others were yet barbarious, the elements of arts and sciences. A race of men now

rejected from society for their sable skin and frizzed hair, founded or study of the laws of nature, those civic and religious systems which still govern the universe... It would be easy to multiply citation upon this subject; from all which follows, that we have the strongest reasons to believe that the country neighbouring to the tropic was the cradle of sciences, and consequence that the first learned nation was a nation of blacks; for it is controvertible, that by the term Ethiopians, the ancients meant to represent a people of black complexion, thick lips and wooly hair.[95]

The writer of the biblical genealogy is not mixed up or immersed with what can be called "scholastic racism" like some of the modern scholars. Through the special ability to commit oral traditions into memories, like Africans, they were able to pass it on without much distortion. They preserved the essential historical truth (that is, the Sumerians and African are related and the origin of the Sumerian civilization is Africa) in the tradition, while using it to express their theological truth. This theological truth is the fundamental unity of mankind. That all mankind originated from one source and are one, family is the purpose of Genesis chapter ten.[96]

This central teaching of Genesis 10, that mankind is of one family, is also affirmed not only by the biblical writers but also by modern science and scholars who have not allowed prejudice and racism to distort their scientific findings. The founder of the science of anthropology and a professor in Gottingen University, Johann Friedrich Bluemenbach, using a comparative anatomy and craniemotrical research, did not only emphasize the essential unity of mankind, he recognized and unequivocally stated that the classification of the so called "varieties" of mankind are arbitrary. He says:

> Very arbitrary indeed both in number and definition have been the varieties of mankind accepted by eminent men... no variety of mankind exists, whether of colour, countenance, or stature, etc., so singular as not to be connected with others of the same kind by such an imperceptible transition, that it is very clear they all related or any differ from each in degree.[97]

Conlin Edwin, after his systematic research, generally agreed that "there is, at present, but one species of man, namely, homo sapien and that all races and varieites have arisen in the first instance from a common human stock." [98] Also at the scientific congress on race, van Luschan declared: "fair and dark races, long and shortheaded, intelligent and primitive, all come from one stock."[99] Finegan reported one of the great American physicians, Dr. Thomas Dooley, as saying the following concerning the unity of mankind.

> I have examined many sick children in America, in Africa, and in Asia. I have been struck by the fact that all of these children have hearts, lungs, kidneys and other organs that are absolutely identical—that even the pattern of veins on the back of their hands is the same the world over. We are all made on the same pattern, and we are molded in the same image.[100]

Such are the unanimous voices of scholars in accord with the teaching of Genesis chapter ten that mankind is of one family.

AFRICAN IN THE EXODUS PERIOD

African Wife of Moses
(Num. 12:1-9)

Throughout the period of Exodus, what appears to be the only reference to an African is in Numbers Chapter 12:1. The treatment of this passage shall involve the analysis of the passage, the identification of this Kushite woman and of what might be considered to be the probable role of this woman in the leadership role of Moses. During the fortieth year of the Israelites coming out of Egypt while encamped at Hazeroth, an important event took place. Moses, the leader of the Children of Israel married a Cushite woman (*KUSITH ISSAH*). This brought disagreement among Moses, Miriam and Aaron and punishment.

Analysis of the Passage

Many scholars, for several reasons, propounded the view that Numbers chapter twelve is not a single literary unit. This is, as noted by scholars, because there are two different oppositions to Moses—one to his marriage and a second to his uniqueness. The fact that punishment was restricted to Miriam while Aaron was equally guilty, and the use of the feminine singular *watedabar* "and she spoke," shows that Aaron may be an addition. The double summons (4-5) and the double departure (9b-10) are used as evidence for a disunity. Thus some also conclude that there may be a base narrative which was later supplemented by other materials.[101] However, no unanimous agreement among scholars exists concerning the extent of supplementation. While Martin Noth considers it to be limited to verses 2-8, G.W. Coats believes this supplement to be verses 2-9 and 11b,[102] V. Fritz finds it in verses 2-9b, 10b-12. W. Rudolph detects additions in verses 2-8, 10a, and 11.[103]

Mostly on the basis of prophetic interest detected in the passage, some scholars assigned the base narrative to the Elohist source (E).[104] O. Eissfeldt makes a distinction between E (the verses most scholars believe to be supplementary), and the source L (the verses which most scholars consider to be the base narrative). F.M. Cross proposed the possibility of a priestly controversy lying behind the entire story, and that this first stratum functions to affirm the legitimacy of the Mushite priesthood (Mosses) and the second stratum the superiority of the Mushite priesthood over Aaron.[105]

Most scholars assign this passage to the Yahwist (J) on the basis of the appearance of some words and phrases characterized by J.[106] The phrases, "the face of the earth" in verse 3, and "O my Lord" in verse 11 are said to be characteristic of J. Noth contends that since Miriam is a Kadesh figure (Numbers 20:1), this passage should be considered J's.[107] S.R. Driver sees a combination of J.E. in the narrative.[108] When Numbers chapter 12 introduces the marriage of Moses with the Cushite woman and it appears as if that would be the subject of the entire story, the subject seems to suddenly change and was not directly mentioned again. This sudden shift from this problem to the question of Moses' prophetic authority in verses two through sixteen is an evidence "that the Yahwist has built the story from a brief isolated data in tradition," according to Budd.[109] All these approaches of dividing the text into such fragmentary materials is not necessary. One can read a definite sequence in the story. But many scholars, preoccupied with separating the sources, do not see the possibility of a definite sequence and a unity in the story.[110] The narrative can be imaginatively reconstructed.

(1)   Moses needed a wife and consulted God.

(2)   God appeared to Moses, his servant, and spoke to him "face to face" telling him to marry a Cushite woman.

(3)   Moses then declared to his people that God had commanded him to marry an African woman.

(4)   Miriam, the prophetess, unhappy with the incident, persuaded Aaron to join her, and they spoke against Moses' marriage

(5)   Miriam also claimed she had seen a vision that Moses should have not done that. This vision of Miriam is highly probably because of the statement in verse 2 and Yahweh's reply in verse 7 and 8. Note the intensity in Miriam's question: "Has the Lord indeed spoken only through Moses?" The expected answer is supposed to be no because the next question, "Has he not spoken through us also?" implies that Miriam was claiming that as God has spoken through Moses (probably to marry a black African woman), so also he has spoke through them that Moses should not have married her."[111] Note the way Yahweh answered Miriam and Aaron. Speaking of Moses he says, "He is entrusted with all my house. With him I speak mouth to mouth, clearly, and not in dark speech; and he beholds the form of the Lord." (Num. 12:7-8)

Miriam alone was punished with leprosy because, since she was a prophetess who claimed to have seen a counter-vision, she was the leader and mouthpiece of her group. If the passage is examined this way it is possible to see it as one story and one event and probably written by one author.

Identification of the Cushite Woman

Like other passages where the exact geographical identification of the term "Cushite" was not given by the Hebrew writers, scholars have spent much energy to identify the Cushite woman Moses married. Many scholars identified her with Zipporah, the Midianite (Ex. 21:7).[112] Ibnu-Ezra and Augustine[113] are early scholars who did this. J.J. Owen compares the Cushite in Numbers 12:1 with "Cushan" in Habakkuk 3:7 which he identifies with Midian, and concluded on the basis of parallelism that the Cushite woman in Numbers 12:1 must be Zipporah.[114] Elliot Binns also identifies the Cushite woman with Zipporah. He said that Miriam was jealous, because it may be that when Zipporah was away to Midian there was no challenge, but when she returned, Miriam's prestige diminished.[115] This has no basis whatsoever. Even though John Marsh admits the difficulty involved with the identification of the Cushite woman with Zipporah, he is emphatic that the Cushite woman cannot refer to an African, but Zipporah.[116] Martin Noth denies that the Cushite woman refers to an African or the Midianite because Egypt is far removed from Moses sphere of activity and that the woman belongs to the tribe or confederacy of tribes parallel to Midian.[117] However, what the name of the tribe or confederacy is, he does not say. G.B. Gray does not even attempt to identify the Cushite woman, because he thinks that the verse is an editorial insertions.[118] What you have seen above is the evidence of de-Africanization of the Cushite woman by most Euro-American biblical scholars.

A close examination of this passage (Numbers 12) and other related passages which dealt with *Kush*, Miriam and Midian shows that the Cushite woman cannot be Zipporah, but an African woman for the following reasons:

(1)   The passage does not make any atempt to associate the Cushite woman with Zipporah or a Midianite, therefore such should not be assumed.

(2)   It does not make sense for Miriam to speak against Moses because of a wife (Zipporah) whom Moses had married so many years ago. Yet the reason for Miriam's anger cannot be because the Cushite woman was black. There is no idea of prejudice against black people throughout the scripture as the modern Western prejudice against black and other world races. What is the likely reason for the anger is that the Cushite was a foreign woman who did not actually know Yahweh.

(3)   Midian and Zipporah were never referred to as *Kush* or Cushite in all the biblical record. Midian and *Kush* or Midianite and Cushite were never used interchangeably in either the biblical, the Egyptian, or the Assyrian records. Jethro was never called a Cushite. Josephus differentiated between Midian and *Kush*.[119] In this regard the margin note of Dake's Annotated Reference Bible which says that the land of Midian in Arabia was the land of *Kush* "Midian was a son of Abraham through Keturah" and that "Moses married a descendant of the son of Abraham and not a member of a Negro race" is misleading.[120]

(4)   The Hebrew clause *al-odoth haissah haklusseth eser lagah, Ki-issah Kusith lagah* ("because of the Cushite woman which he married" (literally took), "for he had married a Cushite woman") strongly implies a recent marriage. Therefore the Jewish tradition of equating the Cushite woman with Zipporah has no basis. It was probably an apologetic device to keep Moses a monogamist.[121]

(5)   In every reference in the Biblical, Egyptian and Assyrian records where the word "*Kush*" is used with a clear geographical or personal identification, it always refers to Africa. An Egyptian inscription as

early as the sixth Dynasty, under Pepi II has the earliest reference to
`Kush'. This monument, the inscription of Ameni, tells us that the king
travelled south, overthrew his enemies, "the abominable *Kash*,"
obtained tributes, past the boundary of *Kush*, to the end of the earth.[122]
King Ahmose, who reigned just before the eighteenth Dynasty, says
in the Carnarvon Tablet I:

> Let me understand what this strength of mine is for! (One)
> Prince is in Avaris, another is in Ethiopia (*Kus*), and (here)
> I sit associated with an Asiatic and a Negro (*Nehesi*)! Each
> man has his slice of this Egypt, dividing up the land with
> me. I can not pass by him as far as Memphis.[123]

Another Egyptian monument relating to *Kush* is the annals of
Thutmose III at Karnak, which had three lists of the Cushite cities under his
domain. These three lists contain seventeen, fifteen, and four hundred names
respectively.[124] Assyrian documents referred to Africa and Africans as
"*Kush*" or "*Kusu*." The annalistic texts of Esarhaddon, says:

> In my tenth campaign I directed my march I ordered...toward the
> country which is Nubia (*Kusu*) and Egypt (*Musur*).... In my
> campaign, I threw up earthwork for as against Ba'lu, king of
> Tyre who had put his friend Tirhakah (*Tarqu*), king of Nubia
> (against called...course of siege) s trust upon (*Kusu*)....[125]

Rasam cylinder of Ashurbanipal, found in the ruins of Kuyunjik also
referred to Tirhakah as the king of *Kusu* and Egypt. He says:

> In my campaign, I marched against Egypt [Magan] and Ethiopia
> [Mullah]. Tirhakah [*Tarku*], king of Egypt [Musur] whom
> Esarhaddon, king of Assyria, my father had defeated.[126]

II Chronicles 12:2-3 mentioned Shishak who invaded Judah with
twelve hundred chariots and sixty thousand horsemen as the king of Egypt.
Among his military men were Cushites, Egyptian and Sukkim. J.A. Wilson
maintains that the Cushites, also called *Wawat* and *Medjay*, were originally
the policemen protecting the Egyptains.[127] II Kings 19:9 mentioned King
Tirhakah as the king of Cush. As far as scholars and ancient records are
concerned, Tirhakah is unquestionably from Africa.

(6) The Rabbinical interpretation of the Cushite woman is "beautiful."
     This was based on the proverbial beauty of the Ethiopians in the
     ancient world.[128]

(7) The Tarqum of Jonathan associated the Cushite wife of Moses in
     Numbers 12:1 with the queen of Ethiopia.

     And Miriam and Aharon spake against Mosheh words that were not
     becoming with respect to the Kushaitha whom the Kushace has caused
     Musheh to take when he fled from Pharaoh but whom he had sent
     away because they had given him the queen of Kush, and he had sent
     her away. (JERUSALEM). And Miriam and Aharon spake against
     Mosheh about the Kushaitha whom he had taken. But observe, the
     Cushite wife was not Zipporah, the wife of Mosheh, but a certain
     Kushaitha, of a flesh different from every creature.[129]

(8) There is a tradition which says that Moses married an Ethiopian
     woman and this Ethiopian was associated with Ethiopia south of Egypt
     whose capital was Meroe (Saba). This tradition says that when the
     Ethiopians oppressed the Egyptians, the Egyptians pleaded with Moses
     to lead their army against the Ethiopians. Moses agreed and he became
     the Egyptian general. When Moses and the Egyptian army besieged
     the capital city of the Ethiopians, Meroe, (Saba) the daughter of the
     king of Ethiopia, Tharbis, fell in love with Moses. She asked Moses
     to marry her. Moses agreed on the condition that she delivered the
     Ethiopians into his hand. Tharbis did and after Moses destroyed the
     Ethiopians, he married Tharbis.[130]

Although no one can be sure how solid these traditions are, they should
not be dismissed outrightly without looking at the facts. One important fact
which the traditions point out in agreement with the Bible, is that Moses
married an African woman.[131] Despite all the ancient and modern scholars'
attempts to identify *Kush* in this passage to a place other than the most
commonly accepted place—Africa [Ethiopia], Josephus did not hesitate to
identify *Kush* with African Ethiopia.

In this light it is highly probable that after Moses' wife died or after she
was divorced, Moses needed another helpmate fit for him in his leadership
responsibility. Of all the women there including the Israelitic women, why
did Moses choose to marry an African woman. The reason may not only be
because Yahweh instructed him, but also because African women were
beautiful and held in high esteem. In Isaiah 18:2 Africans were described as

"tall and smooth." Herodotus also described Africans as "tallest and handsomest men in the whole world." (Herodotus II:20; III:14).

Therefore, it is relatively certain that the Cushite woman in Numbers is an African. It is probable that she is a daughter of one of the sympathizers with the children of Israel who left Egypt with the Israelites. However, the Bible is silent about how she got there.

Although the Bible is silent concerning her contribution to the life of Moses, she likely held an important place in the leadership role of Moses. The research into the role and identification of African women in the Bible is relatively new. I hope that further research will be forthcoming to be able to identify the presence and the role of Africans in the Bible.

Endnotes

1. I will like to appreciate the permission by Howard University Press to use my article published in the Journal of Religious Thought for this book.
2. J.L. Mckenzie, "The Literary Characteristic of Genesis 2-3" *Theological Studies* 15 (1954) 491-572, for a summary of the analysis of this passage.
3. Gerhard von Rad, *Genesis* (Philadelphia: Westminster Press, 1972), 79. See also Culbert A. Simpson, *The Interpreter's Bible*, vol. 1, (IB) (Nashville: Abingdon Press, 1952), 95; U. Cassuto, *A Commentary on the Book of Genesis*, trans. Israel Abraham Jerusalem: Magness Press, 1961), 114; Walter Brueggemann, *Genesis* (Atlanta: John Knox Press, 1982), 46. Claus Westermann, *Genesis* 111 Trans. by J.J. Scullion (Minneapolis: Augsburg Publishing House 1984) 212-213.
4. Westermann, Genesis 1-11, 216.
5. Ibid.
6. G.C. Aalders.
7. Ibid. p. 89.
8. G.W. Coats, *Genesis*, vol. I (Grand Rapids: W.B. Eerdmans Publishing Company, 1983), 51.
9. Ibid.
10. McKenzie, 558.
11. E.A. Speiser, *Genesis The Anchor Bible*, 3rd ed. (Garden city, N.Y.: Doubleday and Co., 1979), 19.
12. Coats, *Genesis*, 58-59.
13. Morris Jastrow, *Religion of Babylonia and Assyria* (New York: Charles Scribner's Sons, 191), 57.
14. Ibid.
15. Ibid.
16. John S. Mbiti, *Concepts of God in Africa* (London: SPCK 19?5), 164, 172, 17.

17. Ibid., 174, 175.
18. Ibid., 162.
19. Ibid.
20. Ibid., 173.
21. E.B. Idowu, *Olodumare God in Yoruba Belief* (London: Longmans, 1962), 20.
22. J.A. Wilson, *The Culture of Ancient Egypt* (Chicago: Chicago University Press, 1951), 137-138. The term *Wawat* and *Medjay* refer to the African people South of Egypt (black people).
23. J. Pritchard, *Ancient Near Eastern Text Relating* to the Old Testament (*ANET*), (Princeton: Princeton University Press, 1969), 268-269.
24. Ibid. Some scholars argued against locating Magan and Meluhhan in Africa, but Sir Henry Rawlinson, maintain contact among them. C.J. Gadd, maintained that the subject of trade during the Third Millenium among the Magan and Meluhhans and the Sumerians are said to be the main produce known Africa for (gold, logs, ivory). (Rawlinson, *History of Herodotus, Book I*, translated by Professor Rawlinson, with Essay VI in its Appendix, Book I, C.J. Gadd, "The Dynasty of agade and the Gutian Invasion," *Cambridge Ancient History* vol. I, Cambridge: Cambridge University Press, 1980) Part 2A, 453-54.
25. The term "*Hiddeqel*" in Hebrew is the same as the Akkadian word *Idiglat*, the shortened Deglat in Aramaic, Tigras in Persian, and Dijlat in Arabic. (Speiser, *Genesis*, 17, and Aalders, Genesis, 91). The Hebrew word is the same as the Old Persian word *Uffatu*, Babylonian—Assyrian *Burattur* or *Puratur*. The Semitic etymology is unknown. (G.J. Spurrell, Notes on the Book of Genesis (Oxford: Clarendon Press, 1895, 31). Scholars therefore have no doubt that *Hiddeqel* and *Perath* refer to Tigris and Euphrates respectively.
26. Friedrich Delitzch thinks Pishon should be a Canal which runs west and south of the Euphrates river. Therefore the Garden of Eden is in the plain of Babylon. Professor A.H. Sayce says, that Pishon is in Pallakopas. See S.R. Driver, *The Book of Genesis* (London: Methuen & Co., 1904), 58-59, op. cit. Josephus says Pishon is Ganges. Fineganidentified it with Indus. Jack Finegan, *In the Beginning* (New York: Harper and Bros. Publishers, 1962), 122, op. cit.
27. Driver, *Genesis*, 58-59, op. cit.
28. S. Cohen believes that this last passage is corrupted and should be amended to Hachilah, a hill in south of Judah since Saul was in the Judean locality at this time S. Cohen, "Havilah," *The Interpreters Dictionary of the Bible* (Nashville: A ingdon Press, 1962), vol. II, 537.
29   Ibid., 537. The following are some scholars who locate Havilah in Arabia: J.A. Montgomery, *Arabia and the Bible* (Philadelphia: University of Pennsylvania, 1993), 39: J.L. McKenzie, S.J., "Havilah," *Dictionary of the*

Bible (Milwaukee: Bruce Publishing Co., 1965), 3 1. TIC. Mitchell, "Havilah," *New Bible Dictionary*, Second Edition (Wheaten, III.: Tenderly House Publishers, 1982), 455. F. Brown, S.R. Driver and C.A. Briggs after a summary of different identification say that the location is undecided. *Hebrew and English Lexicon of the Old Testament* (New York: Clarion Press, 1977, reprint), 296.

30   Ibid., 96.

31.   According to the ancient Egyptians, inscription of Queen Hatshepsut, most of their gold, precious stones, resin, and woods came from Kush and Punt. The Sumerians as early as third millenium B.C.E. emphasized the fact that they obtained gold in dust form, precious stones and wood from Africa (if *Melahha* is accepted as meaning Africa south of Egypt inscriptions of Gudea of Lagash and Sargon of Agade. The ancient Greeks emphasized the fact that gold is so plentiful in Ethiopia, they use it to bind their prisoners (Herodotus III. 23, 114). From this writer's researches, no ancient record has ever referred to Arabia or India as famous for gold, incense and precious stones in antiquity as that of Africa south of Egypt (*ANET.* 269-69).

32.   Speiser calls the identification of Kush with Africa in Genesis 2:13 and 10:8 a mistaken identification. George Rawlinson refused to identify *Kush* in Genesis 2:13 and 10:8 with Africa (Speiser, Genesis, 14-20; George Rawlinson, *The Origin of Nations* (New York: Charles Scribner's Sons, 189), 192-19, Claus Westernmann, *Genesis* 1-11, 208-220.

33.   Aalders, *Genesis*, 91. C.T. Francisco, *Broadman Bible Commentary*, vol. I, p. 127.

34.   Gihon derived from Push meaning "to jump or run to and from" Gihon was formed with the help of the termination on from the root *guh* "to flow." Cassuto, *Genesis*, 116.

35.   The earliest Egyptian reference to the term *Kush* or *Kash* is in the inscription of Ameni written during the reign of Sesostri's I. Other references include the Carnarvon Tablet I, the Annals of Thutmose III and others. See James Breasted, *Ancient Records of Egypt* Vol. I (Chicago: University of Chicago Press, 1906), 251. Gaston Masperso, *The Dawn of Civilization* Vol. I, Trans. by M.L. McClure, (New York: Frederick Unger Publication Co., reprinted 1968) 488. It always refer to Africa. See Pritchard, *ANET*, and Daniel David Luckenbill, *Ancient Records of Assyria and Babylon*, New York: Greenwood Press, 1968), 2 Vols.

36.   Julian Morgenstern says any attempt to locate the garden is due to a misunderstanding of the origin and nature of Biblical history and therefore is valueless and fanciful, *The Book of Genesis* (New York Schocken Books, 1965), 56, Ralph Elliot says that the Hebrew writers were not intending to indicate an actual place, but suggesting a setting for their message. *The Message of Genesis* (Nashville: Broad-mann Press, 1961), 34. Modupe Oduyoye of the University of Ibadan, Nigeria, concludes that the inclusion

of such a river (Gihon), which flows around all the land of Kush, as one of the four branches of the river that flows out of Eden, makes Eden "a place that never was," *The Sons of Gods and the Daughters of Men: An Afro-Asiatic Interpretation of Genesis 1-2* (Maryknoll, New York: Orbis Books,1984), 43. Cassuto says that this text describes a state of affairs that no longer exists since the Garden of Eden according to the Torah was not situated in this world. (Genesis, 118). J.L. McKenzie says the "Garden of Eden is altogether unreal locality answering to the description of Eden exists nowhere on the face of the earth," and "this text is dealing with a real semi-mythical geography" (Genesis: International Critical Commentary (New York: Charles Scribner's Sons, 1910),6.

37.   Clyde T Francisco, *"Genesis," The Broadman Bible Commentary*, Clifton J. Allen (Nashville: Broadman Press, 1973)., Vol. I, 127.

38.   This theological truth is that God created all mankind in a certain locality where there were abundant rivers and green vegetables. From this locality humankind and civilisation spread to the entire known ancient world (Gen.1-3).

39.   NASA, "lost River System, " Aeronautics and Space Report, 4:30 (Sept. 1984).

40   Ibid.

41.   Ibid.

42.   *Dallas Times Herald*, Dec. 31, 1986.

43.   Ibid.

44.   Ibid.

45.   Genesis 10:6-10.

46.   Diodorus Sicilus, 3.11; 3.2-3.7.

47.   This section was first published in *Journal of African Religion and Philosophy*, Vol. 2 no. 2, 1993, 138-143. I acknowledge the permission to use it.

48.   Von Rad says that it is a Priestly Table of Nations which reveals the Priestly world view based on an older Yahwistic Table of Nations which the final redactor worked out with the Priestly Text. Von Rad identifies verses la, 2-7, 20, 22-23, 31-32 as the Priestly account. Von Rad, *Genesis*, (Philadelphia: Westminister Press, 1972), 140-41.

49.   According to Pfeiffer, R. was a pious Jew scholar with antiquarian propensities who "was eager to include in JEDP an ancient document whose foreign origin was obscured by its Jewish supplement (S') *Introduction to the Old Testament* (New York: Harper & Row Publishers, 1948), 286-87.

50.   J. Simons, "The Table of Nations (Gen. X); Its General Structure and Meaning," *Oudtestamentlicho Studien x* ed. Pieter de Boer (Leiden: E.J. Brill, 1952), 170.

51. James Grau, Jr., "The Gentiles in Genesis: Israel and the Nations in the Primeval and Patriarchal Histories." Ph.D. dissertation Southern Methodist University, Dallas, 1980.

52. Ibid. 31.

53. Francisco, *The Broadman Bible Commentary*, (Nashville: Broadman Press, 1969), 140-150.

54. Ibid., 150.

55. Ibid., 150. Hermann Gunkel, *The Legends of Genesis*, trans. W. A. Smith (New York Shocken Books, 1964), 23.

56. U. Cassuto, *A Commentary on the Book of Genesis*. Part I (Jerusalem: Magness Press, 1961).

57. Gerald Massey, *Book of Beginnings*, Vol. 1, Secaucus, N. J.: University Books, 197), 4.

58. Ibid., 4-5.

59. S. R. Driver, *The Book of Genesis, Westminster Commentaries* (New York: Edwin S. Gorham, 1904) 119-20.

60. Ibid., 120. Skinner differentiates between J's *Kush* and P's *Kush* Kassites. *A Critical and Exegetical Commentary on the Book of Genesis*, ICC. Edinburgh: T & T Clark, 1910), 208.

61. These traditions will be discussed fully in the Section of Nimrod. Most scientists, anthropolo-gists and others unanimously agreed with the fact that Africa is the place of origin of the human race.

62. Gerald Massey, *Book of Beginnings*, Vol. I, (Secaucus, N.J. University Books, 1974), 2.

63. Ibid., 4.

64. F. Brown, S.R. Driver and C.A. Briggs, *Hebrew and English Lexicon of the Old Testament*, 806. They call Put Libya see also Put, IDB, Vol. 3., 971.

65. Prophet Jeremiah mentioned *Kush* and Put as men who handled the shield and Lud who was skillful in bow during his prophecy concerning the conquest of Egypt by Nebuchadnezzar (Jer. 46:9). Ezekiel also mentioned Put along with Tyre, Persia and Lud (Ez. 27:10). In another occasion Put is mentioned along with Egypt, Ethiopia, Lud and Arabia and (Ez. 30:5) Put, Gog and Persia, and Kush are mentioned together (36:5). Put is also mentioned in I Chronicles 1:8 and Nahum 3:8. In Isaiah 36:19, there is a textual difficulty. The word Put was amended by scholars to Put.

66. Ibid.

67. Simpson, "The Book of Genesis," *Interpreter's Bible* (Nashville: Abingdon Press, 1952), Vol. 1, 261.

68. Elliot, *The message of Genesis*, (Nashville: Broadman Press, 1961), 3.

69. Skinner, *The Book of Genesis*, 189.

70. Grau, "The Gentiles in Genesis." 28.

71. Francisco, *Broadman's Bible Commentary*, 150.

72. Rad, *Genesis*, 146.

73. Ibid.
74. G. Aalders, *Genesis*, Vol. 1 (Grand Rapids: Zondervian Pub 1. House, 1981), 224.
75. Ibid.
76. Ibid., 224.
77. The Torah, *Genesis, A Modern Commentary*, 92, Spinfeld and Freedman, *Archaeology of the Bible*, page 91, Speiser, Genesis, 72.
78. Skinner, *The Book of Genesis*, 209. Von Rad considers Nimrod a legendary document which attracts several traditions to himself. *Genesis*, 147.
79. Aalders, *Genesis*, 224.
80. G. Cornfeld and D.N. Freedman, *Archaeology of the Bible Book by Book* (New York: Harper and Row, Publ. 1976), 9.
81. Gunkel. *The Legends of Genesis*, 90.
82. Ibid., 90.
83. Grau, "The Gentiles in Genesis" 54.
84. Von Rad, *Genesis*, 143. He says that the association of Nimrod and the Canaans with Kush is probably due to the fact that Egypt dominated that area.
85. W. Brueggemann, *Genesis*, (Atlanta: John Knox Press 1982), 91-92.
86. G. Rawlinson, *The Origin of Nations*, (New York: Charles Scribuers Sons, 189), 168-69.
87. If Israel had been using the political reality of Israel period, "she would have included herself, and other nations that were excluded (e.g. Moab, Edom).
88. E. B. Redlich, *The Early Traditions of Genesis* London: Gerald Duckworth & Co., 1950), 15. Redlich calls it historical legends. 134.
89. Johnson, *The History of the Yorubas* (Lagos, Nigeria: CMS Bookshops, 1921) 5-6. Oduyoye, T*he Sons of God and the Dauhters of Men: Afro-Asiatic Interretation of Genesis 1-11*, (Maryknoll, N.Y. Orbis Books, 1974) 96-97.
90. Runoko Rashidi, "The Nile Valley Presence in Asian Antiquity," in *Nile Valley Civilizations*, ed. Ivan Van Sertima (Brunswick, N.J. *Journal of African Civilization*, 1985), 211.
91. Jackson, *Man, God, and Civilization* (Secaucus, N.J. Citadel Press, 1972), 190. 92.
92. *Ancient and Modern Man in Southwest Asia* (Coral) Gables: University of Miami Press, 1956), 84-85.
93. C. H. Hapgood, *Maps of the Ancient Sea Kings* (New York: Chilton Book Co., 1966), 193.
94. A. H. L. Heeren, Historical Researches into the Political Intercourse and Trade of Carthage' Ethioians, and Egyptians, (New York: Negro University Press, 1969).
95. C. F. Volney, *The Ruins of Empires* (New York: peter Eckler, 1890, 17.
96. Jack Finegan, *In the Beginning'*, (New York: Harper and Brothers Publishers, 1962) 68-70.

97. J. P. Blumenbach, *Anthropological Treatise*, trans. T. Bendyshe (London: Anthropological Society, 1965). 98-100. 98.

98. Conklin Edwin, *The Direction of HUMAN Evolution*, (New York: Charles Scribuer s Sons, 1921), 3.

99. G. Spiller, (Editor) *Papers on Inter-racial Problems* Presented to the First Universal Races Con the University of London, July 26-29, 1911 (London: King and Son, 1911), 21.

100. Finegan, *In the Beginning*, 69.

101. Martin Noth, *Numbers A Commentary y*, trans. by J.D. Martin (London: SCM Press, 1975), 92-96, G. W. Coats, *Rebellion in the Wilderness* (Nashville, Abingdon Press, 1968), 261-6.

102. Ibid.

103. Philip J. Budd, *Numbers Word Biblical Commentary*, Vol.5 (Waco, Texas: Word Books, 1984), 133.

104. W. Jenks, *The Elohists and North Israelite Traditions* (Missoula: Scholars Press, 1977), 5-55. 105.

105. F.M. Cross, *Canaanite Myth and Hebrew Epic* (Cambridge: Harvard University Press, 1973), 203-4.

106. W. Rudolph, cited by Budd, 134 Noth, 92-96; 261-24.

107. Martin North, *A History of Pentateuchal Traditions* (Englewood Cliffs; Prentice Hall, 1972), 20.

108. S. R. Driver, *An Introduction to the Literature of the Old Testament*, (New York: Meridan Books, 1956), (Originally published in 1897).

109. Budd, 133-35.

110. However, it is possible that the unity may have been a result of several centuries of editorial work after which the final redactor brought the text to its present condition.

111. This case of two prophets opposing each other is not unusual in the scripture. Prophets Jeremiah and Hananiah opposed each other (Jer. 26-28) until Hananiah was later exposed.

112. W. Gunther Plant, *Numbers, The Torah A Modern Commentary*, Vol. IV (New York: Union of American Hebrew Congregations, 1979), 116-17.

113. Ladislas Bugner, *The Image of the Black in Western Art*, (New York: William Morrow and Company, Inc. 1976), 13.

114. J.J. Owen, *Leviticus, Ruth: The Broadman Bible Commentary*, Vol. 2, (Nashville: Broadman Press, 1970), 118-119.

115. Elliot Binns, *The Book of Numbers* (London, Methuen and Co., 1927), 75-76.

116. *Interpreters Bible*, Vol. 2, (Nashville, Abingdon Press, 1952), 200-201.

117. North, Numbers, 94.

118. George B. Gray, *Numbers. The International Critical Commentary* New York: Charles Scribners Sons, 1910), 121-122.

119. Flavius Josephus, *Antiquities of the Jews*, Book II, 10-11. See also Exodus Chapter 2.

120. Finnis Jennings, *Dake's Annotated Reference Bible* (Lawrenceville: Dake Bible Sales, 1978), 169.
121. Noth, 77, Gray, 121-122.
122. J. Breasted, *Ancient Records of Egypt*, vol. I. (Chicago University of Chicago Press, 1906), 251.
123. James Pritchard, ed. *Ancient Near Eastern Text Relating to the Old Testament* (Princeton University Press, 1969), 232.
125. Pritchard, 2992.
126. David Luckenbill, *Ancient Records of Assyria and Babylonia,* Vol. 2 (New York: Greenwood Press, 1968), 292. See also Pritchard, 294.
127. J. A. Wilson, *The Culture of Ancient Egypt* (Chicago: University of Chicago Press, 1951), 137.
128. Tarqum Onkelos translates the Cushite to "Beautiful" See Gray, 121, and H.H. Rowley et. al. eds. *Leviticus and Numbers, The Century Bible* (London: Thomas Nelson R. Sons, 1967), 23.
129. J. W. Etheridge, *The Targums of Onkelos and Jonathan Ben Uzziel on the Pentateuch* (New York: KTAV Publication House, 1968), 367-77. Numbers 12:1.
130. Josephus, *Antiquities of the Jews*, Book 11:10 There are other Jewish traditions concerning the story of Moses' campaign in Ethiopia in the Medieval Jewish Texts. *Sepher ha-hashar, Parashar Shemoth* and the Byzatine Chronicle, Palea Historical. Moses was described defending the Ethiopians from an usurper named Balaam after which he married the princess of Ethiopia. Donna Runnalls. "Moses Ethiopian Campaign" *Journal for the study of Judaism in the Persian Hellenistic and Roman Period*, vol. 14, No. 2, (1983), 135-56.
131. Josephus, Book II:1.1.

Chapter 4
Africa and Africans in the Nebiim

This chapter is concerned with references to Africa and Africans in the second division of Hebrew Canon (the Former and "Latter" prophetic books). As generally agreed upon by many biblical scholars, these passages, to be dealt with below, are concerned with events which took place approximately during the period of the Israelite monarchies, and the exile.

AFRICA AND AFRICANS IN THE PERIOD OF THE UNITED MONARCHY OF ISRAEL (1020-922 B.C.E.)

Several factors brought the Tribal League of Israel to an end, thus leading to the establishment of the monarchy in Israel. The crucial and commonly recognizable factor took place toward the eleventh century B.C.E.[1] This crucial event was the crisis of the military threat of the Philistines which brought about the realization of the failure of the tribal organization.[2] Since this destructive Philistine's threat was such that the "ill-trained, and ill-equipped" Israelite tribes had never faced before, there was a need on the part of Israel for "a countervailing unified military defence."[3]

Another important factor was Israel's social and economic inequality among the tribes.[4] Some tribes (Manasseh, Ephraim, Benjamin and Judah) were prosperous, while others were poor. There were reports of priestly abuses by Eli's sons (I Sam. 2;12-17), bribery and perversion of justice (I Sam. 8:1-3).

Another factor which led to the institution of the monarchy in Israel was Israel's desire to be like other nations (I Sam.). This desire to be like other nations may also be connected with the military threat of the Philistines.

These three factors mentioned above brought about "a chain of events" which eventually transformed Israel and made her one of the greatest powers of that period. This period of the united monarch, therefore, can be regarded as one of the most significant periods in Israels entire history.[5] This period was the period when the first three kings of Israel (Saul, David and Solomon) were said to rule over a united kingdoms[6] where people of African descent appear in the period called the United Kingdom. These two occasions shall be dealt with below.

African Military Man in King David's
Army (II Sam. 18:21-32)

Although the period of the so called "United Monarchy" (1020-922 B.C.E.) was regarded as one of the most significant periods in Israel's history, the period was marred with serious internal crisis. The crisis was so serious that many scholars argued against calling that period "a United Kingdom" because the Kingdom was not really united. There were so many internal crisis between Saul and Samuel, Saul and David, David and Eshbaal, David and Absalom, David and Sheba, Solomon and Adonijah, and Jeroboam and Rehoboam.[7] King Solomon's oppressive policy actually widened the more tensions among the tribes. The fundamental problems of tribal independence and jealousy remained. The monarchy as a whole never escaped tension, despite all the brilliance of David and Solomon.

Concerning these tensions and jealousies, our main concern in this chapter is the tension between David and his son, Absalom. The crisis was so serious to the extent that David had to flee from Jerusalem for his life. The presence of a military man of African descent in King David's army for his defence against Absalom is also our concern. While some scholars deny the existence of such an African military man, others who accepted such military figure in King David's army refused to give him any status of great importance. This writer's main concern is the examination of the actual identity and status of the *KUSI* who was present in David's army for his defence in II Samuel 18: 21-22, 32-33.

The Historical Background

Several factors brought the Tribal league of Israel to an end, thus leading to the establishment of the monarchy. The most crucial factor was the Philistine's threat which brought about the actual failure of the tribal organization. The Philistines, though not very numerous people, were "formidable fighters with a strong military tradition."[8] They were well-disciplined soldiers with superior weapons and chariots. They moved very swiftly to conquer the entire Western Palestine.[9] Since this destructive threat was so great that the ill-trained, and ill-equipped Israelite tribes had never faced before, there was a need on the part of Israel for "a counter-vailing unified military defence."

Another factor was Israel's social and economic inequality among the tribes. Some tribes (Manasseh, Ephraim, Benjamin and Judah) were prosperous, while others were poor. There were several reports of priestly abuses, bribery and perversion of justice. Other factors include Israel's desire to be like other nations. These three factors brought about a drastic change in Israel's political history during the united monarchy when the first three Kings (Saul, David and Solomon) ruled over Israel (1020-922 B.C.E.).[10] This period was full of internal crises as discussed in the introduction of this chapter. The crisis with King David's family appear to be exceptional. David had some crisis with Saul, Eshbaal, Sheba and Absalom his son by an Aramean woman from Greshur. It became one of the most serious crisis in David's life.

The trouble actually began when Amnon raped Absalom's sister and David did not take any action against the offence for about two years. Absalom murdered Amnon in cold blood (II Sam. 13:20-29) and was forgiven only after spending three years in exile in his mother's country. When he returned home, he plotted to seize the throne of his father, David. After much preparation, Absalom went to Hebron, where he was anointed King over Israel. He marched to Jerusalem against David and his forces. David, caught by surprise, fled to the east of Jordan.

Eventually, David's forces, led by Joab, gathered. Absalom met his death at Joab's hand, in spite of David's warning to Joab to spare his son, Absalom. Ahimaaz, anxious to deliver the news to David was restrained from delivering the news of Absalom's death. After the Kushite had left to deliver the news to the King, Joab allowed Ahimaaz to overtake the Kushite probably because of his persistence. The news of his son's death caused David great sorrow for which he was rebuked by Joab. After Absalom's death, David was restored to his throne.

Analysis of the Passage

The existence of tensions, repetitions and parallel narratives in the book of Samuel has led some scholars to regard the book as a product of continuous source or originally independent fragmentary materials later gathered together to achieve its present stage."[11] As early as 1800, Budde, including Eichhorn and Wellhausen, expressed the hypothesis that the books of Samuel are made up of two continuous sources (J and E) which were later combined by a Deuteronomistic redactor, and were expanded by a later hand.[12]

Eissfeldt postulated three parallel narrative strands, (L, J and E).[13] According to Eissfeldt, the story of Absalom against David (II Sam. 18), which is part of the Court history of David (II Sam. 9-20, 1 Kings 1-2 belong to J.[14] R. A.[15] Garison Is considers II Samuel "a Deuteronomistic work based on a David Epic in which Chapters 2-7 describe David under the blessings and 9-24 describe David under the curse."

For a long time scholars have considered II Samuel 18 (including the entire Court History of David) as a historical document, an "unequalled masterpiece of ancient Near Eastern historiography undoubtedly written by an eye-witness author.[16]

> ...a historical source equal in importance to the narrative of David's rise, has rightly been rated an unequalled masterpiece of ancient Near Eastern historiography. Besides the realistic and true-to life portrayal of people and events, the artful and dramatic structure of the narrative contributes much to its success. The author was undoubtedly an eye witness to the events and a member of the royal court.[17]

This review of the Court History of David as a historical eye witness account provided the linchpin for understanding the reign of David. Gradually, however, this view has become questionable in the light of its actual genre, its extensive use of conversations, and scenes that some scholars thought that it could scarcely have been eye witness accounts of David's life. In the light of this, three major new interpretatations have been advanced:

(1)   that the document is a political propaganda;[18]

(2)   that it is narrative wisdom writing with didactic purpose of teaching good virtues like friendliness, loyalty, judicious speech and humility;[19]

(3)   and finally, that it was a story, "traditionally or conventionally narrated as a work of art and for serious entertainment.[20]

These new interpretations that consider the Court History of David as a political propaganda, wisdom didactic writing for teaching good virtue and work of art for entertainment is not convincing. The nature of the writing has no doubt supported the historicity of the passage as Sellin Fohrer, Gottwald and other biblical scholars have rightly maintained.

The African Among David's Military Men

The account of David's military men who were his protectors in II Samuel 18 are historical account. Among these military men is a man referred to as

"*Kushi*." In this passages, Western scholars do not have problem with the possible identification of the man called *Kushi* as they did in the other biblical passages where Kush were mentioned. The majority of scholars rightly agreed that the *Kushi* referred to in the passage is a man of African descents.[21] However, his position or function is disputed. McKane, Caird, Hertzberg, Ullendorf, and Smith consider the *Kushi* to be David's negro slave from Africa South of Egypt.[22] Gopher calls him a mercenary from Africa recruited into David's army.[23]

A careful examination of the passage shows that the idea that the Kushite is either a slave or mercenary from Africa has no basis. The Kushite (African) could not be a slave because if he had been a slave, he would not have been the right military man to send to the King. Normally it is not a military man of the lowest rank that people usually sent to the King. If he had been a slave or a mercenary, he would not have known the Court language so well. Ahimaaz was refused at first when he requested the permission to deliver the news of victory to the King. This is probably because he lacked the appropriate court language. He was only reluctantly allowed to go later after the African had been chosen instead to deliver the message of victory to the King. After much persistence by Ahimaaz, he was allowed to go with the hope that he could not overtake the African. A careful comparison of the way Ahimaaz and the African delivered the message of victory will certainly reveal that Ahimaaz has not really mastered the court diplomatic language. When the King asked, `Is it well with the young man Absalom?' Ahimaaz answered, "When Joab sent your servant, I saw a great tumult, but I do not know what it was"—(18:29). The African man answered, "May the enemies of my Lord the King, and all who rise up against you for evil, be like that young man." (18:32) While Philbeck believes that Ahimaaz knew of Absalom's death but deliberately lied, Caird believes that Ahimaaz knew about the death of Absalom and wanted to break the news gently, but lacked enough courage like the African when he faced the King.[24] The African's courage to face the King, with absolute truth of what had happened in the battle and his form of address support the fact that the African was one of the royal military officers in the King's court and that he held a high position. Another fact which supports the view that the African was not a slave or a mercenary is the various meaning given to the Hebrew word *ebed* in various biblical passages. The word *ebed* which appears 799 times in the Old Testament can mean a vassal (II Sam. 10:19), a tributary nation (I Chron. 18:2, 6, 13), a person in the service of the King including all his royal officers, officials and ambassadors (Gen. 40:20, I Sam. 19:1, II Kings 22:12, and Num. 22:18). Although this term could also mean slave or servant, it could as well mean a reverence when addressing a superior (II Kings 8:13, II Sam. 9:8). This term could also have a messianic meaning as it is in the case of the servant passages of Deutro- Isaiah (Isa. 42:1-4; 49:1-6; 50:4-9; 52:13; 53:12). What this writer is saying is that the phrase "servant of the king" or "servant of the Lord," in the text does not necessarily mean that the bearer is a slave or literally a servant who holds the lowest position. McKane and Mauchline' idea that the reason for Joab's refusal to send Ahimaaz to the King is that Joab knew that the King would take violent action against the messenger and since he did not want the wrath of the King to fall on Ahimaaz, he chose a negro slave who was suitable for an unpleasant task has no basis.[25] These scholars who did not regard Ahimaaz who also ran to King David like the African to give the same report as a slave, but insisted that the Kushite must be a slave because he was of African descent, are influenced by the presence of black people who were forced to slavery among them. Such scholastic prejudice has dominated biblical interpretation of passages with references to Kush and Kushite by Eurocentric scholars. The Kushite in David's army is therefore an African who probably became an Israelite. He became one of the most trusted military man who was in-charge of protecting David, the King of Israel. From the above discussion, the presence of an African in David's army is undoubted. It is also reasonably clear that he was not a slave or servant of the King in its literal sense, but a protector of the King of Israel. He was a man of courage and truth. He was not merely a protector, he was an exemplary of courage and truth. Such virtues are characteristics of the African (Kushite) people as demonstrated by the biblical writers. When one of the most important prophets of the Old Testaments Jeremiah, was thrown into a cistern to die by the princess, Ebedmelech, the African (Kushite), was the only person who had the courage to face King Jehoiakim, challenged the people before him for the evil they had committed. He was the one responsible for justice for the deliverance of the man of God (Jeremiah) from the cistern (Jeremiah 38:7-13; 39:15-17). In the days of King Hezekiah, when Assyrian threatened Israel, Israel had nowhere to run, but to the Africans for protection. The biblical record mentioned the African King, Tirharkah in defence of Israel against Assyrian power (II Kings 19:9). Africans became the only hope for King Hezekiah (Isa. 20: 1-6). The Annals of Sennacherib recorded how the king of Judah sent a message to Africa for a military protection and their military encounter with them.[26] Therefore, it is certain, that unlike some of the Western biblical scholars, the people of the ancient Near East, especially, ancient Israel, have no prejudice against African people. To this writer's knowledge such record has not been uncovered either in the biblical text or other ancient Near Eastern records. Instead they were held in a very high esteem.

The African Queen (I Kings 10:13-13
II Chronicles 9:1-12)

I Kings 10:10-13 and II Chronicles 9:1-12 represent the earliest and the briefest account of the visit of the Queen of Sheba to King Solomon of Israel in the tenth century. This brevity has probably led to many variant and further elaboration in several traditions.

According to Islamic tradition in the Quran (sura 27: 15-45) the queen is a worshiper of the sun-god. King Solomon sent a letter through a hoopoe to the Queen. After the Queen had read the letter she consulted her nobles. A decision was made and several presents were sent to King Solomon. When these gifts were not well appreciated, the queen herself went to Israel to visit King Solomon. When the Queen of Sheba arrived at King Solomon's house, the well polished floor of the King's house was mistaken to be water. As a result, she uncovered her legs to prevent her cloth from being wet. During this consultation, the queen of Sheba and King Solomon surrendered to Allah and became Muslims.

According to Jewish tradition,[27] King Solomon usually summon all the beasts, birds, reptiles and spirits to entertain him and his fellow Kings from the neighbouring countries. One occasion, all the entertainers were present except a hoopoe. When asked why, the hoopoe was not present, the hoopoe said that he was searching for a city which might not be subjected to the King's authority and that he had found the city of Qitor, which is full of gold and silver, and trees watered from the garden of Eden. The Queen of Sheba was the ruler of that city. King Solomon sent a letter through the hoopoe to the Queen of Sheba summoning her to present herself before the king. The queen complied and went to the king. At the queen's arrival, she thought that the king was sitting on water. To get to the king she lifted her cloth and her hairy legs were exposed. King Solomon was disappointed and remarked that her beauty was the beauty of a woman, but her hair was the hair of a man. However, the queen ignored this remark and proceeded to recite her riddles and questions.

The Talmud has only one reference to the Queen of Sheba. In this Talmud (Baba Batra 15a) Rabbi Nathan discussed the book of Job that Job lived in the days of Sheba and that Sheba was not a woman but a Kingdom. In Ethiopian tradition, Tamnin who was the head of Sheba's caravans was engaged in trading with Solomon. Having been so impressed with King

Solomon's wisdom reported this to the Queen of Sheba when he reached home. The Queen decided to see this herself. King Solomon had a banquet in honour of the queen. After the banquet, the king invited the queen to spend a night with him. The Queen of Sheba agreed on the condition that she would not be taken by force. The King agreed provided the queen promised not to take anything from his house. However, in the night the queen woke up because she was thirsty for the king has overseasoned the food she ate at the banquet. She discovered that some water was beside her bed and she drank the water. Solomon then accused her of breaking her promise and did as he pleased with her. The queen went back home to Ethiopia and had a son called Menelik. When Menelik grew up, he visited his father in Israel and was well received. When Menelik returned home, king Solomon commanded that the first born son of Israel be sent with Menelik to find an Israelite colony there. When these men left Israel they took along with them the Ark of the Covenant to Ethiopia which became the second Zion.[28]

The Biblical accounts (I Kings 10: 1-13) state that the Queen of Sheba heard of King Solomon's wisdom and decided to visit him and to test his wisdom. She went to Solomon with great quantity of gold, precious stones and spices. She gave all these to Solomon. She tested Solomon's wisdom. Woods were given to King Solomon for making lyres and harps and to support the house of the "LORD." The Bible reported that before the queen went home, the King gave her all that she desired.

The story of the Queen of Sheba is duplicated in II Chronicles 9:1-12 with some variations. While in I King 10:9, the "LORD" was delighted in Solomon and set him on the throne of Israel because He loved Israel forever, in II Chronicles 9:8, the "LORD" was delighted in Solomon and set him on the throne of the "LORD" as king for the "LORD" and would establish them forever. While in I Kings 10:7, the queen said "Your wisdom and prosperity surpass the report which I heard, in II Chronicles, 9:6, it was reported that half of "the greatness of your wisdom was not told me." While in I Kings 10:1 the narrative ended with "And King Solomon gave to the Queen of Sheba all that she desired whatever she asked besides what was given her by the bounty of King Solomon, in II Chronicle 9:12,"... King Solomon gave to the Queen of Sheba all that she desired, whatever she asked besides what she brought to the King."

The Nature of the Biblical Narrative

R. H. Pfeiffer considers the entire story of the visit of Sheba in I Kings 10:1-13 a "successive additions" later revised by the author of Kings.[29] Driver also considers this section as part of the few additions to the pro-Deuteronomistic narrative of Solomon's reign. Some scholars consider the story as a product of the imagination of an [30] oriental story teller and "tribute to his hero." To support the view that the story is legendary are the presence of many superlatives, a characteristic of folktales (e.g. "a very great quantity of spices," very much gold and precious stones and "such abundance of spices," vs. 10), the vagueness of "Queen of Sheba," without mentioning her actual name, the great distance between Jerusalem and the supposed location of Sheba (southern Arabia, 1,400 miles of rugged desert), the theme of foreign pagans admiring, praising and blessing Israel's achievement which is commonly used to polemical purposes in the Bible (Gen. 14:18-20; Pharaoh, Ex. 9:27; Rahab, Joshua 2:9-11 Naaman the Syrian, II Kings 5:15) are cited.[31] After a careful study of the themes and wording of the Queen of Sheba's story related passages, Scott concluded that this story is not only legendary, but also late in origin, written about five hundred years after the time of Solomon.[32] Burke O. Long,[33] in discussing the genre concludes that the story is legendary for the purpose, not so much of telling about the meeting of the Queen and Solomon "but to show just how far Solomon's fame had spread; just how fabulous his "wisdom" and wealth really were, and how his wisdom withstood every test."[34] Long finds three forms of speeches in the legend, eulogy (vss 6-7, 9b and 23), praise speech (vs. 9), and beatitude (vs. 9).[35]

A careful examination of the Islamic and Jewish traditions, unlike the Biblical account, clearly revealed the legendary character of the story, while the Biblical record mentioned nothing about the Queen's religion, the Islamic tradition said that the Queen was a worshiper of a son god and that she later became a Muslim. One Jewish tradition says that King Solomon summoned all the beasts, birds and reptiles and he and the Queen becoming muslims, cannot be taken otherwise, but the great legendary character and of late origin. While the Biblical account, says that when the Queen heard of Solomon's wisdom she decided to go and test his wisdom, both Islamic and Jewish traditions recorded that King Solomon sent a letter through a hoopoe inviting the Queen.

Another closer look at both the Ethiopian and the Biblical accounts, shows that they are not so much embellished with legendary characteristic like that of the Islamic and Jewish tradition. That is probably why other reputable Biblical scholars are strongly opposed to the dismissal of the story of the visit. R.K Harrison,[36] G. Fohrer,[37] Edward Ullendorf,[38] John Gray,[39] John Bright,[40] William F. Albright[41] and James B. Pritchard,[42] consider the story historical. John Bright says that, "It is an incident by no means to be dismissed as legendary... [43] After William F. Albright had concluded his excavation in south Arabia he said:

> In the light of the numerous striking archaeological confir-
> mations of the episodes and references in the Biblical story of
> Solomon, it does seem hazardous to treat this particular episode
> as though it were legendary.[44]

Edward Ullendorf has gathered several arguments favouring the historicity of the visit of the Queen of Sheba

(1)   the Assyrian records have attested to several Queens of Arabia (north Arabia), so it is not impossible that one of them could have visited Solomon;[45]

(2)   the mention of the commercial and seafaring[46] activities in the southern area of the Red Sea appears to corroborate the historicity of the queen's visit.

From the above discussion, it seems that there is no reason to doubt or deny the story of the Queen's visit, though it may be reasonable to question whether the visit actually took place in the exact way the story is told.[47] A shadowy history might have lain behind the earliest version in I Kings 10:1-13, which first appeared in *The Book of Acts of Solomon* (I Kings 11:41), and later got lost except for the title.[48] It is probably that an oral tradition preceded the first written account and finally appeared in I Kings 10:1-13.[49]

Location

Another problem is the exact location of Sheba, the home of the queen who visited Solomon. Many scholars do not hesitate to locate Sheba in southern Arabia.[50] The location of Sheba in southern Arabia were given,

(1)   Both Assyrian and southern Arabian inscription testify to the presence of queens in Arabia as early as the eighth century B.C.E.[51]

(2)   domestication was widespread about two centuries before Solomon's reign.[52]

(3)   Recounting of riddles was part of the cultural conversation among the Arabians.[53]

Of equal importance and of the greatest probability is the location of Sheba in Africa (Ethiopia). Without denying the possibility that Sheba could be located in southern Arabia. Edward Ullendorf favours the belief that it was located on the Horn of Africa.[54] Josephus referring to Africa south of Egypt, states that the Queen of Sheba is the queen of Egypt and Ethiopia.[55] Father Mveng argues that the Queen is the queen of Saba, which, as early as the twelfth dynasty of Egypt was the capital of the Kingdom of Kush, therefore Saba should be understood as Meroe.[56] William Leo Hansberry[57] and Jacob A. Dyer maintain that the Queen was the Queen of Ethiopia, south of Egypt, but that her kingdom included south east of Arabia.[58]

The reasons for locating Sheba exclusively in Northern or Southern Arabia appear unconvincing when carefully examined. Although both Assyrian and Arabia inscriptions attest to the presence of queen in Arabia, none of these inscriptions mentioned any queen contemporaneous with the reign of Solomon.[59]

The presence of domesticated camels and the recounting of riddles as part of Arabian culture is too general to use as evidence for locating Sheba exclusively in Arabia. Hansbery and Dyer's view, that the Queen of Sheba was the Queen of Ethiopia, with her Kingdom including south-western Arabia, appears to be more reasonable in the light of the following facts.

(1)   The area of Ethiopia or specifically, as believed by this writer is noted for frankincense and myrrh trees.[60]

(2)   Another closer examination of the Assyrian record seems to confirm the idea that the kingdom of the Queen of Sheba might include some part of Arabia. The Annalistic Records engraved upon slabs found in Calah written during Tiglath-Pileser III's (744-727) campaigns against Syria and Palestine, say that Arabia is in the country of Sheba. He says, "Samsi, the queen of Arabia who had acted against the oath (sworn) by Shamash and had .. town...to the town I'zasi...Arabia in the country of Sheba.[61]

(3)   In I kings 10:11-12[62] the reference to Ophir from which gold, precious stones and almug wood were brought to Jerusalem for the temple, is

probably a reference to Africa where there was a thick forest, and which was also the source of gold in ancient times.[63]

(4)   The New Testament references in Matthew 12:42 and Luke 11:31 identified the queen who visited Solomon as Queen of the South and said that she came from the ends of the earth. The phrase "end of the earth" is usually used to refer to Africa (Ethiopia).[64] Kebra Nagast identified Candace as the "Queen of the South."

(5)   Although the story of the meeting of the Queen of Sheba and Solomon has enjoyed great elaboration in many parts of the world, yet nowhere is the story is "as important, vital, and as pregnant with practical significance" as in the country of Ethiopia in Africa.[65]

Edward Ullendorf, an authority in Ethiopian Studies, said that it is only in Ethiopia that the lengend of Solomon and the Queen of Sheba enjoy such fame and that it penetrated into the entire society and the constitution. It is considered a monument and not a literary invention.[66] He says further, "..as the Old Testament to the Hebrews or the Hebrews or the Qu'ran to the Arabs--it is the repository of Ethiopian national religious, perhaps the truest and most genuinely indigenous expression of Abisinian Christianity. The King's throne is the throne of David and he himself is the son of David and the son of Solomon, King of Zion.[67]

Purpose of the Visit

Although many scholars place much emphasis on the trade agreement "as the main reason for the queen's visit, it appears that equal emphasis should be given to other purposes when the biblical text is carefully examined. In other words, the visit may be multipurpose. First, verses 1, 2, 4-7 seem to suggest that one of the main reasons for the visit is to test[68] Solomon's wisdom. It is noteworthy that in verse 1, 3, 4-7 the queen meant to attest the might, splendor and wisdom of Solomon. She came to test with "hard questions (vs. 1); Solomon demonstrated his wisdom ("And Solomon answered all her questions: there was nothing hidden from the king which he could not explain to her" vs. 3) by being able to answer all her questions; she saw" all the wisdom of Solomon (vs.4); the report she heard concerning the affairs and wisdom of Solomon was true (vs. 6); and Solomon's wisdom and prosperity surpassed the report she heard (vs. 7). In this encounter it seems to me as Dr. Bailey has maintained, that the writer and the editor of the materials used the story to established and reaffirm that Solomon is the wisest in the world and even wiser than Africans whose wisdom is of high value throughout the ancient Near East.[69] Thus an African woman is used to validate Solomon's

Second, verses 2, 10, 11-13, also seem to suggest that another main purpose of the visit was to give some gifts to King Solomon. She gave to the king talents of gold[70] unnumbered quantity of spices and precious stones—such that never came to Solomon again (vs. 10). Such enormous gift could not be accidental, but were probably well planned part of her visit.

Third, there is a possibility that such great gifts may have resulted in diplomatic trade between Solomon and the Queen, or that it may be that the gifts were given to entice Solomon to establish diplomatic trade with her.

A fourth suggested major purpose of the Queen's visit may be the establishment of close personal relationship with the popular king. Some phrases in the text and in later traditions seem to suggest this motive. The phrase, "and she came to Solomon" (vs. 2), could be translated in various ways. It could mean entering a house in an ordinary manner. It could also mean "to come in" implying an intimate relationship. The Hebrew verb *bo* generally means "to come in" and is used in the Bible in several places to refer to a sexual relationships.[71] Another phrase that relates to this interpretation is "all that she desired" (vs. 13). This phrase was interpreted in the Jewish legend as an expression of the Queen's desire to have offspring by Solomon.[72] The Ethiopian tradition in Kebra Nagast, is that the visitor had a son by Solomon. The sexual life of King Solomon, according to the Biblical account definitely supports this view. We are told that Solomon had 700 wives and 300 concubines (I Kings 11:3).

In the light of the foregoing discussion on the Queen of Sheba and the Qur'anic, the Talmudic and especially the Biblical and the archaeological confirmation of the episode and the Ethiopian traditions, the story should not be dismissed as fables for entertainment.

This writer believes that it is also reasonably certain in the light of the evidence cited above that the Queen lived in Africa and from there went to visit King Solomon of Israel for diplomatic trade purpose and to test his wisdom. Since according to the records of ancient Egyptians, the Assyrians, Mesopotamians and other ancient peoples, Africa was the main source of gold, timber and other precious stones for the ancient world, it is appropriate to conclude that Africa had trade interaction with ancient Israel. Therefore, the great quantity of gifts of gold, timber and all kind of precious stones that was carried to Israel by the queen as a gift for king Solomon could be samples of African products to entice Israel for trade.

Although some scholars regard I King 10:11-12 as an interpolation and therefore out of place, the inclusion of this passage appear very significant to me. It was inserted here to complete a full description of some of the abundant wares which came to Solomon that were briefly mentioned in I Kings 9:26-28 and chapter 10:10. Since Ophir is regarded as a region in Africa, south of Egypt, these passages above were meant to reveal African economic and religious contribution to ancient Israel. These products from Africa, that is, the timbers, were used to support the temple; the precious stones were used to decorate the same temple which was one of the most important and powerful institutions in ancient Israel. These type of timber called "Sandalwood," we are told, are "bright, redish in color, they were heavy and closedgrained." They were also therefore admirably suitable for decorative carving" and making of musical instrument.

AFRICA AND AFRICANS IN THE PERIOD OF THE DIVIDED MONARCHY (922-587/6)

Solomon, toward the end of his reign (about 935 B.C.E.), had a friendly relation with the Twenty-First Dynasty of Egypt. After Solomon's death, the ruler of the Twenty-First Dynasty was over thrown by a Libyan noble called Shishak (Shoshong), who founded the Twenty-Second (Bubastite) Dynasty.[73] Shishak, anxious to reassert Egyptian authority in Asia, invaded Palestine in the fifth year of Rehoboam's reign (918 B.C.E.)[74]

King Solomon's death led to the splitting of his so-called united kingdom.[75] Perhaps the split might have been avoided had Rehoboam, the son of Solomon, been sensitive to the cry of his people. However, he was not. Rehoboam, who was accepted as King of Judah without question refused to honor a request that the heavy burdens imposed by Solomon be abated as the price for accepting him as King over Israel. Rehoboam's refusal led to the immediate rejection of his kingship over Israel and consequently to the division of the kingdoms. The northern kingdom then elected Jeroboam son of Nebat, as their king. This division brings a lack of unified military force as deterrent for outside invaders. This was especially the case when Shishak of Egypt with his Libyan, Sukkim and African army invaded Judah and Israel.

Africans Invasion of Judah: (I Kings 14:25-28)
(II Chronicles 12:2-3)

> In the fifth year of King Rehoboam, because they had been
> unfaithful to the LORD, Shishak, King of Egypt came up against
> Jerusalem with twelve hundred chariots and sixty thousand
> horsemen. And the people were without number who came with
> him from Egypt, Sukkim, and Africa.

The biblical references to this invasion are extremely brief. In I Kings
14:25-26, Shishak invaded Jerusalem and took all the treasures of the temple
and the royal palace. However, II Chronicles 12:1-12 provides additional
information which may mean that the Chronicler probably had access to a
more detailed account of the invasion. The Chronicler supplies statistics of
the size and diverse make-up of the Egyptian forces and the work of prophet
Shemaiah. According to the Chronicler, the invasion was occasioned by
Rehoboam's sin of forsaking the law of Yahweh. The Chronicler's additional
detail of I Kings 14:25-26 that Shishak's forces contained twelve hundred
chariots and sixty thousand horsemen has been dismissed by Curtis and
Madsen as part of the "magnifying character of Jewish "midrash."[76] Kitchen,
while arguing for general acceptance of the Chronicler's figures, suggests
that the number six thousand may have been a scribal error.[77] However, the
Chronicler's account of the number of chariots and horsemen" were
relatively in agreement with archaeological evidence.[78] However, the biblical
account of Rehoboam's giving enormous tribute to Shishak to induce him to
withdraw, led the reader to conclude that the attack was against Judah only.
Shishak's inscription at Karnak, however, listed many cities (about 150
places) conquered in both Judah and Israel. John Bright describes the
process of this devastation of the cities:

> The Egyptian armies devastated Palestine from one end to the
> other. They ranged through the Negeb, reducing the Solomonic
> forts in that area (Arad and Ezion-geber were apparently
> destroyed at this time), and penetrated as far as Edom. Various
> towns in the southern hill country and the Shephelah of Judah
> were attacked and in some cases destroyed. Then having
> approached Jerusalem by way of Aijalon, Beth-horon and
> Gibeon and having forced that city to capitulate, the Egyptians
> pressed on into north Israel, spreading destruction everywhere.
> Their farthest advance took them eastward into transjordan

(Penuel, Mahanaim) and northward as far as Esdraelon, at Megiddo (mentioned in the list) a fragment of triumphal stele of Shishak has been found. The blow laid both Israel and Judah low and undoubtedly forced a postponement of their private quarrel.[79]

The nature of the ethnic composition of Shishak's army as reported by the Chronicler is, of course, what warrants the inclusion of this passage in our examination. This composition includes the Libyans, the Africans (Kushites) and the Sukkiim. Kitchen commends the authenticity of the Chronicler's report of the make-up of Shishak's army.[80] The Libyans were an obvious element of the army mentioned by the Chronicler because Shishak (Shosheng I) was a chief of the Meshwesh, one of the Libyan tribes, who came to the throne of Egypt about 945 B.C.E. and founded Twenty-Second Dynasty.[81] The Nubians (Kushites) were also obvious elements. Although there is no clear account of a survival of a military campaign in Africa south of Egypt, two literary references seem to suggest a military action in that region during the period of Shishak's reign. The first is a fragment of a dedicatory inscription of Shishak (Shosheng I) listing Nubian products presented to Amun.[82] The second is the biblical account (II Chr. 12) listing the Africans as part of Shishak's army. It is possible that the Africans were the largest number in Shishak's army when he invaded Palestine. As discussed in chapter two of this book they seem to have been the largest number of military and police men employed for the security of Egypt and their eventual taking over of the throne of Egypt (Nubian Dynasty). The identification of the Sukkiim has been of considerable difficulty. T. E. Peet identifies them as Tjukten Libyans of the western Delta.[83] However, it appears there is no satisfactory identification of these people. We have to wait for further discoveries for satisfactory identification.

Africans and King Asah (II Chronicles 14:9)

After Shishak invaded Judah, further warfare continued in Palestine. Abijah (Abijam 915-913 B.C.E.), son and successor of Rehoboam defeated Jeroboam I and occupied Bethel (II Chron. 13). Later, Asa also had to defend himself against Zerah the African (Kushite). This encounter between Asa of Judah (913-873) and Zerah, the African recounted by the Chronicler has no parallel in Kings. Although the historicity of this incident has been questioned, many scholars maintained that the event is historical.[84] However, the exact identification of Zerah has been a subject of debate. However, in discussing the identity of the leader of the African raid (Zerah), many scholars consider Zerah's raid as an Egyptian operation.[85] Therefore Zerah must have been Osorkon I, son and successor of Shishak I. Petrie gives three reasons why he considers Zerah's raid Egyptian and therefore identifies Zerah with Osorkon I[86]

(1)   After Zerah was defeated he withdrew toward Gerar which is on the road toward Egypt and not toward Arabia;

(2)   The combination of Zerah's forces (Kushites and Libyans, II Chronicles 16:8) is an unlikely combination to have been assembled by an Arabian Sheikh;

(3)   The presence of chariots in the army suggests Egyptian rather than Arabian origin. Olmstead explains that the reason why Osorkon I was called "Cushite" was because of his family's long sojourn in Nubia.[87]

Peet,[88] Albright,[89] Kitchens[90] and Montet[91] reject the above idea of equating Zerah with Osorkon I on several grounds. It was argued that there is no philological relationship between the name Zerah and Osorkon.[92] Kitchen argues that Osorkon would have been too old then since the period of the military action would have fallen in the twenty-eighth year of Osorkon's reign.[93] Moreover, the Chronicler did not call Zerah a king, but simply a Cushite, Osorkon was a king.[94] What appears most likely to this writer is that Zerah was probably the commander of the Nubian colony stationed in Gerar by Shishak as part of Egypt's security plan.[95] Perhaps, when Asa began to build fortresses (Chronicles 14: 6-8), the colony and the Egyptian overlord felt threatened. Zerah therefore might have been instructed by Osorkon to attack Asa. Asa's victory probably influenced him to institute a reform.

In the above passage there is a recognition of African military might. The Chronicler demonstrates that no matter how powerful an army is, including African military might, Yahweh can destroy it. In other words, Yahweh is even more powerful than African military force which is recognised in ancient Israel as mighty and fierce.

The Prophet Amos: Comparison of Israelites with Africans (Amos 9:7)

For a proper understanding of Amos 9:7-8, it is important to examine the historical context which warranted the prophecy.

The editorial note of Amos 1:1 identifies the monarch (Uzziah and Jeroboam I) who were reigning during Amos' prophetic work. From the above notice scholars generally date Amos' work to 760 B.C.E.[96] Although he was from the south, his work was done in the northern Kingdom during the days of Jeroboam II (Amos 1:11).

By the time of Jeroboam II, the powerful Assyrians had totally crushed the Arameans who were Israelis frequent enemies. This total humiliation of the Arameans city states was described on a stone fragment from the royal archieves of the Assyrian King, Adad-nirari: "I shut up Mari, King of Damascus in Damascus, his royal residence. The terror-inspiring glamor of Ashur, my lord, overwhelmed him, and he seized my feet, assuming the position of a slave."[97]

The Assyrians themselves could not challenge Jeroboam II of Israel because Adad-nirari was followed by weaker kings who had all they could handle in defending their territory against other enemies.[98] As a result of this, Syria-Palestine area was free of danger from Assyria until the reign of Tiglath-Pileser III (745-727). From the biblical record, it appears there was no sign of interference from the southern Kingdom at this period.

Jeroboam, taking advantage of this period of peace, began his aggressive and expansionistic policy (2 Kings 14:23-29). He extended his borders in the north as far as Damascus and Hamath and in the south as far as the Dead Sea. His military   and political power resulted in increased commerce and wealth, but the wealth was not equally shared among the people (Amos 4:1 and 6:1), the poor became poorer.[99]

Moreover, Israel's religious worship was flamboyant and full of hypocrisy (mere sacrifice, 4:4, 5:5, 5:21-24). The Israelites interpreted their prosperity as a sign of God's approval and blessing. They thought that Israel was in a special relationship to Yahweh, and therefore that she was secured.

In this time of religious and social decadence came a radical prophet, (Amos) with a radical message from Yahweh:

Are you not like the (Africans) to me, O people of Israel?' says the LORD. `Did I not bring up Israel from the land of Egypt, and the Philistines from Captor and the Syrians from Kir? Behold the eyes of the LORD GOD are upon the sinful Kingdom, and I will destroy it from the surface of the ground; except that I will not utterly destroy the house of Jacob,' says the LORD. (Amos 9:7-8).

Although source critical studies of the book of Amos maintain that the book has been reworked by many editors, much of its content has been assigned to Amos himself.[100] Amos 9:8 has been regarded as the end of genuine materials.[101] Robert B. Coote,[102] emphasizing the fact that the book of Amos is the end result of many series of compositions of the original words of the prophet, says that those compositions are in three stages:

(1)   Stage "A" is the first record of Amos himself;

(2)   Stage "B" is the work of an editor called Bethel who worked on Amos' record;
(3)   Stage "C" is the work of the closing editor who is a Jerusalemite.

Redaction critics make a more complicated analysis of the composition of the book of Amos by pointing to six stages of composition.[103] In this case chapter 9:78 (which is the main concern here) belongs to the fifth stage of the development of the book of Amos.

A close analysis of the materials in Amos shows that they contain judgment speeches, vision reports, hymnic doxologies, admonitions, laments, brief narratives and promises of salvation.[104] However, in chapter 9:7-8 a controversy with opponents is apparent. The two interrogative questions in 9:7 and 9:7 seem to reflect an opponent's questioning the announced reversal of the holy war against Israel. The children of Israel could not understand why Yahweh suddenly became Israel's enemy rather than its protector.[105] Those two interrogations lead scholars to classify this passage as a disputation form.[106] Many scholars, except Coote,[107] agree that the Cushites referred to in Amos 9:7 are the people of Africa south of Egypt.[108] Referring to the comparison of Africans with the Israelites, some scholars say that it was because the Africans (Cushites) were despised nation; they were a "darkskinned," and "uncivilized" people whom the Children of Israel had known mainly as slaves.[109] A close examination of this passage (Amos 9:7-8) will convince any honest and well-informed biblical scholar that those explanations given above have no basis in the context. The fact that throughout the Old Testament, there is no single reference to the Africans (Cushites) as slaves, shows that such an idea is without foundation. In fact, there is no place in the Old Testament where the color of their skin is at issue.[110] Norman H. Snaith was emphatic on this fact. He says, "There is, of course, no slightest suggestion that the color of their skin (Africans) is the point at issue; there is no warrant anywhere in the Bible for that kind "of idea."[111] The reason they were used as a means of comparison with Israel is that they were seen as "representative" of foreign people living in the remotest or far-distant part of the world, yet with whom the Israelites were well-acquainted.[112] Hans Walter Wolff was also vehemently opposed to the kind of prejudice demonstrated by Harper, Ullendorf, Mays and others. He says:

> To compare the Israelites with the Cushites probably does not in itself mean to say anything disdainful, much less anything reprehensible, about them. They are mentioned simply as representative of foreign and remote peoples who live on the outermost periphery of the known world. If Israelite is the same as they in the sight of Yahweh then it cannot claim any kind of privileged position[113]

This passage should be regarded as a refutation of "an implied objection" from the listeners who boasted that Yahweh's election automatically secured them from punishment. Amos, therefore, in denying that Israel had a special more privileged position than the other nations, put the Exodus on the same level as the migration of other peoples.[114] The same Yahweh who guided the Israelites from Egypt also guided other nations' destinies. The same God who guided Israel from Egypt also put the Africans where they were and brought the Philistines from Caphtor and the Syrians from Kir.[115] God's special relationship is bounded by justice and righteousness. He is, therefore, not exclusively bound to one nation, but is master of all and has a special relationship to all.[116] According to some scholars in Amos is one of the finest expressions of universalism. The passage above is one of the occasion where African nations are used "in terms of their norm for valuation."[117] The comparison demonstrates that Israel is as precious as Africans before Yahweh.

AFRICA AND AFRICANS, THE HOPE OF JUDAH
(Isaiah 20: 1-6; 18:1,2,7; II Kings 19:9)

Africans in Defence of Judah in the Battle of Ashdod (Isa. 20:1-6)

In the year that the commander in chief, who was sent by Sargon the King of Assyria, came to Acceded and fought against it and took it, at that time the Lord had spoken by Isaiah the son of Amaze, saying, "go, and loose the sackcloth from your loins and take up your shoes from your feet," and he had done so, walking naked and barefoot—the LORD said, "As my servant Isaiah has walked naked and barefoot for three years as a sign and portent against Egypt and (Africa), so shall the king of Assyria lead away the Egyptians captives and barefoot, with buttocks uncovered, to the shame of Egypt. Then, they shall be dismayed and confound because of (Africa) their hope and of Egypt their boast. And the inhabitants of this coastline will say in that day, `Behold, this is what has happened to those in whom we hoped and to whom we fled for help to be delivered from the king of Assyria! And we, how shall we escape?'

In order to understand this passage properly, it is important to discuss briefly the historical background, that is, the external and the internal situation which brings about one of the most dramatic prophecies. After the death of Shalmaneser V (722 B.C.E.), Sargon II scarcely mounted the Assyrian throne when he was greeted with rebellion.[118] Marduk Apal-iddina (Merodach- baladan of the Bible),[119] with the help of the King of Elam, rebelled, and Sargon II (722-705) lost the control of Babylon.[120] There was also another revolt in Asia Minor under the leadership of Mita, King of Phrygia Mushki.[121] Sargon also had to crush another revolt in Urartu (714) to establish the Assyrian authority.

Around this period, Egypt experienced a radical change in the royal leadership. After Egypt had been weakened by a power struggle (especially between the 22nd and 23rd Dynasties) and the collapse of the Twenty-fourth Dynasty, a powerful leader from Africa south of Egypt (Cush), Piankhi, overran Egypt and established the Twenty-fifth Dynasty, commonly called the "Ethiopian Dynasty" (716-715 B.C.E.).[122] This powerful king was then able to unite Egypt with Africa south; thereby a powerful kingdom emerged again in Africa which Hezekiah believed could match the power of Assyria. For that reason he looked up to the African power for deliverance (Isa. 20:5-6).

About this same period, Asuri, King of the Philistine's city, Ashdod, undertook anti-Assyrian campaign and also sent messenger to Judah for support. For this reason Sargon II reported not only in his annals, but also in his Display Inscription, that he removed Azuri, King of Ashdod, for sending ambassadors to the neighboring kings for revolt. He says in his annals,

Azuri, king of Ashdod, had schemed not to deliver tribute (anymore) and sent messages (full) of hostilities against Assyria to the Kings (living) in his neighborhood. On account of the misdeed which (thus) committed, I abolished his rule over the inhabitants of his country and made Ahimiti, his younger brother, king over him.[123]

With Babylon having revolted successfully and having sent a messenger to Hezekiah,[124] the leader of the anti-Assyrian campaign, the Ashdodites, also sent messengers to Judah. With the emergence of a new powerful ruler in Africa (Piankhi), who Hezekiah believed could equal Assyrian power, Hezekiah probably believed it was the most appropriate time to revolt. The secret messengers sent to Hezekiah from Egypt made it seem as if King Hezekiah sent a secret messenger to the African King (Shabaka who succeeded Piankhi)[125] for deliverance thinking that prophet Isaiah of Jerusalem would not know. However, Yahweh revealed the whole plan to Isaiah, who reacted very sharply against such a plan. Thus his symbolic prophecy of doom (Isa. 20: 1-6).[126] The prophet Isaiah, in order to demonstrate that such reliance on the African military power would be in vain and that Egypt and Africa would be taken into captivity, walked naked and barefoot for three years (Isa. 20:1-6)[127] Sargon II eventually turned to Palestine. In the three accounts of this campaign found in the annals of Sargon, the great inscriptions and the Prism A[128] it was recorded that Sargon first directed his invasion toward the Ashdodites. Sargon deposed Azuri, King of Ashdod and replaced him with his brother, Ahimiti. Later Ya-ma-ni, the Ionian, established himself on the throne of Ashdod with the help of the people of the city. But at the approach of Sargon, Yamani fled to Egypt. No one is exactly sure of the roles which Egypt, Africa south and Judah play. However, from the Assyrian annals, the Display inscriptions and the Broken Prism,[129] it is clear that when Ya-ma-ni fled to Egypt, the African King Piankhi handed him bound to the Assyrians. It was reported that tributes were also sent to Sargon.[130]

Scholars are divided as to whether Hezekiah heeded the warning of prophet Isaiah. While John Bright[131] believed that in fact, Judah escaped harm, that Hezekiah heeded the words of Isaiah, H. Tadmor believes that Hezekiah participated in the revolt, but was forced to submission by the terror of Assyrians when Ashdod was destroyed.[132] A close examination of the Assyrian records seem to confirm Tadmor's opinion. The Nimrod Inscription reports that Sargon was the "subduer of the country of Judah (la-u-du)...[133] It is evident that Ashdod was totally destroyed in 711 B.C.E.[134]

Africans in Defence of Judah in Eltekeh:
(Isaiah 18:1-2, 7)

Ah, land of whirring wings which is beyond the rivers of (Africa); which sends ambassadors by the Nile, in vessels of papyrus upon the waters! Go you swift messengers, to a nation, tall and smooth, to a people feared near and far, a nation mighty and conquering, whose land the river divides...At that time gifts will be brought to the LORD of hosts from a people feared near and far, a nation mighty and conquering whose land the river divides, to Mount Zion, the place of the name of the LORD of hosts.

Unlike the previous text just discussed (Isaiah 20:1-6), several scholarly controversies surround this text (Isa. 18:1-7). It will therefore be necessary to discuss these divergent scholarly opinions before getting into the actual historical events that surround this text. Gray,[135] Hayes[136] and Winward[137] consider Isaiah 18:1-7 as part of the authentic oracle of Isaiah. Scott considers only 18:1-6 as authentic.[138] A. S Herbert's, [139] divides this passage into three sections. Verses 1-3, 4-6, and 7. Verse 7 is considered as a post-exilic commentary of Isaianic community. Marti[140] sees 18:1-6 as directly linked with Isaiah 17:1-11. According to him, verse 3 is a later interpretation and verses 5 and 6 are the original conclusions of chapter 17:1-11. Kaiser considers the entire text (18:1-7) as belonging to a late post-exilic redactor.[141]

Another problem concerning this particular text is the proper identification of the subject and the object of this prophecy. Scholars have divergent opinions as to whether the prophet was asking Judah to send messengers to the Assyrians or addressing the African messengers to return home to their people.

J. Hayes[142] considers the entire passage as not so much as judgment against a foreign nation, but as an oracle mainly intended for the prophet's own people—Judah. According to Janzen the prophet Isaiah was summoning divine messengers to go to Assyria to tell the Assyrian ruler what was happening in Jerusalem.[143] Clements, however, thinks that the prophet was summoning the African (Kush) ambassadors to go to Assyria against which their plan is directed.[144] As Gray,[145] Scott,[146] Kaiser, and Bright[147] have maintained, a very close examination of the text in question shows that the prophet was addressing the African messengers sent by King

Shabako who were present in Jerusalem to go back home empty-handed, because Judah did not need their alliance.[148]

Otto Kaiser thinks this passage refers to Africa south of Egypt (Ethiopia) and gave several reasons for not believing otherwise.[149]

The Hebrew travellers probably brought the news of wealth of that distant land, the fast light papyrus boats on the Nile, the physical characteristics (height, and body) of the people, and the conquering power of the nation of Africa south when they conquered Egypt.[150] Thus the prophet Isaiah, a well-informed prophet, describes the land as "whirring wings" and the people as "swift messengers." He describes the boats on the Nile, because when they sail, they spread and resemble birds with wings.[151] The prophet was probably familiar with the people of Africa and admired the physical make up of the people, describing them as "tall" and "smooth."[152] Like the Father of History, Herodotus, who describes the African people as "the tallest and the most beautiful people in the world," (Her. III.20) travellers to the land of the Dinka people of Africa have described them as "giants," about seven feet tall, who, like the Nile cranes stand on one foot in the river for hours looking for fish.[153]

Problems still exist as to the exact event in which to place this passage. While some scholars place it in the period of the Philistines' revolt shortly before 711 B.C.E.[154] others place it in the period shortly before Sennacherib's invasion of Palestine in 705-701 B.C.E.[155] Although it could be placed in either event, 701 B.C.E. appears more appropriate because, according to the Sargon inscriptions, Hezekiah sent an envoy to Africa for aid shortly before the event of 711 B.C.E. In the event of 705-701, however, it is more likely that it was Egypt who initiated the revolt and sent an envoy to Jerusalem.[156]

One of the most vexing problems in the book of Kings is also found in the Sennacherib invasions. The main question is whether there "was a single or a double" invasion of Sennacherib. Several scholars believe there was a single invasion, but others believe there were two invasions.[157] Although there is no clearcut or easy answer to this problem, this writer accepts a double invasion theory as a working hypothesis in this book.[158]

After the death of Sargon II in the battle in 705, Sennacherib became his successor. Immediately he was also greeted with rebellion in Babylon. Marduk-Apalidina revolted again and Sennacherib had to face him.

In the west there was also a revolt. Philistia, Ashkelon, and Ekron were active in the revolt.[159] Perhaps while Hezekiah of Judah was contemplating what to do, the Africans under the leadership of King Shabako (710-696) sent envoys (Isa. 18:1-7) to Hezekiah promising to help him fight the Assyrians.

At this point, it seemed as if a revolt should be successful. With the backing of the African army, King Hezekiah made an expedition to the country of the Philistines (2 Kings 18:8). In Ekron, Padi, the king of Ekron, who was loyal to the Assyrians, was delivered to Hezekiah as a prisoner in Jerusalem. With the assurance of the cooperation, not only of the Africans but also of Ekron and Ashkelon, and knowing that the invasion of Sennacherib would surely come, Hezekiah embarked on further defence (II Chronicle 32:3-5). They strengthened existing fortifications, built walls and raised towers upon them. He made weapons and shields in abundance and set commanders over the people (2 Chr. 32:5-6). In case of a siege against Jerusalem, he embarked on the provision of water supply. He undertook a construction of a tunnel which brought water from the spring of Gihon underneath the hill of Jerusalem (II Chr. 20:20; 31:30) to the lower end of the city wall.[160]

In 701 Sennacherib attacked the land of "Hatti" (Assyrian term for the western countries), after conquering Marduk-Apal-idina going southward, he destroyed Tyre and the King of Sidon (Luli) fled to Cyprus where he died. In terror, Arvad, Byblos, Ashdod, Moab, Edom and Ammon quickly sent tribute[161] Sennacherib then moved against Ashkelon and Ekron. Meanwhile the African army under the leadership of Shabako upon whom Hezekiah placed his trust for deliverance, marched to aid Ekron. Shabako, King of Meluhha, with his archers, numerous chariots and horses unnumbered met the Assyrian forces in Eltekeh. The Annals of Sennacherib report the encounter.[162]

According to the Sennacherib annals, the battle of Eltekeh was a total defeat for the Africans, and he destroyed Eltekeh and Ekron. He said that he personally captured the chariots of the king of Egypt and Ethiopia.[163]

Then Sennacherib turned to Judah. He said that he captured forty-six cities of Judah and deported their population, "drove out (of them) 200,150 people, young and old, male and female, horses, mules, donkeys, camels, big and small cattle beyond counting and considered (them) booty.[164] Although not mentioned in the Sennacherib annals, Lachish was one of the cities destroyed (2 Kings 18:17 and 19:8). While besieging Lachish, Sennacherib sent messengers to Hezekiah to surrender (2 Kings 18:14). Sennacherib demanded heavy tribute from Hezekiah. King Hezekiah answered and said to the King of Assyria: "I have done wrong; withdraw from me; whatever you impose on me I will bear" (II Kings 18:21). The Assyrian King required from Hezekiah "three hundred talents of silver and thirty talents of gold" (II

Kings 18:21). But in order for Hezekiah to pay all these levies, he had to give the King of Assyria "all the silver that was found in the house of the LORD, and in the treasuries of the King's house." He also gave Sennacherib "the gold in the temple and from the doorposts (II Kings 18:15-16).

Africans in Defence of Judah in Jerusalem's Siege (II Kings 19:9)

And when the King heard concerning Tirhakah, (the African King), Behold, he has sent out to fight against you, he sent messengers again to Hezekiah, saying,

In II Kings 19:9 we have the biblical evidence that African nations were in defence of Hezekiah throughout his days.

As mentioned earlier, the interrelationship of several narratives in II Kings 18:13-19:37 has been one of the most vexing problems in the book of Kings and probably in the Old Testament as a whole. It has also been said that in an attempt to solve these problems scholars have suggested a single or double Sennacherib invasion. The genuineness of II Kings 19:9 has also been another main question. Although it is generally accepted that Tirhakah was from Africa south of Egypt, most scholars who accepted a single Sennacherib invasion consider this passage as an "error" or "an anachronism," and therefore "unhistorical.[165] Otto Eissfeldt[166] sees this passage as having its origin from Isaiah's legend.

If this passage is not to be dismissed (as believed by this writer and other scholars), there was probably another invasion of Palestine by Sennacherib after 701 B.C.E.[167] The fact that the entire II Kings 18:17-19:37 (and probably Isaiah 36f.) fit too poorly into the event of 701 B.C.E. and the fact that the international situation after 701 B.C.E. favours a rebellion in Judah and another invasion by Sennacherib make it reasonable to accept the two invasion hypothesis by Sennacherib. After 701 B.C.E., Sennacherib had to deal with another opposition in Babylon. In dealing with this opposition he replaced the rebellious king, Belihni, with his own son, Asshur-nadin-shum (700 B.C.E.). The Elamites also rebelled and by 691 B.C.E., the coalition of Babylonians, Elamites and other people rebelled against Sennacherib. Since at this time it seems as if Sennacherib was losing his control over these people, Judah might have taken this opportunity to rebel still trusting the powerful African king, Tirhakah, who probably was not ready to accept Assyrian defeat of Shabako his predecessor.[168] Perhaps when Sennacherib was able to master the rebellion in Babylon about 689

B.C.E., he turned to Judah in 688 B.C.E., thus the event recorded in II Kings 18:17-19:37.

When Sennacherib was in Lachish, thinking that Hezekiah would submit as he did earlier during the siege of 701 B.C.E., he sent the Tartan, the Rabshakeh to Hezekiah (II Kings 18:17-35). Unfortunately this tactic did not work (18:36-19:7). Instead of submitting to terror, Hezekiah consulted the aged prophet (Isaiah) who assured him that Sennacherib would not take Jerusalem (19:6-7).[169] While Sennacherib was fighting against Libnah, he heard that the young energetic African King, Tirhakah, was on his way to defend Judah (19:8-9). The King of Assyria, knowing he would have to fight on two fronts at the same time tried his tactic once again to terrify Hezekiah to submission (19:9-13). This time he put it in writing probably to make sure that Hezekiah understand the seriousness of his message. Hezekiah understood the seriousness of the matter. But, instead of submitting, he opened the letter to Yahweh to read. Perhaps he also sent for Isaiah who assured him again that Yahweh heard his prayer.

While the King of Assyria was getting ready to besiege Jerusalem, perhaps three things happened that forced him to withdraw back home as predicted by the prophet Isaiah.

(1)   He heard the rumour of insurrection, the insurrection that eventually led to his assassination.[170]

(2)   It is very likely that he was also attacked by the young African king, Tirhakah, while trying to besiege Jerusalem or the mere rumour of the advance of the African king also frightened his forces, thus realizing the futility of fighting the Africans and Judah (II Kings 19:9). Although there is no Assyrian record of the second invasion of Sennacherib toward the end of Hezekiah, except the invasion of the Arabs, there is an Egyptian legend which tells of a great defeat which Sennacherib suffered in the hand of the Egyptians.[171] It may also be possible that when Tirhakah was approaching, Sennacherib had no time for so tedious a siege.[172]

(3)   The third possibility that has been suggested is that of the miraculous destruction of the Assyrians. This destruction may have been bubonic plague carried by mice as mentioned by Herodotus II:141 and Egyptian tradition.[173] Admittedly, the above combination of these factors could have been responsible, the African factor (Tirhakah) seems to be more realistic considering the report of II Kings 19:9. In

other words, Jerusalem would have been destroyed by the Assyrian forces in approximately 688 B.C.E. instead of 587—86 B.C.E. by the Babylonians. Judah however survived 100 more years. Perhaps, due to the intervention of Africans.[174]

Throughout the eighth, seventh and even sixth centuries, African nations (Egypt and Ethiopia) were the political and military hope of Israel. They dependent on them for protection. That is the reason why Isaiah of Jerusalem vehemently objected to such dependence of African military might and prophesied against them.[175]

> `Woe to the rebellious children,' says the LORD? `who carry out a plan, but not mine and who make a league, but not my spirit,... who set out to go down to Egypt without asking for my counsel, to take refuge in the protection of Pharoah, and to seek shelter in the shadow of Egypt' (Isa. 30: 1-2). Woe to those who go down to Egypt for help and rely on horses, who trust in chariots because they are many and in horsemen because they are very strong but do not look to the Holy One of Israel or consult the LORD. The Egyptians are men, and not God; and their horses are flesh, and not spirit. (Isa. 31:1-3).

The prophet Ezekiel who spoke during the pre-exilic and exilic periods also prophesied vehemently against Africa (Egypt) that Yahweh will make them so small so that they will never rule over the nations and they will never again be the reliance of the house of Israel"...The vehemence with which these prophets spoke against Israel's dependence on Africa instead of Yahweh, shows the extent and seriousness of this continues dependence.

The Proverbial Use of Africans Skin
Color for Israel (Jer. 13:23)

> Can Africans change his skin or the leopard his spot? Then also you can do good who are customed to do evil!

After the death of Hezekiah, his son Manasseh, who was judged as one of the wickedest Kings in Judah, succeeded him. He turned Israel into an idolatrous community. Unfortunately, his reign over Judah was one of the longest of all the Hebrew kings. Manasseh was succeeded by Amon. However, there came a turning point during the reign of Josiah. The decline of the Assyrian empire began immediately after the death of the Assyrian King, Ashurbani-pal (627 B.C.E.). In 727—26 B.C.E., one of the greatest Old Testament prophets (Jeremiah) was called into the prophetic ministry.[176] The discovery of the temple scroll became the basis for reformation in Judah (622—21) In 612 came the end of the Assyrian power when Nineveh fell to the Babylonians.

The death of King Josiah during his attempt to turn back the Egyptian invaders brought Jehoiahaz, who was later deposed by the Egyptians for Jehoiakim, to take the throne in 609 B.C.E. It was during the reign of Jehoiakim that prophet Jeremiah was very active in his ministry.

His book, the second of the four scrolls called the Latter Prophets, contains the record of his preaching and activities from the days of Josiah through Jehoiakim, Jehoiachin and Zedekiah till after the fall of Jerusalem.

The date of the above passage (13:23) was probably about 605 B.C.E., shortly before or after the battle of Carchemish.[177]

Several scholars believe that 13:23 is a misplaced verse.[178] Hyatt thinks that verses 23-24 might have originally stood after verse 27. In that case verse 27 would have been the answer to the question raised in verse 23.[179]

Jeremiah 13:23 is a disputation form of prophecy.[180] Two questions were first asked, then followed by accusations. A negative answer is automatically expected to these questions. The main purpose of such strong expression is not to despise the skin color of the African people, but to express very vividly that there is a deep-seated wickedness in Judah which has been ingrained into the blood of the people by several years in the school of wickedness. Therefore, Judah will be punished, since wickedness has become part of their permanent nature. They will be scattered like chafs. This penetrating, pictorial portrayal of the power of habit (evil) is saying that, if it is possible for an African to wash away his color and the leopard his spots, then it would be possible for Judah to do good and then escape punishment. According to Newsome, this is the central theological concept of prophet Jeremiah.[181]

Jehudi's (the African Princes) Reading of Jeremiah's Scroll (Jer. 36:1, 21, 23)

In the fourth year when the arrogant and evil king,[182] Jehoiakim, succeeded his father Josiah who was a reformer, the word of Yahweh came to prophet Jeremiah to put his prophecies into writing. Even though the prophet probably could not read or write,[183] without hesitation, he employed a secretary (Baruch), dictated the words of the Lord to him, and he put it into written form (36:2-4).

After Baruch had completed the writing, Jeremiah sent him to read it in the temple during the day of fasting when people throughout the land gathered together in the temple, probably due to some national distress or emergency in December 604 B.C.E. The reason for this fast was not given in the biblical text, but several suggestions have been put forward. D. J. Wiseman has suggested that the presence of the Babylonian army in the Philistine city of Ashkelon occasioned the fast.[184] Others maintain that they fasted because there was no rain as attested in the Mishnah (Taanith 1:5) that if there is no rain by the first day of Kislev (ninth month) fasting must take place.[185] During what might probably be the most memorable day of Baruch's life, he read Yahweh's words dictated to him by prophet Jeremiah in the temple.[186] Although there is no record of any reaction to the words read, one will probably be right to infer that the people were greatly moved. Micaiah immediately reported the matter to the princes (36:11-13) who were anxious to hear the words of the scroll themselves, probably because they could not believe that a man who was banned from the temple and almost killed could have written such a thing. The princes sent "Jehudi, the son of Nethaniah, son of Shelemiah, son of (Africans)," to bring Baruch and his scroll (36:14). However, when they heard the words and ascertained that they were Jeremiah's words, they were greatly distressed and prepared to consult the king immediately. Knowing what the reaction of the king would be, they advised Baruch and Jeremiah to hide themselves.

After the words had been reported to King Jehoiakim, he sent "Jehudi, son of Nethaniah, son of Shelemiah, son of (African)," to bring the scroll and read it to his hearing. For the third time, this scroll was read. However, after "three or four columns" were heard, the king, instead of reacting with reverence like King Josiah, in fury "cut them off with a penknife" and burnt them in the fire (36:23). He went further by ordering the arrest of Baruch and Jeremiah, but "the LORD hid them" (36:26).

In this account, the writer of Jeremiah 36 has a list of the important personalities involved.[187] Among the important participants identified personally is "Yehudi *ben* Nethaniah *ben* Shelemiah *ben* "African" (36:14, 21, 23). There are several unusual features about the personal identification of Yehudi. It is very unusual and remarkable that Yehudi's ancestry was traced to the third generation.[188] Literally his name means "Jew," However, his great-grandfather means "African." [189]

In an attempt to clarify these unusual features mentioned above, several explanations have been suggested. One explanation is that the tracing of Jehudi's ancestry to the third generation is an answer to fulfil the requirement of the Deuteronomic law (Deut. 23:7-8)), that is, only the Egyptians of the third generation will be qualified to enter the Lord's assembly. A close examination of Deuteronomy 23:7-8 shows that the text does not mention Africa south of Egypt or Ethiopia. A careful examination of the same passage also reveals that the names of African's (*Cushi*) son (*Shelmayahu*) and grandson (*Nathanyahu*) indicate that they were already followers of Yahweh. That is why their names were compounded by the ending *Yahu*. Since Jehudi means Jew, Jehudi has become also a full fledge Jew.[190] Therefore the above explanation is unsatisfactory and unacceptable.

Another explanation offered is that African's (Cushi's) father who was a native Israelite was on a mission to Africa at the time of his birth Yehudi was then given to his grandson to celebrate his grandfather's return from abroad and to distinguish him from his brother, who was probably born to a non-Israelite mother.[191] This explanation of course, has no basis in either the biblical text or extra-biblical tradition.

Some scholars see this long trace of genealogy so exceptional that they call for an emendation of the text so that two personalities instead of one will be involved.[192] J.P. Hyatt, accepting the opinion of Cornill and Rudolph, thinks that in the phrase (*Yehudi ben Nathanyahu ben Shelemayahu*), the original *waeth* might have become *ben*.[193] Thus, the phrase would have originally read "Yehudi *ben* Nathaniah and Shelemiah *ben* Cushi." E. P. Volz suggested another similar explanation that the Nethaniah *ben* Shelemiah referred to in Jeremiah 36:14 as Africans (Chushi) is distinct from and has no relationship with Yehudi of Jeremiah 36:21, 23.[194] The above emendation is questionable on the ground that there is no ancient version to support it. Moreover, such textual emendation changes the author's intention and leaves the reader with the impression that since Yehudi seems to play such an important role in the whole incident, his ancestors cannot be from Africa. There is a possibility that this is the purpose of such emendation which leads some scholars to assume that Yehudi was a messenger or petty official or ordinary clerk. Looking at the text, at a glance, it is easy to rush into the conclusion that Yehudi is one of the subordinate officials. The princes sent Jehudi to bring Baruch; Jehoiakim sends him to bring Baruch's scroll; Yehudi also reads the scroll before the king (36:21, 23). However, a careful examination of the role he plays shows that he is probably the most trusted and the most "respected man on the scene."[195] That was probably why he was called upon by the king's ministers and the king himself at the time of such a serious threat and impending crisis (Jeremiah's letter). It is possible that he was the only one among the king's ministers "who transcended party strife."[196] If it is remembered that during the discovery of the temple scroll in the days of Josiah (621), Shaphan, the secretary of state, read the newly discovered scroll which led to the national reformation, the only logical conclusion is that Yehudi is not only of African ancestry, he was probably one of the highest and most educated royal state officials.[197] This conclusion is strengthened if one notices that out of so many officials present, he was the only one asked to read such an important and disturbing document. This can also be supported by the fact that the business of writing and reading belonged to the professional in those days.[198] I should also add that the writer and the final editor of the book of Jeremiah want to demonstrate why Africans were so greatly respected throughout ancient Israel. That is because of their wisdom.

Ebed-Melech and the Deliverance of Prophet Jeremiah
(Jeremiah 38:7-10, 12-13 and 39:15-17)

Although King Jehoiakim was subjected to Babylonian rule after the Battle of Carchemish (605), he was not willing to give up his reliance on Egypt which had existed since the days of Assyrian invasion.[199] Late in 601 B.C.E., Nebuchadrezzar, who succeeded his father after the battle of Carchemish, suffered a setback during a military encounter with the Egyptians.[200] He went back home to reorganize his army. Encouraged by this, Jehoiakim revolted against Babylon (2 Kings 24:1). Although Nebuchadrezzar could not respond immediately, he eventually gathered some Babylonian contingents and together with some guerilla bands of Moabites, Ammonites and Arameans marched against Jerusalem in December 598 B.C.E. King Jehoiakim died in that very month[201] and was succeeded by his eighteen-year old son, Jehoiachin (II Kings 24:8). In 597, Jerusalem surrendered and King Jehoichin and the high officials and the leading men were carried to Babylon.[202]

Zedekiah, Josiah's son, was given the charge to lead his nation. However, King Zedekiah was a man unwilling to learn either from the past or from Jeremiah's strong warning that Yahweh was against Jerusalem and that they should surrender to the Babylonians. Soon Zedekiah, probably influenced by his nobles, revolted, and Jerusalem was again under siege in 588 B.C.E. When the siege was temporarily lifted during the approach of the Egyptians (Jer. 21:1-10; 34:1-22; 37:1-10), the false prophets interpreted the lifting of that siege as a sign of peace for Jerusalem.[203] However, Jeremiah accepted the siege as God's judgment and interpreted it as temporary. Jeremiah counseled submission to the Babylonians.

At that time (588 B.C.E.) when any criticism or opposition to the policy of the militant group of nobles which was determined to carry on the revolt was considered treason, Jeremiah continued to preach submission to Babylon and the destruction of Jerusalem. During this period Jerusalem was dominated by the militant nobles, who considered Jeremiah to be anti-Judah. As Jeremiah was leaving the city (probably to attend to some family business), he was arrested and charged with treason. The nobles demanded that Zedekiah put him to death.[204] Although Zedekiah was friendly with Jeremiah, he did not want to offend the militant nobles. He evaded his responsibility by leaving the whole matter to the nobles to do as they saw fit (Jer. 38:5). Consequently they made use of the king's evasion of responsibility and threw the prophet into a cistern to die (Jer. 38:6).[205]

At this critical moment when Jerusalem was under the Babylonian siege and Jeremiah was between life and death, an African called Ebed-melech, whose name literally means "king's servant,"[206] made his appearance. When Ebed-melech the African, heard of this murderous act, he immediately sought King Zedekiah who was at the Benjamin gate of the city. While the king was probably settling some legal matters or busy overseeing the preparation for the defence of the city, Ebed-melech confronted him. Ebed-melech not only informed the king about the fate of the prophet, he also charged the people who were responsible for such an act with the great crime of attempted murder (38:8-9). This action was a risk for Ebed-melech.[207]

Although King Zedekiah had evaded his responsibility when the aggressive nobles demanded Jeremiah's death from his hand, this time, the challenge of Ebed-melech's courage and sense of right made him act swiftly to save Jeremiah.[208] The king put Ebed-melech in charge of the men who were to rescue Jeremiah (38: 10)[209] Ebed-melech, the African, got rags from the storeroom, carefully and gently let them down to the cistern and instructed Jeremiah: "Put the rags and clothes between your armpits and the ropes" (Jer. 38:12). So Ebed-melech, the African, rescued one of the greatest Old Testament prophets. When some scholars examined "Ebed-melech's courage, dispatch, compassion, and his ability to bring out the best in" one of the kings of Israel, they considered this story in Jeremiah 37:7-13 as "one of the fairest stories in the Old Testament.[210] "Moved to save the life of another and acting without calculation or counting the cost, an unknown black man emerges `from obscurity to immortality.'"[211] Sometime after the prophet was rescued, he sent some words to Ebed-melech (Jer. 39:15-18),[212] promising that he will survive the fall and also be saved from those seeking his life. The basis for this prophecy, according to the prophet, was that he trusted Yahweh instead of following the popular opinion.

As far as the racial identity of Ebed-melech is concerned, scholars do not have any problem identifying him as a black man or his ancestor as from Africa south of Egypt. However, his position in Judah during Zedekiah's time is greatly debated. On the basis of the fact that Ebed-melech was designated as *Saris*, several scholars concluded that he was "a eunuch" keeping King Zedekiah's wives.[213] However, others have seen him as either one of the royal officials, or courtiers.[214] There are several reasons which make it more probable that Ebed-melech was one of the highest royal officers and not a eunuch as some have maintained. If Ebed-melech is a practicing Israelite who worships Yahweh as suggested by the prophet Jeremiah's saying (Jer. 39:15-18) that he trusted in Yahweh, he could not have been a eunuch. Israelite law prohibits a eunuch from their congregation (Deut. 23:1, Lev. 21:17-21). It seems unlikely that Zedekiah would have placed his troops under Ebed-melech's command if he had been a eunuch. If Ebed-melech had been a eunuch, Jeremiah would probably have condemned him according to Israelite law. Consequently, Ebed-melech would not have offered to rescue him.

The original meaning of the word in question and its usage in several other Old Testament passages seem to support that Jeremiah 38:7 does not mean eunuch. The word *saris* comes from the Assyrian word *sa rest* which literally means "he who is at the head of the king" or "he goes before the king, one of his confidential advisors."[215] In the Old Testament the word appears about forty-five times. In most of these places where the word is used, they carried the meaning "officers" or a person of great importance or great wealth.[216] In the few places where the word seems to mean "a eunuch" it appears primarily in the material dating much later than the time of Jeremiah and in most cases in non-Israelite setting.[217]

Although no one can be certain why the Septuagint omits the word *saris*, it could be that it is for the sake of avoiding confusion (since the word can mean both eunuch and officer since in this context of Jeremiah 38:7 it appears to mean "officer."

In the light of these reasons mentioned above, it is more likely that Ebed-melech, the African, was one of king's officers, who was highly respected by the King and the prophet Jeremiah as African nations were held in high esteem and used for valuation in ancient Israel. He was also one of the most trusted of all the officials that must be the reason why the king allow him to lead the team of rescuers.

The Acknowledgment of
African Military Might (Jer. 46:9)

After the collapse of the Assyrian Empire and the death of King Josiah (609), Africa reasserted her dominion over the Syro-Palestinian people and forced Judah into a state of vassalage. During the encounter between the Africans and the Babylonians in the Battle of Carchemish (1605 B.C.E.), the prophet Jeremiah composed this poem (46:1-12) either as a prediction or in celebration of the victory of the Babylonians over the Egyptian army under Pharoah Neco.[218] Lawrence Hay suggested that this oracle was compiled during the second invasion of Palestine in 588-586.[219]

The majority of scholars accept the authenticity of this oracle against foreign nations in Jeremiah 16:1-12. In fact, according to Hyatt, this oracle has a greater claim to authenticity than any other in the oracular collection of Jeremiah.[220] Its language attests to this.[221] Eissfeldt, though, accepts the possibility of its Jeremianic material, was skeptical.[222]

A notable feature of this oracle is the employment of "speech forms which are common in the holy war."[223] There appear "summons to battle" and the "command to flee."[224] Verse 2 was a preface providing the background or the occasion for the poem. Perhaps when the prophet Jeremiah heard of the defeat of the African army at the battle of Carchemish, he was deeply moved, and he composed the poem in verses 3-17.[225]

This poem is regarded as unsurpassed in its vividness and power by any other poem in the book of Jeremiah. The address falls into two strophes (3-6 and 7-12).[226] In both strophes the scene is described in a lively manner: in the first strophe the African armies advance to the battle when the officers issue their sharp orders, then panic and attempt to flee. Their destruction is set forth in short sentences. In the second strophe (7-12), the prophet taunts Pharoah Neco for his great pride and courage, and then shows the inevitable collapse of the cavalry, chariots and infantry. Despite the re-enforcement of the powerful armies of the Africans (Kush and Put are described as *gibborim* and the Ludim, all are destined to perish because it is the judgment of Yahweh.[227]

The above passage like others already discussed (Isa 18, 20, 30:1-2; 31:1, 3) is also another evidence of the degree of Israelite military and political dependence on African nations. It also represents the high degree of the prophetic battle to counteract such military and political dependence on the African nations. This passage also made clear the reason for Israelite military and political dependence. Ancient Israelites recognized that these African nations (Ethiopia, Put, Egypt and Lud) are great warrior and were exceptionally good in handling shield and bow. If they were not highly respected for their military power Israelites would have not so much dependent on them. The prophets (Isaiah, Ezekiel, Amos, Jeremiah) would not have spent so much time prophesying vehemently against these African nations and their military men. Randall Bailey recognized this fact in his article when he argued rightly that the degree of the reliance of Israel on African military protection was responsible for the extremism and bizarre quality of some of the prophets actions and speeches against the African nations.[228]

Zephaniah, the African Prophet
(Zephaniah 1:1-2:10)

After the assassination of Amon, Josiah became king when he was eight years old (640 B.C.E.). At this period, the Scythians invaded the Assyrian Empire and attempted to invade Egypt but were bribed back by Pharaoh Psammeticus. This Scythian invasion of Palestine probably occasioned the call of Zephaniah to the ministry. Zephaniah saw these invaders as the forerunners of Yahweh's judgment.[229] Zephaniah is generally dated to the period between 663 and 612 because the book referrred to the Assyrian invasion and anticipated the fall of Nineveh.[230] Thus the ministry of Zephaniah should be dated 630 B.C.E.[231]

The name Zephaniah means "the Lord protects." Not much is known about the prophet apart from his message and his unusual extended genealogy (1:1). Seven of the Hebrew prophets (Amos, Obadiah, Micah, Nahum, Habakkuk, Haggai and Malachi) left their prophecies without their family history. Just the father of six others were named (Isaiah, Jeremiah, Hosea, Joel, Jonah and Ezekiel). Only the prophet Zephaniah's ancestry was traced to four generations in the Old Testament. The tracing of Zephaniah's ancestry to four generations is not without reasons. However, that exact reason for this unique and long genealogy has been a subject of dispute among scholars.

One group of scholars believe that the reason for Zephaniah's long genealogy is to avoid the misconception that the prophet Zephaniah is a foreigner (African) but a full Israelite.[232] That this could be true was demonstrated by calling the readers' attention to the fact that all the great-grandfathers' names ended with "yah."[233] Others believe that the sole reason for the unusual long genealogy is to show that Zephaniah's great-grandfather is no other than Hezekiah King of Israel.[234] Both reasons put forward above could be true when understood in conjunction with another unique feature in Zephaniah's long genealogy. This unique feature is that all the great-grandfathers of Zephaniah ended with "*Yah,*" the name of the covenant God of Israel, except "Kushi." In the light of the above, I think that the mention of "Kushi" is significant in giving such extended genealogy to Zephaniah. The main purpose therefore may be to show to the readers that the prophet Zephaniah is a full Israelite with a royal status, he is also of African ancestry.[235]

Several objections have been put forward against the above reasons for the unusual genealogy.[236] The first objection is that, on the basis of chronological ground, it is impossible for Zephaniah to be related to King Hezekiah because there are three generations (Hezekiah, Manasseh and Amon) between Hezekiah and Josiah. But four generations were given in the case of Zephaniah who prophesied during the reign of Josiah. The second objection is that Hezekiah was not referred to as king. The third objection is that the name of Hezekiah, Amariah, Gedaliah and *Cushi* are later additions. The fourth objection is that the name "Kushi" cannot be considered a proper name. The fifth objection is that, the name "Cushi" is a common name in the ancient Near East during the time of Zephaniah and does not imply African (Ethiopian) ancestry.[237] Two examples are given: that since a certain Cush from the Assyrian province of Haran was known to have a brother and father with genuine Aramaic names; that since a certain Cushi from Abu Simbel had to write the Phoenician language; such names could not be African origin.[238]

The first objection (chronological impossibility) appears invalid if some facts are well considered. It is possible, though not certain, that Manasseh, the eldest son of Hezekiah, was born in 698 B.C.E. and Amariah, who was Manasseh's brother, was born in 697-696 B.C.E.[239] The fact that Manasseh's son, Amon, was not born until when his father was about forty-five years old (2 Kings 21:1-19) does not necessarily mean that Amariah's son Gedaliah was not born until he was forty-five. What seem probable in the light of the history of that century is that Gedaliah was born when his father Amariah was fourteen or sixteen years old and that the Prophet Zephaniah might have been born when his great-great grandfather Amariah was forty-eight or fifty years old.[240] If Josiah was born when his father was sixteen; Jehoahaz, when his father Josiah was sixteen; Jehoiakim when his father Josiah was fourteen; Jehoiachin when his father was eighteen, and his great-great grandfather was forty-eight, there is no reason why Zephaniah could not have been born when Amariah was forty-eight or fifty years old.[241] Thus, Zephaniah's royal ancestry traced to King Hezekiah is very probable.

The second objection (that the title "King of Judah" was not mentioned) also appears invalid. This could have been deliberately omitted for several valid reasons.

(1)   At that period, Hezekiah as the former king of Judah was well remembered, especially for his reformation.

(2)   There was no need to mention "King of Judah" because the name Hezekiah was uncommon during the pre-exilic time, and, as such, it could not be confused with any other Hezekiah. In fact, no other Hezekiah is mentioned in the Bible.[242]

The third objection (that this was a later addition) has no foundation because these names are not missing in any important ancient manuscript. Moreover, it is not uncommon to mention the name of a man's father and grandfather (Jer. 4:1f; 2 Kings 22:3, 14), although it is in the case of a prophet.

The fourth objection (that the name Kushi can not be considered as a proper name) also has no solid foundation if Gadi, King Menahem's father (2 Kings 15:14), Hachmonie (I Chr. 27:13) and Buzi, Ezekiel's father (Ex. 1:3) could be considered as proper names.[243]

The fifth objection (that the name Kushi was common throughout the ancient Near East and therefore could not mean a man from Africa) cannot be taken seriously in the light of the history of African diaspora. Because a person can speak or write other people's language does not mean he could not belong to any other nation. The fact that African people have scattered to all parts of Mesopotamia as early as third millenium B.C.E. and that they were referred to by the Egyptian as *Kash* or *Kesh*, by Assyrians as Kushi, and by the Hebrew as *Kushi* or *Kushit* has been demonstrated in Chapter two of this book. The political and military alliance between the Africans and King Hezekiah of Judah is a very important reason that Zephaniah could have had African ancestry.[244] This fact also raises the question whether King Hezekiah has an African ancestry or not.

Although there is no clear statement, King Hezekiah could have had African ancestry. Another possibility is that he married an African woman who gave birth to Zephaniah's grand fathers. It is logical to think this way considering the fact that King Hezekiah had more interaction with African nations than any other King of Israel. Throughout his life he made Israel dependent on African nations both militarily and politically.[245] As discussed early, this great dependence on African nations was responsible for the prophets antagonism. I hope that further research will make this fact clearer.

Zephaniah's oracle against the foreign nations chose Philistia to represent the West, Moab and Ammon the east, Assyria the north, and Africa south of Egypt (Ethiopia) instead of Egypt to represent the south (Zeph. 2:4-15). Why Africa instead of Egypt or Africa and Egypt as usual?[246]

Just as striking as the preference of Africa south of Egypt to Egypt in the oracle of judgment, so also is the preference to name only Africa south of Egypt in Zephaniah 3:10 for salvation. The Prophet Zephaniah, in chapter 3, tells about the conversion of all people and gives them pure speech. In this oracle of salvation, no nation was mentioned except Africa south of Egypt. "From beyond the rivers of (Africa) my suppliants, the daughter of my dispersed ones shall bring my offerings." Why single out Africa? Considering the smallness of Zephaniah's message, one will probably be right to say that he has unusual interest in Africa and this might be because of his ancestral background.[247]

Prophet in ancient Israel had great contribution to the religious, political and military and social life of ancient Israel. They help in shaping the totality of what ancient Israel was. Thus to find an African as one of these prophets means that Africans have contributed to the total development of ancient Israel. It could also show that racial discrimination on the basis of color was not in existence in ancient Israel.

Since Africans and their nations were highly respected, throughout the ancient Near East, it could have been a great advantage and great esteem to have Africans as one of the prophets in Israel.

The Knowledge of the Power of Africans (Nab. 3:8-9)

Are you better than Thebes—(No Amon) that sat by the Nile, with water around her, her rampart a sea, and water her wall? [Africa south] her strength Egypt too, and that without limit; Put and the Libyans were her helpers.

During the reign of Ashurbanipal, Assyrian power reached its zenith. But after the death of Ashurbanipal, (630 B.C.E.), the Assyrian Empire, whose power has been felt far and wide, began to crumble. The Medes under the leadership of King Kyaxares, and the Chaldeans under the leadership of Nabopolassar combined their power and moved against the Assyrians. In about 614 B.C.E. Ashur fell. In 612 B.C.E. the actual capital of the Assyrian, Nineveh, fell woefully. That was the end of Assyrian domination.

Although scholars are divided as to whether the book of Nahum should be dated before or after the fall of Nineveh, there exists a general agreement that this book should be understood in the light of the international event describe above because the content of the book concerned the fall of Nineveh.

R. H. Pfeiffer[248] thinks that even though the description of the fall of Nineveh is vivid, unexcelled, and with "a sense of reality" and "concreteness" that makes it seem as if it is an eyewitness account, a redactor who lived about 300 B.C.E. was responsible for the present work. This redactor quoted I Kings 11 :39, Jeremiah 30:8, Isaiah 52:7 as he vaguely remembered them. P. Haupt thinks that the book was written as a festival liturgy for the celebration of the Day of Nikanor on the thirteenth of Adar in 161 B.C.E.[249] A. Haldar believes that the book was written as a form of political propaganda against the enemies (Assyrians) shortly before the fall of Nineveh.[250] S.J. De Vries, sees the book of Nahum in its present form as a material shaped by a confused redactor who, working from memory, inserted his own words into the original poem of Nahum between 663 and 253 612 B.C.E.[251] B. S. Childs, interpreting the book of Nahum from a canonical perspective, sees the threat against Nineveh in Nahum not as an expression of personal hatred of the Assyrian, but as a psalm meant to establish the theological context of a particular historical event of the 7th century.[252] According to Childs, the author is merely expressing the fact that no nation, no matter how powerful can withstand Yahweh. The event is therefore an illustration of a divine power against "human evil and nationalistic arrogance.[253]

A close examination of the book of Nahum shows that the depiction of the fall of Nineveh is not a judgment oracle as such, but an expression of intense feeling of the oppressed people against the oppressor, expressed in songs and poetry.[254] These feelings expressed in the yearly national ceremony, probably enabled the people of Judah to share in the triumph of the oppressed over the oppressor brought about by the mighty power and justice of Yahweh on behalf of Israel (1:14, 3:5-6).[255] Such participation in this national ceremony probably elevated the spirit of the community of faith in Jerusalem. The joyous celebration was echoed all over the world as far as Africa.[256]

Nahum 3:8-10 shows that the prophet Nahum was quite aware of the international situation of his time. Nahum, like Isaiah of Jerusalem (Isa. 18:1-2), was well aware of the conquering power that emerged from Africa during the Cushite dynasty. He was aware of the event in which Africa south of Egypt under the leadership of Piankhi (715?) Shabako, and Tirhakah overran Egypt. The prophet knew that people of Africa (Kush), and the military resources of Egypt proper (subjugated by Africa), was also available for battle against Theban enemies. In fact, he was aware that the strength and the military resources of Africa which were combined to wage war against the Theban enemies were so vast that the prophet described them as "without limit" (Nab. 3:9)[257]

AFRICA AND AFRICANS IN THE EXILIC PERIOD

Although the destruction of Jerusalem and the subsequent deportation of Judah in 587 B.C.E. by the Babylonians did not end Judah's history, it was nevertheless a great national catastrophe in which her institutions and her "national-cultic community" were suspended and never recreated in exactly the same form.[258] Although not all the people of Judah were deported, the event should neither be minimized, nor the biblical account be considered an exaggeration of the actual event as did Professor C.C. Torrey.[259] There was a total disruption of life. Almost all the fortified cities of Judah were destroyed. Apart from the fact that most of the population was deported, many of them probably died in the battle. Others probably died of diseases and starvation.[260] While some fled for their lives, others were executed.[261]

Scholars still do not know precisely what happened in Judah during the exilic period, except that the condition was precarious and miserable as described by the book of Lamentations.[262] However, one can assume that there were few refugees who rejoined the few people who were left in Judah (Jer. 40: 11-12).[263] Despite the fact that the temple was ruined, some Pilgrims possibly continued to visit the temple ground for prayer and sacrifices.[264] All that these poor helpless remnants could do was to mourn and dream of eventual restoration of Judah.[265] The major impulse for restoration came not from these helpless remnants, but from the deported men. Two major exilic prophets were especially important for the encouragement of restoration faith. When it appeared that there was no more hope at all for the restoration of the Jews, the prophet Ezekiel who was probably deported in 597 B.C.E., and the unknown prophet, second Isaiah, began to proclaim a future hope for the exilic Jews in Babylon. These two prophets included in their proclamation of the restoration of faith, Yahweh's dealing with other nations in his process of restoration. According to them Yahweh will punish not only the Assyrians, Babylonians but also the African nations.[266] As part of Yahweh's method of accomplishing this restoration, the riches of these nations shall be given to Israel.[267]

The Prophet Ezekiel and Yahweh's Judgment
on Africa (Ez. 29:10; 30:-5)

The book of Ezekiel is one of the Old Testament prophetic books that has been a subject of great criticism among biblical scholars. In several attempts to solve the problems associated with the book, scholars have proposed several theories concerning the composition, genuineness, the dates and the place of the prophet's activity.

Scholars appear to fall into three camps. The first group considers the book of Ezekiel as a pseudepigraphical book written even as late as the Maccabean period.[268] According to this group the book of Ezekiel was written by a Jerusalem prophet other than Ezekiel, and soon after 230 B.C.E. the book was revised and ascribed to prophet Ezekiel.[269] The second group believes that the book as it now exists contains the prophet Ezekiel's sayings or small collections of sayings which were later composed by several redactors or Ezekiel's disciples who expanded the materials.[270] Although in detail the views of these scholars differ from one another, yet they all regard the book of Ezekiel as "a deposit of the preaching of the prophet Ezekiel who was active in the exile about "593 onwards."[271] The third group of scholars maintain the view that the book was written and compiled by Ezekiel himself who prophesied both in Jerusalem and in Babylon.[272]

The nations occupy a more prominent place in the preaching of Ezekiel than any other Old Testament prophet. The nations are closely associated with Israel in the prophet's preaching. They became the stage against which the prophet proclaimed judgment and salvation to Israel.[273]

Ezekiel 29:10 and 30:4 form parts of the special collection of the oracles against the foreign nations in chapters 25 to 32 which consists of seven oracles against foreign nations.[274] Egypt and Africa south, arranged in a chronological order except 29:17-21. Chapter 29:1-12 contains four oracles joined together and dated to the period of 587 B.C.E. according to Hayes.[275] Chapter 29: 9-16 is considered uniform.[276] Chapter 29:9-16 is a further -6 279 elaboration of certain elements in verses 3-6.[277]

The oracles in 29:1-16 are divided and characterized by three recognizable formulas found in verse 6, 9, and 16. The "summon or encounter formula, the messenger formula and the proclamation of salvation formula.[278] The basis for the threat against Egypt and Africa south of Egypt is given in Ezekiel 29. They are condemned because of the sin of hybris and arrogance. Hayes has suggested that this sin of arrogance referred to is Pharoah's boast and claim of being the `creator' and the possessor of the Nile.[279] This opinion is supported by the phrase in verse 9, *weani asiti* which could be translated "I made myself."[280] This phrase could be a reference to the self-begotten sun god of Egypt with whom the Pharoahs identified themselves. Another basis for this judgment on Egypt and Africa, south of Egypt is that they made themselves available as the false source of hope, thereby causing Judah to revolt.[281]

The oracles in Ezekiel 30:1-19 are the only undated oracles on Africa. They have been considered secondary because of the late eschatological character of the oracles and the fact that they are undated.[282] It is also believed that the original work has been reinterpreted in terms of the `day of Yahweh' which shall come upon the pagan nations.[283] Hayes considers verses 2-5 as the primary oracles with verses 6-8, 10-12 and 13-19 as the elaboration and an extension of the original motif of the day of Yahweh.[284] According to Walther Zimmerli, 30:1-19 contains three oracles (1-9, 10-12 and 13-19) introduced by the messenger formula.[285] These oracles against the foreign nations of Egypt and Africa represent a prophetic pronouncement of doom upon Egypt and her allies. The judgment against Egyptian allies, especially, Africa, is well understood since most of the time, (especially from the 8th century onward 25th Dynasty) Egypt seemed to depend on Africa. In fact, Africa, south of Egypt supplied Egypt her ruler and protection. Egypt never seemed to act alone without these Africans south. Since Egypt did not act alone, the terror and destruction, which von Rad called "the sacral panic"[286] will fall upon Africa south, and other Egyptian allies.[287] What appears very significant in the threat and the prophetic funeral dirge (Ch. 25-32) against these foreign nations, is the purpose or the motive for this condemnation. The purpose is not to glorify Israel or for Israel to rejoice in the fall of her enemies, but that these nations may finally honour and recognize Yahweh, God of Israel.[288]

Africa and Deutro—Isaiah's Prophecy
(Isaiah 3:3; 5:1)

> For I am the LORD your God, the Holy One of Israel, your Savior, I give Egypt as your ransom, (Africa south of Egypt) and Sheba in exchange for you. This says the LORD: `The wealth of Egypt and the merchandise of (Africa south of Egypt), and the Sabeans, men of great stature, shall come over to you and be yours they shall follow you; they shall come over in chains and bow down to you. They will make supplication to you, saying: `God is with you only, and there is no other, no god besides him.'

During the departure of the last monarch of Babylon (Nabonidus) who left his kingdom in the charge of Belshar-usar, came the final blow to the Babylonian kingdom.

Approximately 550 B.C.E., Cyrus embarked on the conquest of the Near Eastern empire. Cyrus, overthrowing his grandfather, King Astyges of Media, merged together two nations (Persia and Media). He extended his empire to the Aegean Sea and also to the Ionian Greeks, before turning to Babylon. Soon, in 539 B.C.E., Babylon fell. His conquest of Babylon was recorded in the Persian document called the Cyrus Cylinder:

> Marduk (the most important Babylonian god)...beheld with pleasure his (i.e., Cyrus) good deeds and his upright mind (and therefore) ordered him to march against his city Babylon...going at his side like a real friend. His widespread troops strolled along, their weapons packed away. Without any battle, he made him enter his town Babylon, sparing Babylon any calamity.[289]

Immediately after Cyrus' conquest, he demonstrated great tolerance by allowing the Jews to return to Jerusalem as recorded in the biblical account:

> In the first year of Cyrus the King, Cyrus the King issued a decree concerning the house of God at Jerusalem, let the house be rebuilt, the place where sacrifices are offered and burnt offerings are brought;...And also let the gold and silver vessels of the house of God, which Nebuchadnezzar took out of the temple which is in Jerusalem, each to his place; you shall put them in the house of God. (Ezra 6:2-5).

Shortly before Cyrus' conquest of Babylon when most of the Jews had lost all hope of deliverance, an unknown prophet (Deutero-Isaiah),[290] suddenly began his unexpected prophecy of hope: Yahweh's deliverance of his people through Cyrus' conquest of Babylon and the return of the Jews to their homeland.

With the exception of C.C. Torrey, who dated Deutero-Isaiah to 400 B.C.E., most scholars accepted a date shortly before Cyrus's conquest (538 B.C.E.) as the general date when the Deutro-Isaiah prophesied to the exile in Babylon.[291] This general conclusion is reached on the basis of the theological, stylistic, linguistic and historical differences between Isaiah 1-39 and Isaiah 40-55.

It has been stated that Isaiah 43:1-7 is misplaced.[292] 43: 1-7 is regarded as the conclusion of chapter 42, thus, the chapter divisions between 42, 43 and 44 should not be pressed too hard. While Westermann divided chapter 43:1-7 to two sections (1-4 and 5-7) within a single oracle,[293] Whybray divided it to two sections and two separate oracles (1-3a and 5a, 3b-7).[294]

John Scullion saw a community lament form in the preceding chapter (42:18), including 43:1-7.[295] Isaiah 43:1-7 is regarded as part of the reply to a community lament in which he is accused as being blind and deaf to the cry of the exile.[296] However, Yehezkel Kaufman[297] calls this a lawsuit, a theme also found in chapter 45. A close examination of this 43:1-7 shows that it falls into the category of oracle of salvation.[298] C. C. Torrey thinks that verse 3 should have ended with *mosieka* because a new subject is introduced by the word *natathi*.[299]

What the word *mosieka* actually means here is explained in what follows: "I give Egypt as your ransom (Africa) and Seba in exchange for you because you are precious in my eyes, and honoured, and I love you. I give men in return for you..." (43:3-4). It has been suggested that the actual meaning of this passage is that Yahweh would give all African territories to Cyrus as a price for liberating the children of Israel in exile.[300] Although Deutero-Isaiah has every reason to expect that the next territories to be conquered in Cyrus' agenda would be Africa, there is no evidence of any kind that Cyrus conquered Africa. Egypt was not conquered by the Persians until the time of Cambyses (525 B.C.E.), the successor of Cyrus.[301] One must not press this passage too much by giving it a literalistic interpretation or consider the text as a careful theological statement. Such could lead not only to a false historical conclusion, but also to the same ideas which pervaded the earl, Christian church in the early days of slavery.[302] Deutero-Isaiah seems to be saying, using every symbol and great extravagant language at his disposal, that Israel is loved by Yahweh; Israel has a Saviour who will go to all lengths, even giving the entire world for Israel's deliverance. Here the love of Yahweh serves as a motif throughout the poems.

With "eloquent verbosity," "repetition" and "fanciful hyperbole,"[303] the prophet drew partly from contemporary history, partly from eschatological imagination, and partly from covenantal tradition to express the bond of love which bound Yahweh and Israel.[304] It seems as if there is nothing Yahweh will not give for Israel's deliverance, even the powerful and the very rich nation of Africa.[305]

Isaiah 45:14 is related to 43:3 according to its content. While some scholars consider 45:14-17 as a single unit, others consider the passage as

composed of fragments. Westermann considers 45:14-17 as a combination
of fragments with different styles, vocabularies and intentions.[306] These
fragments are divided into three 45:14, 15 and 16-17.[307] According to
Westermann, verse 14 appears strange where it is now because it has no
connection with what precedes and what follows it. This strangeness and the
similarity of its content to Third Isaiah brings the likelihood that it was
originally connected with Isaiah 60:3-14.[308] Kohler, Begrich and Mowinckel
divided the passage into two sections:[309]

(1)   45:14-17 as the first section in the form of oracle of salvation, and

(2)   45:18-25, as the second section in disputation form.

Other scholars who find a unity in the above passage consider
45:14-15 as representing a peak of theological and poetic intensity with
common themes of the absolute and unique divinity of Yahweh and the unity
of mankind under his sovereignty.[310] Another problem among scholars is the
identification of the person addressed in 45:14. In other words, to whom will
all the wealth of Africa and their men be given? Scholars who consider
Isaiah 43:3 as a reference to the conquest of Cyrus, maintain the same view
in 45:14.[311] It was interpreted to mean that as Africans were led by Cyrus in
chains, passed through Jerusalem on their way to captivity, they confessed
God's presence. The problem with this interpretation is that there is no
historical record of Cyrus' capture of Egypt. More importantly, the Hebrew
pronoun *lak*, "to you," which is used for the person addressed, is feminine.
That rules out Cyrus. This feminine suffix supports the view that Israel or
Jerusalem is addressed.[312]

If this passage is taken literally, it means that all the wealth, and the
powerful men of Africa, would go to Jerusalem for Israel's use. G. A. F.
Knight considers this passage not as a historical statement, but a vision and
hope of other prophets who believed that the whole world would eventually
worship them (not God) with their gifts (Isa. 49:23; 60:9, 10, 16; Zeh. 6:15;
Isa. 2:1-5).[313] This type of vision and hope is what Whybray considers "a
spiritualistic and military imperialistic ambition" of Israel which probably
"harks back" to the days of David and Solomon.[314] C. C. Torrey, eliminates
baziqim "in chains" because it is "metrically superfluous" and therefore is a
gloss.[315]

Endnotes

1. John Bright, *A History of Israel*, Third Edition (Philadelphia: Westminster Press, 1981), 184-85.

2. Norman K. Gottwald, *The Hebrew Bible: A Socio-Literary Introduction* (Philadelphia: Fortress Press, 1985), 319. Bright, *A History of Israel*, 184-85. The Philistines, though not very numerous people, were "formidable fighters with a strong military tradition." They were well-disciplined soldiers with superior weapons and chariots. Perhaps the Philistines sensed in Israel a threat to their security. They moved swiftly to conquer the entire Western Palestine. For a description of Philistine weapons see Y. Yadin, *The Art of Warfare in Biblical Lands* (McGraw-Hill, 1963), vol. 2, 2 8-53, 336-5 and 350-55.

3. Eissfeldt, "The Hebrew Kingdom," *CAH* Vol 2.," Part 2B, 570 and Gottwald, *The Hebrew Bible*, 319.

4. Ibid., 319.

5. A. Alt, "The Formation of the Israelite State in Palestine," in *Essays on Old Testament History and Religion, trans.* R.A. Wilson (Oxford: Blackwell, 1966), 171-237. See also O. Eissfeldt, "The Hebrew Kingdom," *CAH*, vol. 2, Part 2, 537-605. See also Bright, *A History of Israel*, 184.

6. Some scholars have argued that what is called "a united monarchy" should not be because the kingdom was not really united. There were many internal strifes between Saul and Samuel, Saul and David, David and Eshbaal, David and Absalom (which shall be discussed further in this chapter), David and Sheba, Solomon and Adonijah. Jeroboam and Rehoboam. Solomon's oppressive policy widened and brought tensions among the tribes. The monarchy as a whole never escaped tension, despite all the brilliance of David and Solomon. The fundamental problems of tribal independence and jealousy remained. See Bright, *A History of Israel*, 228, and C. T. Francisco, *Introducing the Old Testament* (Nashville: Broadman Press, 1950). For the sake of understanding the term "united monarchy will be used here. 229.

7. Norman K. Gottwald thinks that the number of years which each King of Israel reigned (Saul, David and Solomon,) 40 years each (II Sam. 5.4, I kings 11:42) might be round numbers to express a long and full reigns. Gottwald, *The Hebrew Bible*, 294.

8. Ibid., 319.

9. Yadin, *The Art of Warfare in Biblical Lands* (McGraw-Hill: 1963), 2 8-53, 336-5.

10. Gottwald, 294.

11. Ernst Sellin and George Fohrer, *Introduction to the Old Testament*, trans. David Green (Nashville: Abingdon Press, 1965), 217.

12. Ibid., 217-23 for a summary of the history of criticism of books of Samuel.

13. Eissfeldt also denies any appearance of Deuteronomistic redaction in the Court History of David, Eissfeldt, *Introduction*, 280. Ibid., 278. According to R.H. Pfeiffer, the hand of the Deuteromistic editor is lacking in II Sam 18. He maintains that II Sam. 9-20 is probably an insertion. *Introduction to the Old Testament* (New York: Harper and Row Publ. 19 8). 367.

14. Otto Eissfeldt, *The Old Testament: An Introduction*, Trans by Peter Ackroyd (New York: Harper & Row, Publishers, 1963), 279.

15. *David the Chosen King, A Traditional Historical Approach to Second Samuel*, trans. E.J. Sharpe and S. Rudman (Stockholm: Almquist 6 Wicksell, 1964), 20-37.

16. Sellin-Fohrer, *Introduction*, 222. Gotwald, *The Hebrew Bible*, 317.

17. Ibid. 222. 230.

18. R. H. Whybray, *The Succession Narrative Studies in the Biblical Theology*, (London: SCM Press, 1968), 50-55.

19. Ibid., 56-116.

20.. David Gunn, *The Story of King David: Genre and Interpretation, Journal of the Study of Old* supplementary. (Sheffield: JSOT Press, 1978), 37-60.

21. William McKane, *I and II Samuel* (London: SCM Press, 1963), 267. Peer R. Ackroyd, *The Second Book of Samuel* (Cambridge: Cambridge University Press, 1977), 172; Ben F. Philbeck, Jr., *The Broadman Bible Commentary I Samuel-Nehemiah*, edited by C. J. Allen, Vol 3, (Nashville: Broadman Press, 1970), 129 Edward Ullendorf, *Ethiopia and the Bible* (Oxford: OUP, 1968), Charles Copher, "Egypt and Ethiopia in the Old Testament," in the *Nile Valley Civilizations* (New Brunswick: Transaction Periodical Consortium, 1985), 173; Henry Smith, *The Books of Samuel: International Critical Commentary* (Edinburgh: T & T Clark, 1910),359.

22. McKane, *I & II Samuel*, 267; Caird, *IB*, vol 2, 1143, Ullendorf, *Ethiiopia and the Bible*, 8; Philbeck, *I Samuel to Nehemiah, The Broadman Bible Commentary* vol. 3, 129; Smith, *The Books of the Samuel: ICC.*, 359.

23. Charles Copher, "Egypt and Ethiopia in the Old Testament," in *Nile Valley Civilizations*, 173.

24. W. Kaiser, "Ebed," *Theological Wordbook of the Old Testament* (Chicago: Moody Press, 1980), 639.

25. *1 Samuel-Nehemiah, the Broadman Bible Commentary*, edited by Clifton J. Allen vol. 3, (Broadman Press 1970), 129; G. A. Buttrick, *Interpreter's Bible*. vol. 2 (Nashville: Abingdon Press, 1952), 11 1- 2.

26. 26 James Pritchard, ea., *Ancient Near Eastern Texts Relating to the Old Testament*, 3rd ed. (Princeton: Princeton University Press, 1969), 287.

27. 29 E. A. Wallis Budge, *The Oueen of Sheba and her son Menyelek* (1) (London: London University Press, 19), 37-39.

28. Ibid.

29. 30 R.H. Pfeiffer, *Introduction to the Old Testament* (New York: Harper & Row Publ. 19 8), 33.

30.   S.R. Driver, *An Introduction to the Literature of the Old Testament*, (Gloucester; World Publishing), 19.
31.   S.R. Driver, *An Introduction to the Literature of the Old Testament*, (Gloucester; World Publishing), 19.
32.   R.B.Y. Scott, "Solomon and the Beginning of Wisdom in Israel," *Supplement to Vetus* 2, 1955, 262-9. R. H. Pfeiffer, Introduction also maintains that the book of kings was originally written about 600 B.C.E. and re-edited with some additions half a century later. According to Pfeiffer, the first edition knew nothing about the destruction of Jerusalem 587-86 but the second made "unmistakable" allusion to this event, 377.
33.   Burke O. Long, *I Kings with an Introduction to the History of Its Literature* (Grand Rapids: William B. Eerdmans Publishing Co. 1984), 11 9-20.
34.   Ibid.
35.   Eulogy is a speech praising an individual, living or dead, by citing some of his "praiseworthy attribute." The praise speech used the formula "Blessed be Yahweh your God" and is frequently used in the book of Kings. The beatitude is different from the praise speech. Praise speech always offers praise to God while the beatitude is never to God, but to a person or to Israel, the recipient of God's blessings uses the formula. 232.
36.   Harrison maintained that even though this story may have already acquired a legendary tone the source "unquestionably contained some historical material of great value." "Book of the Acts of Solomon," *Introduction to the Old Testament* (Grand Rapids: William B. Eerdmans Publishing Co., 1979). 726.
37.   Sellin Fohrer, *Introduction to the Old Testament* (Nashville: Abingdon Press 1965, The material is from historical source.
38.   *Ethiopia and the Bible*, 13.
39.   John Gray, *I & II Kings* (Philadelphia: Westminster Press, 1963) 241.
40.   John Brght, *A History of Israel*, (Philadelphia: Westminster Press, 1972), 215.
41.   *Archaeology and the Religion of Israel* (5th edition Double day Anchor Book, 1959), 130-2.
42.   Solomon and Sheba ed. (London: Phaidon Press, 1974) 7-39.
43.   John Bright, *A History of Israel*, 215.
44.   *Archaeology and Religion of Israel*, 130-40.
45.   The Annalishic Records from the "so-called "Annals" engraved upon slabs found in Calah" (ANET) *Ancient Near Eastern Text Relating to the Old Testament* 3rd edition (Princeton: Princeton University Press, 1909), 282-283.
46.   Many scholars maintain that vss 11 and 12 are intrusions into the text, Pfeiffer, *Introduction to the Old Testament*, 384.
47   J. Robinson, *First Book of Kings* (Cambridge: Cambridge Press, 1972) 126.
48.   Pritchard, *Solomon & Sheba*, 7-8.

49. Ibid.

50. John Bright *A History of Israel*, 215, J. A. Montgomery locates the Sabean Kingdom in the northern Arabia. Albright, *Archaeology and the Religion of Israel*, 130-42; Gus W. Van Beck, *The Land of Sheba, Solomon & Sheba*, 40-62. James Pritchard (ed.) *Solomon & Sheba*, 7-15. D. A. Hubbard "Sheba," *New Bible Dictionary* Edited by J. Douglas, Second Edition (Wheaton: Tyndale House Publishers, 1982), 1098. D. A. Hubbard "Queen of Sheba," *New Bible Dictionary*, 1098-99, J. Robinson, *I & II Kings*, 126-27, D. Harvey. "Queen of Sheba," *IDB* VOL., 311-12.

51. The Assyrian King. Tiglath-pileser IV, obtained tribute from an Arabian queen in his campaign of 732-731. B.C.E. and listed Sheba among the tribes of northwest, Arabia. *Interpreters Dictionary of the Bible* ed. George Buttrick (Nashville; Abingdon Press, 1962) vol. 4, 311 (DB). A.

52. D. A. Hubbard, "Queen of Sheba" *New Bible Dictionary*; Ed. J. Douglas (Wheaton: Tyndale House, 1982), 1098.

53. D. Harvey, "Queen of Sheba," *IB*, vol. 4, 311-12.

54. Ullendorf, "The Queen of Sheba in Ethiopian Tradition in *Solomon & Sheba*, 107, Ullendorf, *Ethiopian and the Bible*, 130ff.

55. Jewish Antiquities Book VIII, 6, 5-6. Edward Ullendorf's assessment of Josephus account is as follows: Josephus gives a slightly expanded and somewhat "smartened up version of the Old Testament story; yet he remains specifically faithful to the biblical narrative and is entirely innocent of those accretions which later on attached themselves to the queen and her meeting with Solomon." *Ethiopia and the Bible*, 135.

56. See Copher, *Nile Valley Civilization* (New Bruswick: Transaction Periodical, Consortium, 1985), 1-75.

57. Hansberry, *Africa and Africans as Seen by Classical Writers*, (Washington D.C. Howard Unviersity Press, 1977), 59.

58. *The Ethiopian in the Bible* (New York: Vantage Press, 197), 27ff.

59. Beek, "The Land of Sheba," *Solomon & Sheba*, 61 and 63.

60. Gus W. Van Beck, "The Land of Sheba" *Solomon & Sheba*, 47.

61. In Chapter two of this book I discussed extensively the Greek record which regard south of Egypt (Etiopia) as the place where there is plenty of gold. In fact, the country of Ghana as late as twentieth century was still refered to as Gold Coast.

62. *ANET*, 283.

63. I Kings 10:11-12 has been variously called "editorial insertion," instrusion and misplaced text which should have been read after I Kings 9:26-28, J. Robinson, *The first Book of Kings*, 126 and 128, Long, *I Kings*, 11-20; James B. Pritchard, *Solomon and Sheba*, 10. However, these verses may be part of the story refer-ring to those whom the queen employed to bring additional gift mentioned above. See Ullendorf, *Solomon and Seba*, 107.

64. George Rawlinson identified with southern Arabia. Rawlinson, *Origin of Nations* (New York: Charles Scribners' son, 189), 2 9. Pfeiffer and Gray are not certain. Pfeiffer calls it "mysterious Ophir in south Arabia east Africa or India. *Introduction to the Old Testament*, 385. John Gray locate Ophir in south Arabia, India or Africa because of the mention of apes and baboon in I Kings 10:1 and II kings, 238.

65. *BA* xxxvi (1973), 42-48. According to Beck, Ophir can be identified with Egyptian "Punt" (Arabia or Somaliland). *Solomon & Sheba...*, 47. Herbert "Ophir" *Theological Dictionary of the Old Testament* locates Ophir in Somali-land in Africa where the mentioned products were attested in the ancient Lime. Although there is much possibility that Ophir be identified with Egyptian Punt in Africa, any absolute certainty concerning its location must await further archaeological discovery.

66. E. A. Wallis Budge, *The Queen of Sheba and Her only Son Menyelek* (1) (London: African Publication Society, reprinted in 1983), 42. After the British army defeated King Theodore of Abyssinia in 1868, the British army took to England numerous Ethiopic manuscripts and placed then in the British Museum. Among these manuscript were two copies of an ancient work highly venerated in Ethiopia. This work, *Kebra Nagast or "Glory of the Kings"* was regarded as containing an unshakeable proof that the royal house of Ethiopia descended from King Solomon and the Queen of Sheba. In 1872, King John IV of Ethiopia requested from the British government this venerated ancient document because his people would not obey him without it. Instead of sending the original copies, the trustee of the British Museum sent back one of the two copies, but kept in London the one which date 320 CE. Wallis Budge translated it into English. The phrase "gad of the earth" closely resembles the description of Kush as a remote country by the ancient Near Eastern people.

67. Ullendorf, "The Queen of Sheba in Ethiopian Tradition," *Solomon & Sheba*, 104.

68. Ibid. 104-5. See article II of the revised constitution of Ethiopia, 1955, which said that "The imperial dignity shall remain perpetually attached to the line of Haile Sallassie I, descendant of King Sallassie, whose line descends without interruption from the dynasty of Menelik I, son of the Queen of Ethiopia, the Queen of sheba, and King Solomon of Jerusalem.

69. "Beyond identification: The use of Africans in the Old Testament Poetry and Narratives," in *Story the Road We Trod*, ed. C. H. Felder (Minneapolis Fortress Press, 1991), 181. As intellectual genius who produces at will the answer to all questions is a reference to Solomon of later Religious Tradition.

70. The 120 talents of gold amounted to approximately 1/2 tons, James Pritchard, *Solomon & Sheba*, 9.

71. Gen. 10:13, Gen. 19:34.

72. Robinson believes the phrase "all she desired" could mean a child as wise as Solomon to rule her kingdom. *The First Book of Kings*, 129, has also been interpreted to refer to Solomon's entertainment courtesy and gifts given to the queen with such majesty, Gray, *I & II Kings*, 243.

73. For dates of this dynasty see W. F. Albright *BASOR*, (1953), 4-11. K. A. Kitchen advanced dates for Shishak ten years later in the *Third Intermediate Period in Egypt* (Warminster: Aris & Phillip's 1973), 67.

74. John Bright, *A History of Israel*, 233. Several other reasons for the invasion of Shishak have been given by various scholars. Kitchen, interpreting the statement in the inscription found at Karnak (Bubastite Portal) that "evil things" are being perpetrated by some group east of the Delta, says that the invasion of Shishak was a retaliation against Palestine. The Third Intermediate Period in Egypt, 294. Redford interprets the evil things" as the schism and therefore Shishak acted on the "real" or "imagined" request of Rehoboam to restore order. D. B. Redford, "Studies in Relations between Palestine and Egypt During the First Millenium B.C.: The Twenty-Second Dynasty," *JAOS* 93 (1973): 10ff. According to Redford the gold from temple and palace was a payment for services rendered. Yeivin proposed the motive to be a response by Shishak to Solomon trade policies. Solomon's trade alliance with Tyre to the detriment of his long-time partnership with Egypt caused Shishak to want to invade Paleshne. Since his attempt to invade Palestine during Solomon's reign was unsuccessful, he immediately took advantage of the schism. S. Yeivin, "Did the Kingdom of Israel Have a Maritime Policy? " *JOR* v (1959-60), pp. 207-15. See also S. Yeivin, "Topographic and Ethnic Notes," *JEA* (1962):75-80. 237 48 (1962):75-80.

75. See, the previous discussion of the United Kingdom in this chapter.

76. E. L. Curtis and A. A. Madsen, *A Critical and Exegetical Commentary on the Books of Chronicles, ICC* (New York: Charles Scribner's Sons, 1910), 371.

77. Kitchen, The Third Intermediate Period in Egypt, 295.

78. Shishak's inscription carve on a pylon of the Karnak Temple known as the Bubastite Portal. Breasted, *ARE* IV 709-10. Gray, *I & II Kings*, 344.

79. Bright, *A History of Israel*, 233-34. See also Gottwald, *The Hebrew Bible*, 33. For the list of the towns in Israel and numerous settlements in the Negeb mentioned in Shishak's inscription see Breasted, *ARE* IV: 711-16; and Y. Aharoni, *The Land of the Bible*, trans. A. F. Rainey (Philadelphia: Westminster Press, 1967), 323-30.

80. Kitchen, *The Third intermeediate period in Egypt*, 295.

81. Martin North, "Jerusalem and Israelite Tradition," in *The Laws of the Pentateuch and Other Essays*, trans. D. R. Ap-Thomas (Edinburgh: Oliver and Boyd, 1966) 136f.

82. Breasted, *ARE*, IV 724.

83. T. E. Peet, *Egypt and the Old Testament* (Liverpool University of Liverpool Press, 1924) 159.

84. R. J. Coggins, *The First and Second Books of Chronicles* (Cambridge: Cambridge Unviersity Press, 1976), 200. Coggins doubted the historicity of the episode. G. A. F. Knight, *Nile and Jordan*, 282. W. M. F. Petrie, *A History of Egypt*, vol. 3, 34d ed. (London: Methuen and Co., 1925), 2 2f. A. T. Olmstead, *History of Palestine and Syria* (New York: Charles Scribner's Sons, 1930), 357.

85. G. A. F. Knight, *Nile and Jordan*, 282, W.M.F. Petrie, *A History of Egypt*, vol 3, 34, ed. (London: Methuen and Co., 1925), 242f A. T. Olmstead, *History of Palestine and Syria* (New York: Charles Scribner's Sons, 1930), 357.

86. Petrie, *A History of Egypt*, vol. 3, 242f.

87. Olmstead, *History of Palestine and Syria* 357f. However, this "Long Sojourn' of Osorkon's, family cannot be documented.

88. T.E Peet, *Egypt and the Old Testament*, 161ff.

89. Albright, Egypt and the History of the Negeb, " *JPOS*, 147.

90. *The Third Intermediate Period in Egypt*, 309.

91. Montet, *Egypt and the Bible*, Trans. Leslie R. Reylock (Philadelphia: Fortress Press, 1968), 43.

92. Peet, *Egypt and the Old Testament*, 161.

93. *The Third intermediate Period*, 309.

94. Albright, Egypt and the History of the Negeb," *JPOS*, 147.

95. Ibid., 147. Although the number of the army of Zerah might have been exaggerated, the story should not be summarily dismissed as a mere invention by the Chronicler. He might have magnified the numbers to express the nature of the threat and to express the value and necessity of reliance on the Lord for victory. Peter Ackroyd, *I & II Chronicles*, (Cambridge: Cambridge University Press, 1977), 137.

96. James Newsome, Jr., *The Hebrew Prophet* (Atlanta: John Knox Press, 1984), 17., 281. 239.

97. *ANET*, 281. Adad-nirari was followed by Shalmenesar IV— 783-774, Asshur-dan III—773-756, and Asshur-nirari V— 755-746. John Bright, *A History of Israel*, 256. John bright, *A History of Israel*, 254ff. 1001 James Newsome, Jr., *The Hebrew Prophets* (Atlanta: John Knox Press, 1984) 20. Gottwald, *The Hebrew Bible*, 355.

98. In Judah, Uzziah attacked Philistia and the Arabah, and was therefore able to control the trade routes and the ports of the Red Sea and the Mediterranean. Both Kings also enjoyed long reigns and maintained close friendship which enabled the people of Israel to enjoy a degree of intenational power and prestige unknown since the reign of Solomon. John Bright, *A History of Israel*, 254ff.

99. James Newson, Jr., *The Hebrew Prophets* (Atlanta: John Knox Press, 1984) 20. Gottwald, *The Hebrew Bible*, 355.

100. Ibid.

101. N. H. Snaith, *Amos, Hosea and Micah* (London: Epworth Press, 1956), 49-50, Gottwald, *The Hebrew Bible*, 355.

102. Robert B. Coote, *Amos Among the Prophets* (Philadelphia: Fortress Press, 1981), 2-3. Coote says that toward the transitional period from the Babylonian rule to the Persian, the "B" document had to be updated. Then the final editor added I:9-12, 2:4-5 and 9:7-15, 111.

103. (1) Chapter 3-6 may be the original work of the prophet himself; (2) The oracles against the nations and vision reports added to the beginning and the end of the older collection of judgment speeches; (3) An old school of Amos inserted the Amaziah incident and added the admonitions; (4) During the time of Josiah Bethel expositor inserted the doxologies and enlarged Amos critics of Bethel cult (2 Kings 23:15); (5) A Deuteronomistic redactor in the exile added the oracles against Tyre, Edom and Judah; (6) Later postexilic salvation history was appended to the book. For more detailed analysis see Gottwald, *The Hebrew Bible*, 355. Also see Hans Walter Wolff, *Joel and Amos* (Philadelphia: Fortress Press, 1977), 106-13.

104. Gottwald, *The Hebrew Bible*, 353. 240.

105. The children of Israel did not seem to follow the eloquent styles of Amos. Amos first followed the eloquent styles of Amos. Amos first noted other nations' atrocities and the people agreed. Then after the prophet had secured their approval, he suddenly jumped on Israel and Judah. John Barton points out two advantages for the literary style of Amos. (1) It ensures that his word of doom will be heard since his audience's attention had already been gained by indirectly flattering them. (2) It makes it harder for the audience to dismiss the prophet's message since they had already agreed that sin and judgment go together. Amos's Oracles Against the Nations (Cambridge: Cambridge University Press, 1980), 3-4.

106. Disputation sayings are frequent features in Amos' speeches whenever the arguments of his listeners provoke rejoinder (Cf. 3:3-8; 5:18-20; 6:2). Usually disputation refers to the prophet's own words as he defends his vocation and message, but in this case, Yahweh himself is the one who takes up the debate and makes Disputation sayings are frequent features in Amos' speeches whenever the arguments of his listeners provoke rejoinder (Cf. 3:3-8; 5:18-20; 6:2). Usually disputation saying refers to the prophet's own words as he defends his vocation and message, but in this case, Yahweh himself is the one who takes up the debate and makes the rebuttal. J. L. Mays *Amos* (Philadelphia: Westminster Press, 1969), 152, 156.

107. B. Coote, *Amos Among the Prophets*, 118. According to Coote the Kushite in Amos 9:7 refers to Mesopotamian people and that this verse belong to the "C" stage of recomposition.

108. Erling Hammershaimb, *The Book of Amos: A Commentary*, trans. John Sturdy (New York: Schocken Books, 1970), 134. James Luther Mays, *Amos* (Philadelphia: Westminster Press, 1969), 157. Edward Ullendorf, *Ethiopia*

and the Bible, 9. William Rainey Harper, *Critical an Exegetical. Commentary on Amos and Hosea ICC* (New York: Charles Scribner's Sons, 1915), 192. Hans Walter Wolff, Joel and Amos, 347. N. H. Snaith, *Amos, Hosea and Micah*, 49. R. B. Coote *Amos Among the Prophets*, 118.

109. Erling Hammershaimb, *The Book of Amos*, 134, says that the "dark-skinned" people from Africa were held in contempt by the Israelites. Mays in his commentary, *Amos*, 157, says that Israel knew Africans "mostly as slaves," and that this comparison was meant to humiliate the children of Israel and to reduce them to the role in order of things which the Cushites have played in the society. Ullendorf in his book, *Ethiopia and the Bible*, 9, believes that the only way to appreciate fully what he called "the climatic inference" of these passage (9:7) is to see the Africans serving "as the epitome of a far-distant, uncivilized, and despised black race." W. R. Harper, in his *Critical and Exegetical Commentary on Amos and Hosea*, 192, admithng that there was no reference made to their dark skin, maintains that the fact that slaves were so often drawn from them was a ground for despising them.

110. Pherhaps Hammershaimb, Harper, Mays, Ullendorff and others were influenced by the nineteenth and twentieth century beliefs about black people. They tried to use the Bible to justify the evil act of enslaving Africans from the Bible. Nowhere were the black people held in contempt in the Scripture as a result of their skin or place of origin.

111. Snaith, *Amos, Hosea and Micah*, 49.

112. Ibid. 49; Wolff, *Joel and Amos*, 347.

113. Wolff, *Joel and Amos*, 347.

114. What appears to be a contradiction to Amos 3:1 is not a contradiction as such. The prophet Amos was saying that since the children of Israel have failed to live up to the covenant between them and Yahweh by committing sin perpetually, Yahweh is no more bound to them because they have forfeited that choice and relationship. Henry Mckeating, *The Books of Amos, Hosea and Micah, The Cambridge Bible Commentary y*, eds. P. R. Ackroyd, A. R. C. Leaney, J. W. Parker (Camridge: Cambridge University Press, 1971)

115. James M. Ward, *Amos and Isaiah*, (Nashville: Abingdon Press, 1969), 72.

116. When Hezekiah 2 Kings 20:12-19; Isa. 39:1-8 it is possible that he sent these messengers not only to congratulate him, but also to persuade him to the anti-Assyrian camp. It is also possible that when King Hezekiah showed them his palace treasury, he was trying to demonstrate that his strength could make him a valuable ally against the Assyrians Claus Schedl, *History of the Old Testament*, vol. 4.249.

117. Randall Bailey, Beyond Identification.., 176.

118. For a detailed description of this rebellion and internal affairs during this period see John Bright, *A History of Israel*, 278-88, Claus Schedl, *History of the Old Testament*, vol. 4 (Staten, N. Y. Alba House, 1971), 243-64.

119. 2 Kings 20:12; Isaiah 39:1.

120   For about 12 years, Sargon lost control of Babylon. Bright, *A History of Israel*, 280. Ibid.

121. Ibid.

122. Others suggest the date 720 B.C.E. for Piankhi. However, Bright, following Albright preferred 716-715. Ibid., 281.

123. *ANET*, 286.

124. When Hezekiah recovered from his critical illness and Merodach-baladan sent congratulatory messengers to him (2 Kings 20: 12-19; Isa 39: 1-18) it is possible that he sent these messengers not only to congratulate him, but also to persuade him to the anti-Assyrian camp. It is also possible that when King Hezekiah showed them his palace treasury, he was trying to demonstrate that his strength could make him a valuable ally against the Assyrians, Claus Schedl, *History of the Old Testament*, vol 4., 249.

125. To this writer's knowledge, it was Dixon only who said that Piankhi and Shabaka were Libyan rather than Africans. D. M. Dixon, "The Origin of the Kingdom of Kush—Merge), "*JEA* 50 (1964): 121-32. Other Egyptologists, Breasted, W. Y. Adams, and also Bright and Albright agreed with Dixon.

126. This form of prophecy in Isaiah 20:1-6 can be classified as symbolic act and prophecy of doom or disaster. The Sargon inscription enabled scholars to date the year of the capture of Ashdod to 711 B.C.E. because his capture was accomplished in the 11th year of his reign. It also says that Judah was drawn into the revolt and she appealed to Piru. *ANET*, 287. See Gray, *The Book of Isaiah, ICC*, 342. 43, and *ANET*, 286-87. Until the time of the discovery of the Assyrian inscriptions in 1963, this was the only place where the name Sargon was mentioned. The Sargon inscription was discovered in Ashdod in the 1963 archaeological excavation at the site. D. N. Freedman, "The Second Season at Ancient Ashdod," *BA* 26 (1963), 134-39. See also E. J. Kissane, vol. I *The Book of Isaiah*, 216. The term "Tartan" is not a proper name but generally means commander in chief, governor general, second to the King of the holder of a military rank next to the King. Otto Kaiser, *Isaiah 13-39* (Philadelphia: Westminster Press, 1974), 112-16. J. Hayes considers Isa. 20:1-6 as a text that has been transmitted as a historical narrative describing the activity of the prophet, and that verses 4-6 represent Isaiah's original interpretation of his action which was later recast in the form of a historical description. J. Hayes, "Oracles Against the Foreign Nations in the Old Testament: Their Usage and Theological Importance," 209.

127. According to Kaiser, the idea that the prophet walked naked and barefoot for three years is "inconclusiveable considering the climate of Palestine." Therefore this text is a purely narrative theme composed after the event of 711 B.C.E. and is of interest to scholars, not because it is historical reliable, but because of its theological content. Kaiser *Isaiah*, 13:39, 17. Many of the Near Eastern inscriptions—show pictures of prisoners partially nude. See *ANET* supplementary edition, l07-11. It is unlikely that Isaiah was completely

naked. This oracle must have been uttered three years before the actual fall of Ashdod (715-714).

128. *ANET*, 285-87.

129. Ibid.

130. Ibid. From the above, it seems as if Egypt and Africa helped neither Ashdod nor Judah as prophesied by Isaiah. However, there is no evidence that the Assyrians entered Egypt to the extent of carrying the Africans into captivity as symbolically prophesied by Isaiah. Clement believes that the prophecy of this symbolic action was fulfilled in 701 when the Egyptians were defeated in Eltekeh R. E. Clement, *Isaiah 1-39*, 175.

131. John Bright, *A History of Israel*, 281-82.

132. H. Tadmor, "The Campaigns of Sargon 11 of Assur: A Chronological Historical Study," *Journal of Cuineform Studies (JCS)* Xll (1958):79-84. C. Schedl also believed that Judah did not heed the words of Isaiah and was driven to submission, *History of the Old Testament*, vol. 4, 252.

133. *ANET*, 287.

134. Ibid.

135. G. B. Gray, Isaiah l-XX ICC, XXVii-icix. Excavations in Ashdod attest to a violent destruction of the city, probably by Sargon in 711 B.C.E. Fragments of a victory stele of Sargon were also uncovered there. See D. N. Freedman, "The Second Season at Ancient Ashdod," *BA*, XXVI (1963):138.

136. J. Hayes Oracles Against the Nations, 195.

137. Stephen Winward, *A Guide to the Prophet* (Atlanta: John Knox Press, 1968), 93-95.

138. R. B. Y. Scott, *IB*, vol 5, 160.

139. A. S. Herber, *The Book of the Prophet Isaiah 1-39, Cambridge Commentary to the New English* Bible (Cambridge: Cambridge University Press, 1973), 11 7-19.

140. For detailed analysis of Marti's opinion, see Otto Kaiser, Isaiah 13-39,91.

141. Ibid.

142. Hayes, Oracles, 206.

143. W. Janzen, *Mourning Cry and Woe Oracle* (New York /Berlin: BZAW. 125. 1972), 60-62.

144. Clements, *Isaiah 1-39 NCBC*, 165.

145. *The book of Isaiah l-XXVII ICC*, 310-11.

146. Scott, *IB* vol 5, 276-77. Bright, *History*, 281.

147. Bright, *History*, 281 and Kaiser, *Isaiah 13-39*, 93-94.

148. Kaiser, *Isaiah 13-39*, 93-94.

149. Ibid.

150. Gray, *IsaiahI 1-XXVII ICC* 310-11.

151. Ibid. Pliny xiii, II describes them as swift speedy and light.

152. Isaiah 18:2. From this passage, it is evident that ancient people do not share the modem prejudices of some scholars (some of those scholars are listed in

chapter 3) about the black people. Professor Gray has this to say: "There is no reason why the Hebrew should have not admired the burnished copper colour of the Ethiopians, for even Jer. 13:23 need not be interpreted as though the ancient Hebrew shared the modem white man's objection to colour." *Isaiah ICC*, 311-12.

153. Francis Mading Deng, *The Dinka of Sudan* (New York: Holt, Rinehart, and Winston, 1972). See also Oduyoye, *The Sons of Gods and the Men*, 26-27.

154. John Bright, *A History of Israel*, 2. Clement, *Isaiah 1-39, NCBC*, 173-76. Elmer Leslie, *Isaiah* Nashville: Abingdon Press, 1963), 65-66. E. J. Kissane, *The Book of Isaiah* (Dublin: Richview Press, 1960), 195. Kaiser, *Isaiah 13-39*, 90-96.

155. Gray, *Isaiah ICC*, 310-12. Claus Schedl, *History of Old Testament*, vol 255-64.

156. *ANET.*, 287.

157. Among those who accept single invasion are M. Pierce Matheney, Jr., and R. L. Honeycutt, *I Samuel-Nehemiah BBC*, vol. 3, 272-74; Claus Schedl. *History of the Old Testament*, vol. IV, 255-64; H. I. Hester, *The Heart of Hebrew History* (Liberty, Missouri: Quality Press, 1982), 237-38; Martin Noth, *The History of Israel*, 2nd edition (New York: Harper 4 Row, Publishers, 1960), 265-69; Nomlan K. Gottwald, *The Hebrew Bible*, 368-69. Those who accepted a double invasion theory include John Bright, *A History of Israel*, 284-88; G. W. Anderson, *The History and Religion of Israel* (Oxford: Oxford Unviersity Press, 1979), 104-10; John Tullock, *The Old Testament Story* (Englewood Cliffs: Prentice-Hall, 1981), 223-24.

158. Although accepting the invasions by Sennacherib is far from solving the problem, this writer thinks that it makes more sense as one examines the texts. (1) 2 Kings 19: 13-16 says that Hezekiah submitted and bribed Sennacherib, yet Isaiah maintained that Sennacherib would not take Jerusalem or lay siege to it in 2 Kings 19:32-34 and Isaiah 37:33-35. It was also reported that Sennacherib returned home when the angel of the Lord smote his army. (2) 2 Kings 19:9 says that "Tirhakah, King of Ethiopia" opposed Sennacherib. But when the chronology of the Egyptian kings is examined, Tirhakah who became coregent in Egypt in 690-89 and became king in 685-84 would have been too young to lead the African army against Sennacherib in 701. (3) The idea that the cause of the divergence's of these accounts is that one account belongs to the priestly writer (2 Kings 18: 13-16; Isa. 36:1) while the other belongs to the secular (2 Kings 19:13-16) does not seem valid. This writer thinks that the systematic attempt of some scholars to dismiss any text that seem difficult as "interpolation," "secondary addition," or editorial; mistake is sometimes unjustifiable. That there is no Assyrian or Egyptian record which mentions another Sennacherib invasion after 701 does not prove that there was none. Perhaps, archaeologists will one day uncover such evidence. For the arguments for one and two invasions of Sennacherib

see Gray, *I & II Kings*, 399-604; Bright, *A History of Israel*, 284-88; H. H. Rowley, "Hezekiah's Reform and Rebellion," *BJRL* XLIV (1962):420ff; and Tullock, *The Old Testament Story*, 223-24.

159. *ANET*, 287f.

160. This is the famous Siloam tunnel. The tunnel was dug from both ends and where the crews met was an inscription on the rock. The tunnel was 1700 feet long, and runs in an S-curve.

161. *ANET*, 387ff.

162. Ibid.

163. Ibid.

164. Ibid., 288.

165. Otto Kaiser, *Isaiah 13-39*. 117: Pfeiffer, *Introduction to the Old Testament*, 400; Noth, *History of Israel*, 265-69; Robinson, *The Second Book of Kings*, 182.

166. *The Old Testament: An Introduction*, 296. He maintains that the entire II Kings 18:13-20: 19 originated from Isaiah's legend and was secondarily inserted in the book by Isaiah.

167. Bright, *A History of Israel*, 286-87 and Albright, "New Light From Egypt on the Chronology and History of Israel and Judah," *Pasor* 130 (1953):4-11.

168. Just at this time the young African king who mounted the throne of Egypt 690-680 might have promised and encouraged Judah's revolt.

169. Isaiah was influenced by the inviolability of Jerusalem since it is the city of Yahweh. M. P. Matheney, Jr., and R. L. Honeyoutt, Jr., *I Samuel—Nehemiah, The Broadman Bible Commentary*, vol. 3, 277-88. These also were his words to Ahaz during the Syro-Ephraimite war in 734 B.C.E.

170. Babylonian Chronicle seem to confirm this incident by saying that `Sennacherib King of Assyria departed, and went and returned, and dwelt at Nineveh. And it came to pass, as he was worshipping in the house of Nisroch, his god, that Adrammelech and Sharezer his sons smote him with the sword: and they escaped into the land of Ararat. And Esarhaddon his son reign in his stead.' *I Samuel—Nehemiah*, "BBC," 275.

171. H. Snaith suggested that it "may be that Sennacherib suffered a disastrous defeat in an attempted invasion of Egypt, if not in 701 B.C.E. or in 691 B. C. when he made a successful campaign against Judah's neighbour." *IB* vol 3, 303-4.

172. Gray, *I & II Kings*, 604.

173. N. H. Snaith, *IB*, vol. 303 It should not be a surprise that the proud Assyrians failed to record such defeat. Strabo XV, 687 described Tirhakah as a great conqueror. Tirhakah is also represented on the monuments and on the Pylon of the great temple at Medint-Abu as a king who was cutting down his enemies of conquered lands of Egypt Syria and Tepopa (Tepopa is an

unknown land) before the god of Ammon. C. F. Keil, *The Second Book of Kins Commentary on the Old Testament*, 444.

174. Keil, *The Second Book of Kings*, 445. There is no certainty in the chronology of the reign of Tirhakah. See Ibid. 444.

175. Bailey, "Beyond Identification," *Stony the Road We Trod*, 173. These long dependence was based on African's Egyptian capability of withstanding external military invasion and "its long history of independence." Dr. Bailey has correctly observed that the majority of Euro-American biblical scholars have spent their time on establishing the historical background of this prophesies without seeing or empasizing these extent of Israel's dependence on African nation for political and military protection.

176. Most interpreters accept 267-6 as the beginning of of Jeremiah's prophetic life following Jer. 1:2 and 25:3. Others, however, consider the figure in chapter 1:2 (13th year and 23rd year) as scribal error and therefore placed it in 617-616. See especially T. C. Gording, "A New Date for Jeremiah," *Expository Times* XLIV (1932-33): 262-65. Probably the latest date suggested is 605 by C. F. Whitley, "The Date of Jeremiah's Call," *Vetus Testamentum* XIV (1964): 467-83. He accepts this date (605) because he thinks that the outcome of the battle of Carchemish influenced Jeremiah's call. For a summary of different opinions see J. P. Hyatt, "The Beginning of Jeremiah's Prophecy," in *A Prophet to the Nations: Essays in Jeremiah Studies*, ed. Leo Perdue and Brian W. Kovacs (Winona Lake: Eisenbrauns, 1984), 63-72. James Newsome, Jr., also accepts the 627 date. *The Hebrew Prophets* (Atlanta: John Knox Press, 1984), 124.

177. James Leo Green, *Jeremaih-Daniel BBC*, Vol 6, 88.

178. J. P. Hyatt, "The Book of Jeremiah," *IB* vol. 5, 927; H. Cunliffe-Jones, *The Book of Jeremiah* (London: SCM Press, 1960), 114; James L. Green, *Jeremiah—Daniel BBC* vol. 6, 88.

179. P. Hyatt, "The Book of Jeremiah," *IB*, vol. 5, 927.

180. B. O. Long, The Stylistic Components of Jeremiah 3: 1-5," *Zeitschrift fur die Alttestamentliche Wissenschaff* 88 (1970), 386-90.

181. *The Hebrew Prophets*, 9. According to Jeremiah's central message, the agent of punishment is the Babylonians. Yet he maintains that God still has a future for Judah. To Jeremiah and his audience it is unthinkable for Africans and leopards to ever consider changing the way they look, having learnt "the advantages of being who they are," that is, "rulers of territories who are respected by and awesome to their neighbors." So also Judah having learnt the advantages of sinning has no incentive of changing. Prophet Jeremiah is saying that Judah should use Africans as yardsticks for assessing themselves. Bailey, "Beyond Identification ..."

182. II Kings 23:34-24:6; Jer. 22:13-19; 21:11-14.

183. This can be true because in the days of Jeremiah, reading and writing was probably scarce in Israel. This may be due to the fact that the art of writing

was restricted to professionals. Thus Jeremiah grew up in the "world of speaking and hearing and not of writing and reading" as today. Only important materials were committed to writing. William Holladay, *Jeremiah: Spokesman Out Time* (Philadelphia: Pilgrim Press, 197). See also Eduard Nielsen, *Oral Tradition* (Chicago: Alee R. Allenson, 1954), 64-79. 1985.

184. D. J. Wiseman, *Chronicles of Chaldean Kings* (626-556 B.C.) in the British Museum (London British Museum, 1956), 68-69. See also John Bright, *Jeremiah* (Garden City, N.Y.: Doubleday &: Co., 1965), 182.

185. Gene Rice, "Two Black Contemporaries of Jeremiah, *"Journal of Religious Thought"* (JRT) XXXII (Spring-Summer 1975) 102.

186. The exact content of the scroll has been a subject of debate among scholars. Scholars have generally sought the contents of the original scroll in Jeremiah 1-25. For example, opinion said that 1-6 was included in the original scroll but 8-10 were added later by Baruch during the second edition. William L. Holladay, *The Architecture of Jeremiah* 1-20 (Lewisburg, Pa.: Bucknell University Press, 1976), 169-74. Hyatt considered the original scroll to be 1:4-14, 17; 2:1-37 3:1-5, 19-25; 14:1-8, 11-22, 27-31; 5:1-17, 20-31; 6:1-30; and possibly 8:4-9:1. *Jeremiah The Prophet of Courage and Hope* (New York: Abingdon Press, 195), pp. 37-38. See also "Jeremiah," IB vol. V, 787-90.

187. Jeremiah, Baruch, Blishana, the secretary, Delaiah *ben* Shenaiah, Elnathan *ben* Achbor, Gemariah *ben* Shaphan, Zedekiah *ben* Hananiah (36:12), Jehoiakim, Jerahmsel, Seraiah *ben* Azriel, Shelemiah *ben* Abdeel, Micaiah *ben* Gemariah and Yehudi *ben* Nethaniah *ben* Shelemiah *ben* (African) (36: 14, 21, 23).

188. J. P. Hyatt, "Jeremiah," *IB*, vol. V., P. 1066; R. K. Harrison, *Jeremiah and Lamentation* (Downers Grove: Inter Varsity Press, 1973), 151; J. A. Thompson, *The Book of Jeremiah,* *"The New International Commentary on the Old Testament* (Grand Rapids: William B. Eerdmans Publishing Co., 1980), 625. 251.

189. Gene Rice, "Two Black Contemporary of Jeremiah," XX *JRT* (1975):104.

190. Ibid. See also J. A. Bewer, The Book of Jeremiah II (New York: Harper & Rows., 1952), 37.

191. B. Duhm, *Das Buch Jeremia* (Tubingen & Leipzig: J. C. B. Mohr, 1901), cited by Gene Rice in "Two Black Contemporaries of Jeremiah," XXXII *JTR* (1975):105.

192. J. P. Hyatt, "The Book of Jeremiah," *IB*, vol. 5, 1066.

193. Ibid. See also E. A. Leslie, *Jeremiah* (New York Nashville: Abingdon Press, 1954), 179-80, who also accepted such emendation. Unfortunately, the Jerusalem Bible accepted such translation (see Jerusalem Bible Jer. 36:1-4).

194. Gene Rice, Two Black Contemporaris of Jeremiah, 11 *JRT*, op. cit. 106.

195. Gene Rice, "Two Black Contemporaries of Jeremiah," *JRT*, 107

196. Ibid.

197. R. K. Harrison is probably right when he says that Yehudi must have been a
      man of importance. Jeremiah and Lamentation (Downers Grove: InterVarsity
      Press, 1973), See also J. A. Thompson, *The Book of Jeremiah: The New
      International Commentary on the Old Testament* (Grand Rapids: William B.
      Eerdmans Publishing Co., 1980), 625. Thompson recognizes him as one of
      the state officials. Calvin also infers from his genealogy that Yehudi was a
      man of some pre-eminence." *Commentary on the Prophet Jeremiah and the
      Lamentations*, IV (Grand Rapids Michigan: WM. B. Eerdmans.. Publishing
      Co., 1950), 339.
198. William Holladay, *Jeremiah: Spokesman Out of Time*, 70-71, Eduard
      Nielsen, *Oral Tradition*, 64-79.
199. John Bright, *A History of Israel*, 327. J. D. Newsome, Hebrew Prophets,
      102-3.
200. Ibid.
201. Ibid. He was probably assassinated. See also J. P. Hyatt, "New Light on
      Nebuchadrezzar and Judean History," *JBL* LXXV (1956), 278ff.
202. *ANET*, 564. Babylonian administrative documents found in Babylon by the
      German expedition in Babylon show that Jehoiachin was actually a prisoner
      of Nebuchadrezzar. *ANET*, 308. See also Albright, "King Jehoiachin in
      Exile," *BA* .V (1942), 49-55.
203. When this siege was lifted temporarily, the Hebrew slaves who had been
      freed were immediately repossessed (Jer. 34:8-22).
204. In ancient Jerusalem there existed many cisterns dug to catch rain during the
      rainy season of the winter to be stored for use during the rainless months of
      May to October. Hatti *IB*, vol 1075. This might be the type of cistern where
      Jeremiah was thrown.
205. The officials whose political position differed from that of Jeremiah
      continued their resentment against Jeremiah as their inevitable end predicted
      by Jeremiah drew nearer. Two of these famous officials were Jucal and
      Gedaliah who maintained persistently that Jeremiah must die for the
      following reasons: (1) he weakens the hands of the soldiers; (2) he was not
      seeking the welfare of the people but their harm; and (3) he was defecting to
      the Babylonians. Jer. 37: 11-15 and 38:1-4. See also H. Cunliffe-Jones, *The
      Book of Jeremiah*, 223. Information in the Lachish letter states that almost
      the same charge was made in one of these letters against certain officials in
      Jerusalem. A letter written from the captain of an outpost to Ya'osh, the
      commander in Lachish says: "Who is thy servant but a dog that my lord has
      sent the letter of the king and the letters of the officials, saying, `pray read
      them?' And behold the words of the officials are not good, but only weakened
      your hands and to slacken the hands of the men who are informed about
      them." W. F. Albright, "The Lachish Letters After Five Years," *BASOR* 82
      (Apr. 1941):22.

206. In ancient Jerusalem there existed many cisterns dug to catch rain during the rainy season of the winter to be stored for use during the rainless months of May to October. Hyatt, *IB*, vol. 5, 1075. This might be the type of cistern where Jeremiah was thrown.

207. The term "Ebed-melech" is used for those who serve the royal family. Isaiah bears this title in II Kings 22:12 and 2 Chronicles 34:20 and was mentioned in connection with Shaphan the secretary.

208. Jeremiah 39:17 shows that Ebed-melech, from that time on, lives a life of fear of reprisal. Gene Rice, *JRT* XXXII (Spring-Summer 1975), 97.

209. The Hebrew text of Jeremiah 38:10 says these men were "thirty men," but on the basis of one manuscript support and common sense, the RSV changed this to read three men." See S. R. Driver, *The Book of Prophet Jeremiah* (London: Hoddar R. Stoughton, 1906), 233. C. F. Keil, *The Book of Prophet Jeremiah*, 111-12, objected to this emendation. The idea supporting the emendation, that it is unnecessary to use thirty men to rescue one person from the cistern, is denounced as arbitrary hypothesis. He believes that these thirty men may serve as security against the militant nobles who might try to prevent the rescue of the prophet.

210. G. A. Smith, *Jeremiah* (New York: Harper & Bros., 4th ed. 1929), 281; J. L. Green, *Jeremiah—Daniel, "BBC,"* 171; Gene Rice, *JRT* XXXII (Spring-Summer 1975), 97.

211. It seems more logical that Jeremiah 39:15-18 which proclaims the survival and safety of Ebed-melech should have followed immediately the account of the rescue in Jeremiah 38:7-13 instead of placing it in its present context. Scholars have rightly considered it out of place. Its present position and the presence of Deuteronomic theology of retribution have led several scholars to question its authenticity. Hyatt considered this as a later addition by the Deuteronomic editor who felt that Ebed-melech should not go unrewarded. *IB*, vol.5, 1081-82. Thompson thinks that the editor might be trying to say that Ebed-Melech survived the fall. *The Book of Jeremiah NICO* 648-49. J. L. Green believes that the text may be chronologically out of order, yet it is an authentic oracle on the ground that it meets the fundamental tenet of the biblical faith. *Jeremiah—Daniel BBC* vol. 6, 174.

212. Gene Rice, *JRT* XXXII (Spring-Summer 1975), 97 and R. Calkins, *Jeremiah the Prophet* (New York: Macmillan Co., 1930), 298.

213. C. F. Keil, *Jeremiah Commentary on the Old Testament*, 111-12; H. Cunliffe-Jones, *The Book of Jeremiah*, 224-25; R. K. Harrison, *Introduction to the Old Testament* 155. The RSV translates the word eunuch.

214. J. L. Green, *"BBC,"* vol. 6, 171. Thompson, *The Book of Jeremiah*, 639: Hyatt, *IB*, vol. 5, 1075; H. Freedman, *Jeremiah* (London: Soncino Press, 1949), 254; S. H. Blank, *Jeremiah: The Man and the Prophet* (Cincinnati: Hebrew Union College Press, 1962), 5, 211. This is also true of the

translators of the following versions: *Jewish Version, the New American Bible*, and the *Living Bible*.

215. Thompson, *The Book of Jeremiah*, 639; R. de Vaux, *Ancient Israel* (London: Darton, Longman & Todd, 1961), 121.

216. In Gen. 37:36 and 39:1, Pharoah's captain of the guard, a married man, was called *saris*. The chief baker and the chief cupbearer, were also called *saris* (Gen. 40:2, 7). The officials of Israel are divided into several categories—officials of the tribes, that served the king, commander of thousands, of hundreds, in charge of the properties, and all the warriors (I Chronicles 28: 1). The official sent to bring the prophet Micaiah, ben Imlah (I Kings 22:9, II Chronicles 18:8) and the officer of the king who restored the house and the land of the Shunammite woman (II Kings 8:6) were called *saris*. The high military or diplomatic officer of the Babylonian and Assyrian armies bore *Rabsaris* (II Kings 18: 17; Jer. 52:25). During the fall of Jerusalem, the commander of the Israelite men was called *saris* (II Kings 25: 19; Jer. 52:25). Nathan-melech whose name has the same compound word with Ebed-melech who has his dwelling in the area of the temple was also called *saris* (II Kings 23:11) The fact that those who were deported by the Babylonians were the people in the class of *saris* and were the leading men of Israel shows that the people called *saris* could be people of high rank or of great wealth. See Gene Rice, *JRT* XXXII (Spr.-Sum. 1975), 98-99.

217. However, the following passages are what seem to be the clearest instances where *saris* could mean eunuch: Isa. 56:3, 4, Esther 1:10, 12, 15; 2:3, 14, 15, 21; 4:4, 5; 6:2, 14; 7:9. 256 Daniel 1:3, 7-11, 18. All these passages are later than the period of Jeremiah. However, II Kings 20:18 and Isaiah 39:7 may be earlier, but no certainty for these passages can be attested as meaning eunuch.

218. J. L. Green, *Jeremiah-Daniel, BBC* vol 6, 185. Hyatt, *IB* vol 5, 1105; D. J. Wiseman, *Chronicles of Chaldean Kings*, 67-79. When the site of Carchemish was excavated by a British excavation group, evidence was found that there was a destruction of the town in about 600 B.C.E. and that it was later occupied by the Egyptian army. A large number of Egyptian subjects from the period of Psametik I to Neco were found. Hyatt, *IB*, vol 5, 1105.

219. "Oracles Against the Foreign Nations in Jeremiah 46-51," Ph.D. dissertation, Vanderbilt University, 1960.

220. Hyatt, *IB*, vol. 5, 1105.

221. Ibid.

222. The Old Testament An Introduction, 363.

223. Hayes, "Oracle Against the Nations in the Old Testament, Their Usage and Theological Importance," Princeton Theological Seminary, 1964, 24ff.

224. Ibid. Verses 4 and 9 portrayed Yahweh as gathering another people to fight his people. In the book of Jeremiah, this type of speech forms occur only in

the oracle against the nations and the oracles on the enemy from the North in chapter 4-6.

225. J. L. Green, *BBC*, vol. 6, 185.
226. Ibid.
227. Ibid. See also C. F. Keil, *The Book of Jeremiah*, 181-82. The description of Kush and Put as *giborim* is significant. Perhaps it shows that the Egyptian people were depending on them and the Hebrews recognize their might. 231.
228. The Prophet Isaiah in chapter 20 walked nude for three years. The Prophet Ezekiel in chapter 16 used "sexual innuendo." 257.
229. Winward, *Guide to the Prophets*, 102
230. Gotwald, *The Hebrew Prophets*, 390-91.
231. Sellin-Fohrer, *Introduction to the Old Testament*, 456. J. P. Hyatt dated the ministry of Zephaniah to the reign of Jehoiakim (609-598) and considered the superscription in Zephaniah 1: I regarding the date of Zephaniah inaccurate. "The Date and Background of Zephaniah, " *JNES* VII (1948), 25-29. Smith and Lacheman considered the book of Zephaniah as `definitely pseudepigraphic as Daniel, and should, like Daniel, be read against the background of 200 B.C.E., D. L. Williams followed Hyatt in dating the book to the time of Jehoiakim. "The Date of Zephaniah," *JBL* LXXXII (1963), 77-88.
232. Sellin-Fohrer, *Introduction to the Old Testament*, 456. 1014. (1925):-31., 282.
233. Zephaniah, 1:1.
234. G. B. Gray, *Studies in Hebrew Proper Names* (London: Adam R. Charles Black, 1896), 262. Winward, *A Guide to the Prophets*, 102. Gottwald, *The Hebrew Bible*, 390. Charles Taylor, *IB*, vol.6, 1014.
235. Gene Rice, "African Roots of the Prophet Zephaniah," *JRT*, 36 (1979), 21-31.
236. For a summary of those objections see Gene Rice, "African Roots of the Prophet Zephaniah," *JRT* 36 (1979):21-31.
237. See E. Lipinski's review of A. S. Kapelrud's book, *The Message of the Prophet Zephaniah: Morphology and I deas* in VT 256.
238. G. B. Gray, "The Royal Ancestry of Zephaniah," *Expositor* II (1900):76-80. Unfortunately we are not certain of the exact date of Hezekiah's death, but is probably 686. 258.
239. Ibid.
240. Ibid. see also Gene Rice, *JRT*, 36 (1979) 21-33.
241. J. M. P. Smith, *Micah, Zephaniah and Nahum ICC*, 183. See also G. B. Gray, *Studies in Hebrew Proper Names*.
242. Gene Rice, *JRT*, 36 (1979):21-31.
243. Ibid.
244. The role the Africans have played in the political and military endeavous of the ancient world powers cannot be overestimated. The Africans (Ethiopians)

were important factors in the struggle to expel the Hyksos from Egypt and in Egyptian achievement of her imperialistic expansionism during the period of the 18th Dynasty. See Steindorff and KcSeele, *When Egypt Rule the East*. 27-28; C. B. Copher, " The Black Man in the Biblical World," *JITC* I (1974):17-16; WEB Du Bois, *The World and Africa*, 2nd Edition (New York: International Publishers, 1965), 117-25). As discussed earlier, the Africans were principal component of Egyptian army during their occupation of Palestine.

245. This dependence may not have only been because of African nations military and political might, but also his ancestral or marital connection with Africa.

246. J. P. Hyatt thinks that in Zephaniah 2:12 Ethiopians are used to represent Egyptians. "The Date and Background of Zephaniah," *JNES* (1948):28. However, he thinks that it is for the remembrance of the 25th Dynasty.

247. Rice, *JRT*, 36 (1979):21-23. While As Kapelrud considers Zephaniah 2:12 a later addition, added between 609 and 598, He thinks that chapter 3:10 is not. See *The Message of the Prophet Zephaniah* (Oslo-Berge-Tromso: Universittetsforleget, Naper Bokrykk eri 1975).

248. According to Pfeiffer, this redactor's memory failed him and that was why here existed some traces of incomplete acrostic arrangement in Nahum chapter 1. According to Pfeitffer, Nahum is not a prophet, but a poet. *Introduction to the Old Testament*, 594-97.

249. According to Haupt, the reason why the alphabetic arrangement in Nahum I is not complete is because the rest of the chapter does not fit for reading in the celebration of the Day of Nikanor. So it stopped in 2. "The Book of Nahum," *JBL* 26 (1907):1-53.

250. *Studies in Nahum*, 24. He fails to see any alphabetic in Nahum 1.

251. "The acrostic Nahum in the Jerusalem Liturgy," *VT* 16 (1966):476-81.

252. *Introduction to the Old Testament as Scripture* (Philadelphia: Fortress Press, 1979), 443-44. K. J. Cathcart considered the book of Nahum as a literary work belonging to the category of the "treaty-curses." Cf. Deut. 28:36ff. "The Treaty-Curses and the Book of Nahum," *Catholic Biblical Quarterly* 4 (1963):433-39.

253. Ibid.

254. 256 Hayes 224-25.

255. Ibid.

256. Ibid.

257. W. A. Maier, *The Book of Nahum* (Saint Louis: Concordia Publishing House, 1959), 321-22. J. M. P. Smith, *Micah, Zephaniah and Nahum Habakluk and Obadiah ICC*, says that the phrases and Egypt, and there was no end should be omitted because they are glosses. However, he gives no substantial reason for regarding them as glosses. S. Haupt also considered the above phrases as glosses but gave no substantial reason for them to be omitted. "The Book of Nahum: A New Metrical Translation," *JBL* XXIV (1907):part I.

258. Bright, *A History of Israel*, 343.
259. *The Chronicler's History of Israel* (Yale: Yale University Press, 1954) Bright, *A History of Israel*, 343-44. Excavation in several cities of Judah seems to support very great catastrophic events as described by the biblical account. Examples of these cities are Lachish, and Beth-Shemesh, Tell Beit Mirsim (probably Debir) and Jerusalem.
260. Lamentation 2:11-21; 4:9-12.
261. II Kings 25:18-27; Jer. 42. According to Bright, this is especially responsible for the fact that even after the return of the first exile, the population of Judah which probably exceeded 250,000 in the eighth century, scarcely exceeded 20,000. Bright, *A History of Israel*, 344.
262. Lamentation 5:1-18.
263. Bright, *A History of Israel*, 344.
264. Ibid.
265. Ibid.
266. Ezekiel 29-30.
267. *Isaiah*, 43 and 45.
268. The representative of this theory is C. C. Torrey, *Pseudo-Ezekiel and the Original Prophecy* (New Haven: Yale University Press, 1930). "Certainly Pseudo-Ezekiel," *JBL* 53 (1934):291-320; "Notes on Ezekiel," *JBL* 58 (1939): 68-86.
269. C. C. Torrey, "Pseudo-Ezekiel," *JBL* 53 (1934):291-320.
270. See Fohrer, *Introduction to the Old Testament*, 403-17. Eissfeldt, *The Old Testament: An Introduction*, 365-82; G. A. Cooke, "New Views on Ezekiel, Theology 2 (1932):61-69; Finegan,"The Chronology of Ezekiel, *JBL* 69 (1950):61-66; W.A. Irwin, "Ezekiel Research Since 1943," *VI*, III (1953): 54-66; Orlinsky, "Where did Ezekiel Receive the Call to Prophecy?" *BASOR* 122 (1951):34-36; Mull Weir, "Aspects of the Book of Ezekiel, *VT*, 2 (1952) 97-112.
271. An example of diversity in detail concern the identification of what could be regarded as the genuine passages. Irwin and Seldms believe that the poetic passages in Ezekiel are all genuine and divinely inspired word of Ezekiel. W. A. Irwin, "Ezekiel Research Since 1943," *VT* III (1953):54-66; A. van Selms, "Literary Criticism of Ezekiel as a Theological Problem," *Die Ou Testamentiese Wertgeme-enskap in Suid Afrika (OUTWP)* 1961, 2-37. Another point of divergence among these scholars concerns the place of Ezekiel's prophetic activity. S. B. Frost in *Old Testament Apocalyptic* (London: Epworth Press, 1954), 84, believes that it was in Palestine only. G. R. Berry in "Was Ezekiel in the Exile?" *JBL* XLLX (1930):83-93, accepted this view. While Fohrer, Rowley and others maintained that he prophesied in Babylon only, Spiegel and Pfeiffer maintained that he prophesied in both Palestine and Babylon. Fohrer, *Introduction to the Old Testament*, 406-7; H. H. Rowley, The Book of Ezekiel in Modern study," *Bulletin of John Ryland*

Library BJRL XXXVI (1953-54):146-90. S. Speigel Ezekiel or Pseudo-Ezekiel?" *Harvard Theological Review* (HTR) XXIV (1931):245-321; R. Pfeiffer, *Introduction to the Old Testament,* 518-65. For a survey of the history of the problem, see Sellin-Fohrer, *Introduction to the Old Testament,* 403-17 and Eissfeldt, *The Old Testament: An Introduction,* 365-82. See also Keith Carley, *Ezekiel Among the Prophets: Studies in Biblical Theology,* second series (Naperville, Ill.: Alee R. Allenson, n.d.), 1-3.

272. This view has been abandoned by many eminent scholars. E. Young, *Introduction to the Old Testament* (Grand Rapids: Wm. B. Eerdmans, 1952), 23 ff. Eissfeldt, *The Old Testament: An Introduction,* 368.

273. Hayes, 251-52.

274. Some interesting characteristics of this collection of prophecies against the nations were noticed by Hayes: (1) evidence of mythological influence which tends to transfer Yahweh's activity into the area of trans-historical identifying the enemy of Yahweh with the mythological powers, (2) many of the oracles pronounced were given without any basis for the judgment or condemnation, and (3) where reasons were given they fall into three basic divisions. Hayes, 270.

275. Ibid, 271.

276. Ibid.

277. Ibid.

278. Zimmerli, *Ezekiel,* vol. 2, translated by D. Martin, edited by Hanson with Greenspoon (Philadelphia: Fortress Press, 1983), 102-9.

279. Hayes, "Oracles Against the Foreign Nations," 263.

280. Ibid.

281. The basis for false source of hope probably began in the eighth century in the days of Isaiah as previously discussed in this chapter. The dependence was very extensive.

282. H. G. May, *IB,* vol. 6, 228-29.

283. Ibid.

284. The Association of the day of Yahweh with the day of the battle against his enemies probably goes back to the idea of the Holy War. Hayes, 266.

285. Zimmerli, *Ezekiel,* vol 2, 127.

286. Gerhard von Rad, *Theology of the Old Testament,* Trans. by J. A. Parker, Vol II (Philadelphia: Westminster Press, 1967), 124.

287. What Zimmerli calls the catch phrase is in "these who supported Egypt" in verse 5. They are six in number. They shall all fall along with Egypt by the sword. Walther Zimmerli, *Ezekiel,* vol 2, 129.

288. This sentence, "They will know that I am the LORD," is used frequently in the book of Ezekiel. Zimmerli calls the sayings, which include such formula as "They will know that I am the LORD," the formula of "self-introduction" or "statement of recognition." He tries to derive this form from I Kings 20:13, 28. Walther Zimmerli, *I Am Yahweh,* translated by D. W. Stott, and edited by

Walter Brueggemann (Atlanta: John Knox Press, 1982) It is the words of "Divine Self Manifestation." See also Zimmerli, *Ezekiel*, vol. 2, 127-28. However, Sellin-Fohrer considers the above formula as the work of the Deuteronomishic redactor of the book who puts it there on the basis of Ezekiel's words. To Fohrer, it is not a separate literary type. The formula therefore is for the purpose of providing a proper understanding of the announcement which has been said or about to be said, that Yahweh has or about to act against or for the people. Sellin-Fohrer, *Introduction to the Old Testament*. 409-10.

289. *ANET*, 315.

290. No biography of this important Old Testament character exists anywhere in the biblical record, thus he remains a personality unknown.

291. However there are differences in details among scholars. For example Morgenstern ascribes 40-48 to Deutero-Isaiah and considers 49-55 as part of Trito-Isaiah (56-66). He made chapter 40 later than 48. "Two Prophecies From 520-516 B.C," *HUCA*, XXII (1949):365-431; See especially "The Message of Deutero-Isaiah in Its sequential Unfolding," *HUCA* XXIX (1958):1-67. M. Harran thinks that while 40-46 were written between the liberation edict and the first group of returnee, 49-66 came from his subsequent ministry in Palestine. "The literary Structure and Chronological Framework of the prophecy in Is. XL-XLVIII," *VT suppl.* IX (1963):127-55. There is no unanimous agreement concerning the exact passages of the Servant of the LORD and also his exact identification.

292. J. D. Smart, *History and Theology in Second Isaiah*, (Philadelphia: Westminster Press, 1965) 96.

293. Claus Westermann, *Isaiah 40-66* (Philadelphia: Westminster Press, 1969), 114-19.

294. R. N. Whybray, *Isaiah 40-66, NCB*, 81-82.

295. John Scullion, *Isaiah 40-66* (Wilmington, Delaware: Michael Glazier, 1982), 7-9. *Isaiah 40-66*, (Philadelphia: Westminster Press, 1965) 96.

296. Ibid.

297. *The Babylonian Captivity and Deutro-Isaiah, History of the Religion of Israel*, vol. 4 (New York: Union of American Hebrew Congregation, 1970), 109-110 and 223.

298. Page H. Kelley, *BBC*, VOL.5, 309. Whybray, *Isaiah 40-66, NCB*, 81-82.

299. C. C. Torrey, *The Second Isaiah* (New York: Charles Scribner's Sons, 1928), 33.

300. R. North, *The Second Isaiah* (Oxford: Clarendon Press, 19??), 120.

301. C. R. North, *Isaiah 40-55, Torch Bible Commentaries* (London: SCM Press, 1952), 72.

302. In 1442 when Antonio Gonsalvez and Nuno Tristan brought some Africans and some gold dust to Pope Martin V of Portugal, the Pope Conferred upon Portugal the possession and sovereignty over all countries from Africa to

India because, according to him, the heathen nations have no right to possess any thing on earth for all the treasures belong to the people of the Kingdom. Sir Henry Johnston, *A History of the Colonization of Africa by Al. N. Races* (Cambridge: Cambridge University Press, 1913), 78-79.

303. Robert Pfeiffer, *Old Testament Introduction*, 463. 306 Muilenburg, *IB*, vol. 5, 483.

304. Muilenburg, *IB*. vol 5, 483. such bonds of love is expressed inform of virtual oath when Yahweh used his own personal name.

305. J. Smart, *History and Theology in second Isaiah*, 130.

306. *Isaiah 40-66*, 169.

307. Ibid.

308. *Isaiah 40-66*, 169-71.

309. Muilenburgh, *IB* op. cit. 528-59.

310. Scullion, *Isaiah 40-66*, 73-73.

311. C. R. North, *Isaiah 40-55, TBC*, 9I.

312. Muilenburg, *IB*, vol 5, 529.

313. Knight, *Deutro-Isaiah: A Theological Commentaries on Isaiah 40-55* (New York: Abingdon Press, 1965), 140.

314. Whybray, *Second Isaiah* (Sheffield, England: JSOT Press, 1983), 63.

315. *The Second Isaiah*, 360-61. According to C. C. Torrey, the verse does not fit the sene of voluntary giving of themselves to Jerusalem, a thought Deutro-Isaiah tries to convey. However, Smart sees the wealth of African nations in view. It was consistently stated that Africans were considered one of the most powerful and riches nations by the biblical writers and editors. Isaiah 19.5 refers to Africans as workers in bombed flax..weavers of white cotton. Ezekiel also observed that Africa was a place of fine embroidered linen. Deutro-Isaiah also mentioned the wealth of Egypt and the merchandise of Ethiopia and the Sabeans men of stature (Isa. 45: 14). The writer of the book of Job also referred to the "topax of African which cannot be compared to wisdom" (Job 28: 19). The writer of the book of Daniel also recognized Africans nations as wealthy when he referred to the "treasures of gold and silver, and all the precious things of Egypt and the Libyans and the Ethiopians." Daniel 11:43.

Chapter 5
Africa and Africans in the Kethuvim

The books called the "Writings" compose a third group of books in the canonization process. In the books of this group, Africa and Africans are mentioned twice in the Psalter, twice in Esther and once in Daniel.

AFRICA'S ACKNOWLEDGEMENT
OF GOD WITH THEIR GIFTS
(Psalm 68:31)

> Let bronze be brought from Egypt; Let [Africa spirits] hasten
> to stretch out her hands to God.

It is widely accepted by scholars that Psalm 68 is textually the most corrupt of all the Psalms, and one of the most difficult and obscure of the Psalms, exegetically speaking.[1] A reader can easily detect the confusion and the enigmatism immediately when he examines the chapter because the style of the Psalm changes abruptly. There are many awkward lines and sudden shifts in thought.[2] Words which do not occur anywhere in Old Testament are also used, spellings which are either incorrect or unique, sequence and consonants which seem to be in disarray abound.[3] The difference in translation of this chapter in several versions is a result of these difficulties. These difficulties have also led to diverse interpretations. While some scholars have doubted that it is a psalm at all, others have regarded it as a collection of short songs, or even an index of first or key lines of as many as thirty separate hymns, like a page from the index of a hymnal.[4] Some scholars have also regarded this Psalm as a collection of short songs written and arranged to accompany different actions in some festival drama, part of which have been lost.[5] However, others have regarded this Psalm as a unitary hymn in two parts which review the past and the future of God's people.[6]

The problem of dating the Psalms is complex and has met no unanimous resolution. The most frequent periods assigned to the Psalms range from 1200 to 160 B.C.E.[7] Method of dating the Psalms varies: allusion to historical events; liturgical factors or literary and theological relations with other scriptural passages.[8] According to Albright,[9] Durhami[10] and Sabourin, Psalm 68 is a pre-exilic Psalm. According to Albright it was written during the Solomonic period.[11] According to

Durham, the language and the syntax pointed to the fact that this Psalm was an ancient one.[12] Stuhlmueller considered Psalm 68 as a national epic which belonged to Israelite history. According to him it was first composed during the reign of King Saul, and was later revised during the reigns of David and Solomon with some additions highlighting Jerusalem as the new Sinai (vss. 16 and 35).[13] The petitionary part of Psalm 68 was finally added during the period of the Assyrian crisis (reign of Hezekiah).[14] Other scholars held to the post-exilic date of this Psalm. [15] Taylor considered the fact that the Lord is represented as choosing Zion as his dwelling place after the march through the wilderness, and the allusions to the older literature as evidence that the work is post-Deuteronomic. It specifically resembled the period of imitative writings.[16]

The majority of modern scholars seems to have abandoned the practice of trying to date the Psalms. Instead, more emphasis has been given to the classification of the psalms and their life setting. The classification of Psalm 68 is difficult because it has no counterpart elsewhere in the Psalter.[17] Taylor, Leslie, Drijvers and Mowinckel considered this an enthronement Psalm to celebrate the enthronement festival of Yahweh.[18] This Psalm therefore, served as a liturgical processional book for this festival; The occasion for this enthronement Psalm has been identified in 68:24 by Taylor:[19]

> The solemn processions are seen, O God, the processions of
> my God, my King, into the sanctuary the singers in front, the
> minstrels last, between them maddens playing timbrels: `Bless
> God in the greet congregation, the LORD, O you who are of
> Israel's fountain.'

Weiser, Sabourin and Dahood see this Psalm as a triumphal hymn whose real life setting is the commemoration of the sacral act of salvation during the autumn covenant festival of Yahweh.[20]

Psalm 68:29-33 reflected Deutero-Isaiah's universalism. In the feast at Jerusalem, the cult community, after acknowledging the kingship of Yahweh over the covenant community, from beginning to the present, the congregation expected that in the days to come Yahweh would be King over the universe "world empire" to be established on earth. When this empire is established, all nations will be represented acknowledging Yahweh and bringing homage to him (68:31). In this case, Egypt, Pathros and Africa (the most venerable and also the most remote and exotic of the ancient nations[21] represent the entire world coming to Jerusalem and acknowledging Yahweh with their gifts.[22]

It is noteworthy that only two nations from Africa were mentioned to represent the entire world. It means that the Psalmist know how wealthy and important these African nations were and that it suffice to just mention these two African nations to make the point of how far reaching (geographically) and rich (economically) will be this universal appeal of Yahwism.

UNIVERSAL KNOWLEDGE OF YAHWEH
(Psalm 87:4)

Among those who know me I mention Rahab and Babylon; behold, Philistia and Tyre, with (Africa) `This one was born there,' they say.

The majority of scholars believe that Psalm 87 is one of the most disorganised poems in the Psalter.[23] The fact that this Psalm (87) in Hebrew begins with *Yesudatho beharere godes* (his foundations are laid on holy hills) without any antecedent for "his foundations," and the difficulty encountered in tracing any clear line of thought through this poem, made scholars suggest a disorganization.[24] According to Oesterley, this disorganization is due to the fact that the lines were copied in their wrong order.[25] The process of this disorganization is further hypothetically explained in the following manner:

a scribe, in copying out the Psalm, inadvertently omitted some of the lines, which he subsequently added in the margin; a later scribe, in making his copy of the Psalm naturally wished to include the lines which had been placed in the margin; but this was no easy matter,because there was, presumably, no indication as to where they belong in the text. The later scribe had, there-fore, to do the best he could; but he was somewhat wanting in discernment otherwise he would not, for example, have began the Psalm with a meaningless sentence, as it is in its present form; nor would he have been content with the illogical sequence of the lines as we now have

them; nor does he seem to have realized the great significance
of the refrain: "This one was born there."[26]

For the above reasons, several scholars have suggested various
rearrangements of the verses in chapter 87.[27] Although the beginning of
the poem may be difficult, scholars need to remember that what may seem
logical to modern translators and commentators may be completely
different from what was acceptable to the ancient biblical writers.[28]

Several distinct periods have been suggested for this Psalm. While
Oesterley[29] suggested an exilic period for this Psalm, Elmer Leslie,[30] M.
E. J. Kissane[31] and Anderson[32] preferred a post-exilic date. Dahood
accepted the possibility of either a pre- or post-exilic date.[33]

Since the main theme of this Psalm is the elevation of Zion as the
chosen city and the mother of all nations, scholars have no problem
classifying this Psalm as Hymn or Song of Zion. Although there is no
problem in the classification, difficulty exists in verse 4. Different
interpretatations have been suggested. While some suggested that "Among
those who know me ..." in verse 4 referred to the proselytes who came
to Jerusalem on pilgrimage for worship from various countries for a
particular festival,[34] others suggested that this passage referred to the Jews
in dispersion who were living in Judah.[35] Yet other scholars maintained
that this Psalmist was discussing his future vision of Zion as a world-wide
center of Yahweh's worship for all people as symbolized by Egypt,
Africa, Philistia and Tyre.[36]

In this passage, this writer sees a remarkable concept of the unity of
God's people which transcends nations, languages and color. The
Psalmist, like Deutero-Isaiah, brings out the universalistic[37] doctrine. He
claims Zion as the chosen and most loved by Yahweh of all the nations of
the world.[38] Zion is seen as their mother. As the Psalmist recognizes all
people from every nation, he begins to count: "This one was born there."
Then, the representatives of the nations (of which Babylon, Philistia, Tyre
and Africa receive special mentioning) at the sanctuary would repeat after
the Psalmist in their song of praise and sacred dance: "This one was born
there." This is the "brotherhood of man in the highest sense."[39] Here it is
remarkable that Africa south of Egypt is again mentioned as one of the
representatives of the nations. Weiser gives a vivid and accurate
description of the life situation and the vision of universalism that
impressed itself in the memory of the poets:

The festal throng moves along in solemn procession, in step with the rhythm of the hymns. People from all over the world pass by before the eyes of the singer. It is as if the whole world had arranged to meet in this place. They have come from the Nile and the Euphrates, from the land of the Philistines and of the Phoenicians, and even black figures from distant Ethiopia are not absent from this gathering of the nations in the house of God on Mount Zion. However much they may differ from each other in language and appearance, they are all united in one faith, believing in the one God whom they jointly profess....The hymn which they sing (v. 7) impresses itself deeply on the poet's memory; for all of them the Temple of Jerusalem is their home, though cradled in some remote country. In an imaginative picture of almost visionary power, which at a single stroke embraces things near and far, the poet portrays the thoughts which that vision has awakened in him and around which his song has crystallized, thoughts of the majesty of God, and of Jerusalem's importance as the spiritual centre of the world. It must have been an experience of this kind that led to the composition of the Psalm.[40]

XERXES' RULERSHIP FROM INDIA TO AFRICA
(Esther 1:1 and 8:9)

Like the historical books in the Bible, the book of Esther began with *Wayehi* (It came to past) and ended in the same way the book of Kings and Chronicles ended by appealing to the source in which the reader may do some verification of the facts:

And all the acts of his power and might, and the full account of the high honor of Mordecai, to which the King advanced him, are they not written in the Book of the Chronicles of the Kings of Media and Persia? (10:2)

For the above reason and the fact that there exist, precise dates, Persian names, several Persian customs and court life, and the popularity of the feast of Purim, many Jews and Christians accept the historicity of the book of Esther. However, there are great difficulties for such acceptance.[41] Apart from Xerxes, none of the characters are mentioned in any extra-Biblical historical document.[42] This book is a festal legend to explain the origin of Purim and authorize the continuity of its celebration.[43]

Although there is no accurate historical record in the book of Esther which gives any clear indication of the time of its writing, the period that appears compatible is the period shortly after 161 when the Jews had some temporary success in their revolt against religious oppression of Antiochus Epiphanes.[44] At this time, the Jews were prone to exaggerate their racial pride.[45] A period earlier than the Maccabean period has also been suggested.[46] It is said to have been written as "propaganda for observance in Palestine of a festival, brought home by the Jews from Dispersion."[47]

The phrase, "it came to pass," *Wayehi* in 1:1 is regarded as a conventional open formula to set a stage for the reader.[48] However, Hans Striedl considers it as the author's attempt to archaize his account of Purim.[49]

Although the masoretic text says that the Persian king reigning at that time was Ahasuerus, and the Septuagint calls the King Artaxerxes, there is a general agreement among modern scholars that the King referred to is Xerxes I, the son of Dairus who reigned from 485-465 B.C.E.[50] The measurement of the ruins and treasures in Susa seems to support the book's description of the Persian empire at its height.[51] It is also known that Xerxes divided his empire into districts with many satraps as governors over them.[52] The 127 provinces probably represent an old way of describing his vast empire.[53] According to a foundation tablet discovered in his palace at Persepolis, Xerxes claimed to have ruled over an empire extending from India to Africa. Xerxes describes himself as the king of all kings and the only king of all countries and he listed the countries under his domain from whom he collected taxes.[54] Kush is among these countries.

The closing phrase "... to the Jews in their script and their language," implies that to a certain degree, the Jews retained their autonomy during the days of Xerxes.[55] There is a repetition of chapter 1:1 in chapter 8:9. A decree was sent to every province from India to Africa. This is for the purpose of indicating the power, the might and the greatness of Xerxes I.

AFRICA'S PRECIOUS THINGS AND
ANTIOCHUS IV (Dan 11: 40-45)

He shall become ruler of the treasures of gold and of silver,
and all the precious things of Egypt; and the Libyans and the
(Africans) shall follow in his train.

The book of Daniel is usually divided into two parts by scholars. While
the first part (1-6) contains six stories, the second part (7-12) contains four
visions.[56] The major concern of this writer is in the fourth vision (10-12)
of Daniel where an angelic being revealed to Daniel a survey of the
history of the world from the Persian Period to the reign of Antiochus
Epiphanes. This section on the last vision (10-12) has been regarded as the
climax of the book of Daniel[57] and the first Jewish attempt at a universal
history of the world since the Table of Nations (Gen. 10).[58]

Scholars suggest various sources of the story in chapter eleven of
Daniel. Lacocque considers the eschatological dimension of 11:40-45 as
something borrowed from Isaiah and Ezekiel.[59] It could be that Antiochus
death is an imitation of the enemy falling upon the mountain in Ezekiel
39:4, and other passages.[60] J. C. H. Lebram holds that the historical
material in Daniel chapter eleven was derived from the Egyptian source,[61]
especially the tradition of Cambyses as the evil king.[62]

Ostensibly, the setting of the book of Daniel is in the sixth century
at the Babylonian, Median and Persian courts. This proposed setting has
led to the traditional dating of Daniel to the period between 605-562
B.C.E.. The above date for the book of Daniel is still maintained and
defended by conservative scholars.[63] However, several other scholars have
rejected the traditional date on the basis of the nature of the literary
material, the content and the aim of the book of Daniel.[64] The suggested
alternative date is between 167-164 B.C.E., which was the period of
terror, trial and persecution of the Jews. This Maccabean period appears
to be the most likely period when the book of Daniel was written.
Therefore, the interpretation of the passage which deals with Africa and
Africans in the book of Daniel (11:43) will be discussed in the light of the
historical background of this period.

Different interpretation has been given to Daniel chapter eleven by
various scholars. Those who maintain the exilic date for the book of
Daniel regard Daniel 11:21-45 as a prophecy of the great battle between
the Antichrist and the African great armies of the future world ruler.[65]

According to this group of scholars, the Antichrist will repel all attacks and dominate the world until he meets his end during the second coming of Christ.[66] Other scholars who maintain the Maccabean period for the book of Daniel hold that Daniel 11:21-45 has to do, not with any future Antichrist, but the exploits of Antiochus Epiphanes who persecuted the Jews and their religion.[67] Since this is the position of this writer, a brief historical background of Antiochus Epiphanes will help to elucidate the proper interpretation of this passage.

Antiochus (IV) Epiphanes was the younger son of Antiochus the Great and the brother of King Seleucus IV. In 189 B.C.E., Antiochus IV was a hostage in Rome according to the treaty with his father, Antiochus III, following the Battle of Magnesia.[68] When Seleucus IV offered his son as a replacement, Antiochus IV was released in his twelfth year.[69]

Antiochus Epiphanes succeeded his brother as the ruler of the Seleucid Empire in 175 B.C.E.. In his determination to hellenize the Jews he permitted the helenizing party in Jerusalem to erect a gymnasium on the Greek pattern. Antiochus also sold the office of the high priest to the highest bidder. When he sold it to Jason who offered him money, the Jews maintained their allegiance to the legitimate high priest, Onias III. Jason was later deposed when Menelaus offered Antiochus more money. When Menelaus engineered the assassination of Onias and plotted to steal the temple vessels, riots broke out. Jason took advantage of these riots and the fact that Antiochus was away for a military campaign against Egypt. He came back to the city and drove Menelaus away.

Antiochus returned from his Egyptian campaign in great wrath for two major reasons. First, the Roman authorities had compelled him to withdraw from his Egyptian campaign, barring him from any territorial expansion in the west just as he thought he had Egypt in his grasp. Second, the driving out of Menelaus, his nominee, and the Jewish riots angered him greatly. His reaction was aggressive Hellenization of the Jews and attempts to stamp out their religion and culture.

By December 168 B.C.E., the Jewish sacrifices, circumcision, Sabbath keeping and the possession of the Torah were forbidden. The result of this action was a serious rebellion which began in Modein by the Maccabees who were able to clean and restore the Jewish temple worship in 164 B.C.E..

In the spring of 163, Antiochus marched east to strengthen his frontier provinces against the Parthians.[70] During this campaign, he developed some mental problems and died at Tabac in Persia (163 B.C.E.).[71]

The statement in Daniel 11:40-45 that Antiochus IV would plunder Egypt and Africa, carry her treasure and later meet his death while hurrying back to Jerusalem does not correspond with the known historical facts of Antiochus' career after the desecration of the temple (I Macc. 6; II Macc. 9). The problem of lack of correspondence of Daniel's account of Antiochus' latter career with the known history, has led to some interpretative problems among modern scholars. Some denounced Daniel's account of Antiochus' death as imaginary. Heaton said that since the writer of the Biblical account is ignorant of Antiochus' eastern campaign, which began in 165 B.C.E., he invented another expedition against Egypt and he presented the death of the wicked king in a setting of his expectation and faith.[72] The account of Antiochus' later career is meant to comfort the persecuted Jews.

The writer seems to assure the persecuted ones during the Maccabean period that even though the wicked seem to prosper and conquer even the powerful nations (Egypt and Africa), his (Antiochus Epiphanes') end is at hand. Thus, ancient Africa is recognized as wealthy nations throughout ancient Israel.

Endnotes

1. W. O. E. Oesterley, *The Psalms*, vol. 2 (London: Macmillan Company, 1939), 320-21. John Durham, *Esther-Psalms BBC*, vol. 4, 305. M. Dahood, *Psalms 11. 51-100, Anchor Bible*, edited by J. W. Rogers and J. W. McKay (New York: Doubleday and Co., Garden City, 1968), 133; J. W. Rogers and J. W. McKay, *Psalms 51-100* (Cambridge: Cambridge University Press, 1977) 82-83; Artur Weiser, *The Psalms A Commentary*, translated by Herbert Hartwell (Philadelphia: Westminster Press, 1962) 481.

2. John Durham, *Esther-Psalms BBC*, vol. 4, 305, Rogers and McKay, *Psalms 51-100*, 82-83.

3. John Durham, *Esther-Psalms BBC*, vol. 4, 305. These difficulties were first spotted by Albright's examination of Psalm 68. He laid bare these problems by revealing the new grammatical and stylistic principles unfolded by Ras Shamra Tablets in his famous article, "A Catalogue of Early Hebrew Lyric Poems (Psalm LXV111)," *Hebrew Union College Annual*, 23 (1950-1951):1-39.

4. See Albright, "A Catalogue," *HUCA* 23 (1950):1-39. He analyzed it as thirty incipits or beginnings of poems written during the Solomonic period.

According to Weiser, the style of Psalm 68 moves to and fro, alternating between forms and speech, narration and description, prayer and hymn, are mixed together. Weiser, *Psalms*, 481.

5. Rogers and McKay, *Psalms 51-100*, 82-83.
6. Ibid.
7. Leoplod Sabourin, *The Psalms: Their Origin and Meaning* (New York: Alba House, 1974), 17.
8. Ibid. While Duhm believe that majority of Psalms were written during the Maccabean period' or Hasmonean period, Wellhausen was not sure whether there existed any pre-exilic Psalms. Mowinckel considered the time of the monarchy as the golden age of Psalm writing. For a more elaborate survey of Dubm, Wellhausen, Engnell and Mowinckel, see Sabourin, *The Psalms*, 17-19. R H. Pfeiffer believes that the majority of Psalms were written during the assembling of the Psalter between 400-100 B.C. *Introduction to the Old Testament*, 629. "A Catalogue," *HUCA* 23 (1950):1-39.
9. "A Catalogue," *HUCA* 23 (1950):1-39.
10. Durham, *BBC*, vol 4, 305.
11. "A Catalogue," *HUCA*, 23, (1950), 1-39.
12. *BBC*, vol 4, 305.
13. Stuhimueller, *Psalms*, (Willington, Delaware: M. Glazier, 1983), 307-8.
14. Ibid.
15. W. R. Taylor, *IB*, vol 4, 353.
16. Ibid. This refers to the approximate time of the intertestamental period when many writers were imitating the styles of ancient authors.
17. This Psalm contains no coherent and progressive train of thoughts. There are too many series of allusions which could not be fitted accurately or with assurance into a particular historical facts well known to scholars that could be found in the Old Testament tradition. Weiser, *Psalms*, 481. Even the metres are not uniform but vary. They vary even within a chapter. Lines of 4 + 3 and 3 + 4 predominate in the chapter. The lines in 68:31 is that of 2 + 2. Taylor, *IB*, vol. 4, 354.
18. Taylor, *IB*, VOL.4 `353' Pius Drijvers, *The Psalms: Their Structure and Meaning* (New York: Herder and Herder, 1965), 320. (Mowinckel considers this as enthronement Psalm recited during the annual feast, dedicated to the commemoration of the enthronement of Yahweh in the first month of Tishri and the ceremonies accompanying this festival derived from the Babylonian Marduk feast.
19. Taylor, *IB* .vol 4, 353.
20. Weiser, *Psalms*, 483, Sabourin, *Psalms*, 328. Dahood, *Psalms*, 133.
21. Rogerson and McKay, *Psalms*, 91.
22. Drijvers, *Psalms*, 176. Weiser, *Psalms*, 375. Psalm 68:31 is a favorite verse of the present Ethiopia. It was quoted twice in *Kebra Nagast* 50 and

frequently used as a motto. Ethiopia stretching her hands to God has become a proof-text and a symbol of the country's passionate adherence to the orthodox faith. Ullendorf, *Ethiopia and the Bible*, 9.

23. Oesterley, *Psalms*, 390, McKay and Rogerson, *Psalms*, 182; Weiser, *Psalms*, 379-82; John Durham, "Psalms" *BBC*, VOL. 4, 349; A. A. Anderson, *The Book of Psalms NCB*, 618; *The New English Bible with Apocrypha*, 2nd edition (New York: Oxford University Press, 1970), 687.

24. Ibid.

25. Oesterley, *Psalm*, 390.

26. Ibid.

27. Gunkel suggests the following sequence: 2, 1, 5c 7, 3, 6, 4c, 4a, 4b, and 5ab, John Durham, "Psalms," *BBC*, vol. 4, 349. Oesterley suggests 2, 1, 5', 7, 3, 6', 4', and 5'; J. Durham, "Psalms," *BBC*, vol. 4, p. 349. The translators of the New English Bible suggested, 2, 5', 4, 5˜, 6, 7, 3. A. Weiser merely suggests that verse 6 should be placed before verse 4; *Psalms*, 379-82. However, other scholars like Dahood, McKay, Rogerson, Eaton and Anderson disagree with such a rearrangement. They prefer the order in the Masoretic text because the above suggested rearrangements are based only on mere intelligent guesses. Dahood, *Psalms* 11, 398-99, McKay and Rogerson, *Psalms* 51-100, 182: Eaton, *Psalms*, 214-15, *Psalms NCB*, 618.

28. McKay and Rogers, *Psalms 51-100*, 182.

29. Oesterley says that this Psalm was written toward the end of the exilic period. Like Deutero-Isaiah, the writer of the Psalm envisaged in his mind the re-establishment of the temple worship.

30. *The Psalms* (Nashville: Abingdon Press, n.d.), 34-35. 284.

31. *The Book of Psalms*, vol. 2 (Dublin: Reichview Press, 1954), 81-90

32. *Psalms NCB*, vol. 2, 618-22.

33. *Psalms 1151-100*, 298. The reason why Dahood could not make up his mind is that, as the omission of Assyria implied a late composition so also, the mention of "Kush," Africa South of Egypt, suggest the period of the so called Ethiopian Dynasty (715-663 B.C.E.).

34. Weiser, *Psalms*, 580; McKay and Rogerson, *Psalms*,

35. Leslie thinks it refers to either Jews or the proselytes.

36. Oesterley, *Psalms*, 390.

37. Esther—*Psalms BBC*, vol. 4, 350, Oesterley, *Psalms*, 390.

38. Oesterley, *Psalms*, 390.

39. Ibid.

40. Weiser, *Psalms*, 580.

41. B. W. Anderson, *IB*, vol 6, 825-26.

42. L. H. Brockington, *Ezra, Nehemiah and Esther NCB*, ea., 217-18. All that is known to scholars is Ametus mentioned by Herodotus (VII:114, IX:112) as the wife of Xerxes.

43. Anderson, *IB*, VOL. 6, 825.

44. Brocknington, *Ezra, Nehemiah and Esther, NCB*, 217-18.

45. Ibid.

46. Ibid.

47. Carey Moore, *Esther, AB*, 3, 286.

48. Carey A. Moore, *Esther, AB*, 3. 285.

49. "Untersuchung Zur Syntax and Stillistic des hebraishen Buches Esther," *ZAW 55* (1937):73-108, cited by C. A. Moore in *Esther, AB*, 3.

50. Moore, *Esther Anchor Bible*, 3.

51. R. B. Bjornard, *Esther—Psalms BBC*, vol. 4, 5.

52. *ANET*, 316.

53. Ibid.

54. *ANET*, 316.

55. Ibid. The Septuagint omits "the Jews in their script and language. C. A. Moore, *Esther, AB*, 80.

56. S. B. Frost, "Daniel," *IBD*, vol. 1, 761-68.

57. James A. Montgomery, *The Book of Daniel, ICC*, 421-22.

58. Ibid.

59. Lacocque, *Daniel*, 232-32.

60. Ibid. See also Zephaniah 14:2; Joel 3:2 and J. Collins also believes that the Isaiah 14:25. eschatological dimension has a parallel in Ezekiel 39. *Daniel with an Introduction to Apocalyptic Literature* vol. xx (Grand Rapids; Wm. B. Eerdmans Publising House, 198), 100. Collins, *Daniel*, 99. *BBC*, vol. 6, 456. Lacocque, *Daniel*, 232.

61. C. H. Lebram, "Apocalyptic und Hellenismus im Buch Daniel, *VT*, 20 (1970):503-24, Cited by J. Colins in *Daniel*, 100.

62. Ibid.

63. For example see E. Young, *The Prophecy of Daniel* (Grand Rapids: Wm. B. Eerdmans Publishing House, 19 9). H. C. Leupold, *Exposition of Daniel* (Minneapolis: Augsburg Publishing House 19 9); J. F. Walvoord, *Daniel: The Key to Prophetic Revelation* (Chicago: Moody Press, 1971). 286.

64. J. Collins, *Daniel*, 36; Lacocque, *Daniel*, 232-33. James Montgomery, *The Book of Daniel ICC*, 21-22; N. K. Gottwald, *The Hebrew Bible*, 590-91.

65. Walwoord, *Daniel: The Key to Prophetic Revelation*, 279.

66. Ibid.

67. Gottwald, *The Hebrew Bible*, 590-91; Lacocque, *Daniel*, 232-33; Pfeiffer, *Introduction to the Old Testament*, 7 8-81; J. Collins, *Daniel*, 100.

68. J. J. Owens, *Jeremiah—Daniel BBC*, vol. 6, 451.

69. Ibid.

70.   E. W. Heaton, *The Book of Daniel* (London: SCM. Press, 1956), 240.
71.   Ibid.
72.   Ibid.

Chapter 6
Conclusion

In the preceding chapters, I have examined the role and the contribution of Africa and Africans in the Old Testament and its environment. The examination of the historical, archaeological and literary documents of the ancient Near Eastern people leads to the conclusion that the terms *Wawat*, *Kush*, *Punt*, *Nehesi*, *Magan* and *Meluhha*, and Ethiopia are the main terms used in ancient Near East to refer to Africa and Africans (chapter II).

The examination of the word "*Kush*" in the Egyptian, the Assyrian and the Hebrew documents has established the strong possibility that this term (*Kush*) is the main term used to refer to Africa and Africans in the Old Testament. This has been supported by the fact that everywhere *Kush* is used with clear-cut or definite identification in the Egyptian, the Assyrian and the Hebrew documents, it has referred to Africa and Africans. The examination of the products of the land and people of *Kush* supports that these products (gold, wood, and other precious stones) are the ones frequently associated with ancient Africa.

The evidence uncovered from the examination of the biblical, archaeological and historical documents concerning the place of Africa and Africans in the Old Testament and its environment in the preceding chapters leads to the following conclusions:

First, that Africa and Africaas have made a significant contribution to the religious life and the civilization of the ancient Near East, and particularly ancient Israel. As emphasized by Wallis Budge and Rawlinson, the principal Egyptian gods came from Africa. It therefore follows that there is a great African influence on beliefs, manners, and customs of the Dynastic Egyptians.[1] They both emphasized the tradition which associate the origin of the Egyptians and their writings (hieroglyphics) from the south.[2]

The results of the researches of the "Father of Assyriology," Sir Henry Rawlinson, George Ralinson and Petrie, into the antiquity of the African people are in favour of this my conclusion that the Sumerian religion and civilization may have come originally from the Nile valley.[3]

The presence of Africa and Africans in the biblical tradition concerning the Garden of Eden and the Table of Nations (Gen. 2:10-14 and Gen. 10:6-10) which describe the fall of man and the origin of nations, echo a significant place given to Africa and Africans in the religion of Israel.

Ebed-melech (Jer. 38:1-7, 12-13 and 39:15-17), who is an African or a person of African descent, became an example of courage, faith, compassion and kindness to Israel by delivering one of her greatest prophets. Ebed-melech taught the weak king (Zedekiah) and his people a sense of right and wrong. When the weak king, Zedekiah, could not decide what to do with the prophet Jeremiah (because of the fear of his princes who wanted the prophet to die) and allowed the princes to put the prophet in the cistern to die, Ebed-melech, the African, with great courage and faith, went to the king, challenged him and taught him the sense of right (Jer. 38:1-13). Ebed-melech said to the king, (My Lord the King, these men have done evil in what they did to Jeremiah the prophet by casting him into the cistern ...' The result was not less than a change of mind by the king. King Zedekiah, who had already given the princes permission to do whatever they liked to Jeremiah, realized what he had done wrong. He "commanded" that the prophet be rescued. Ebed-melech had faith in the prophet Jeremiah. That is why he and the other men rescued him from death while the other officials preferred his death. In this, Ebed-melech transcended the party strife which crippled the society of that period.

Prophets played a very significant role in shaping not only the religious, but also the political and economic life of Israelite society. The fact that prophet Zephaniah has been shown to be an African or of African ancestry demonstrates a significant place given to Africans in the religious life of ancient Israel and their struggle for survival.

That the Queen of Sheba came from Africa and that Ophir is one of the tribes in Africa, have been discussed at great length. The temple, one of the most important religious institution in Israel, was built and supported with African wood. This same temple was decorated with African gold, silver and many precious stones which the queen gave to King Solomon as gifts. I Kings 10:1-13 says, that some gold, silver, precious stone and spices were brought to Jerusalem.

One important possibility which should not be overlooked by scholars is that Hezekiah's religious reform may have been influenced or brought about because of the African promise of protection and Hezekiah's trust in the African rulers. This promise of help probably gave Hezekiah the courage to revolt against the powerful Assyrians. This possibility is supported by many facts:

(1)   The prophet Isaiah of Jerusalem emphasized and spoke vehemently against African help and envoy.

(2)   Hezekiah trusted or depended on the African mighty power (Isaiah 18:1-2, 7; 20:1-6; II Kings 19:8-19).

(3)   Hezekiah had constant and close contact with the African rulers.

(4)   Zephaniah, who has African ancestry, was traced back to Hezekiah.

(5)   The period of Hezekiah (715-6 B.C.E.) was the exact period when the African rulers ruled Egypt. It was also a period when they had a very strong army and political influence throughout the ancient Near East (Isaiah 18:1-2, 7; II Kings 19:8-13), to the extent that they were feared far and wide.

Second, the important place occupied by Africa and Africans in the Old Testament and its environrnent is also evident in their political and military influence throughout the ancient Near East and Israel in particular. Their political and military genius led to their being sought as mercenaries, voluntary fighters, princes, and protectors.

Africans from the south were the military police protecting the Egyptians guarding their boundaries.[4] Eventually their power grew to the extent that they were able to rule Egypt (Kushite Dynasty 725-660). Their military intervention, helped to change Assyrian policy toward the west. Although that help failed, Yamani, king of Ashdod, fled to Africa for protection against the Assyrian invasion of Ashdod (711 B.C.E.). During another revolt by Philistia, Ashkelon and Ekron and Judah against the Assyrians, they trusted the African king (Shabako) and his army for deliverance. Although, according to Assyrian records, the Africans were defeated, yet the Africans lived up to the trust by defending the Ekronite, the Ashkelonites and the Philistines in the battle of Eltekeh.[5]

The military and the political role of Africa and Africans in ancient Israel is evident from their intervention during Israel's crisis. An African called Kushi was present in King David's army as one of his protectors. King Hezekiah put his trust on the African rulers for deliverance from the Assyrians. The Assyrians (Sennacherib) were kept busy until bad news of African approach and bad news from home drove them back home. Although the intervention of the Twenty-fifth Dynasty in Palestine against the Assyrians might not be sufficient to prevent the downfall of Israel later, it probably played a significant "part in saving Jerusalem from capitulating to the Assyrian attack under Sennacherib."[6]

The fact that Jehudi, among all the princes, was the only one called upon to read Jeremiah's scroll, demonstrates the genius and important administrative place given to Africans in Israelite society.

Third, Africa and Africans played some significant role in the economic life of the ancient Near East and of Israel in particular.

The Egyptians acknowledged the fact that they depended on the African people for most of their economic products. The inscriptions of Hatshepshut acknowledge the fact that the source of the Egyptian ebony, ivory, gold, incense, myrrh and precious stone, was Africa south of Egypt.[7] Professor George Rawlinson listed some of these Egyptian products as balsam, precious metals, costly stones, rich beasts, camelopards, panthers and apes, and woods.[8]

As early as the third millenium B.C.E., the Sumerians acknowledged the fact that Africa had been the source of their gold, "stone logs," ivory, wood and pearls.[9] Evidence of trade contact between Africans and Sumerians has been discussed in chapter two of this book.

In ancient Israel, the economic contribution of Africa and Africans was evident in Sheba's visit. The majority of scholars believe that the main purpose of Sheba's visit was for trade relation with Solomon. Like Pharaoh Necho, who employed the Phoenicians to circumnavigate Africa, King Solomon employed the Phoenicians to ship African products to Israel (II Kings 10). Although the Biblical record is silent concerning any trade relations between Hezekiah and Africa, it is most natural that their strong alliance probably involved not only military, but also marriage and trade.

Fourth, it is remarkable that of all the nations and peoples known to the children of Israel, Africa and Africans are among the very few nations and peoples mentioned as representatives of far away nations. They are mentioned in both the prophetic books and the psalter. The reason for this is the expression of the important place of Africa and Africans among the ancient Israelites who saw them as one of the most ancient, most venerated and mighty nations in the ancient Near East."[10]

Fifth, the realistic fact that Africa and Africans hold an important place in almost every aspect of the life of the ancient Israelites is further demonstrated by the fact that Africa and Africans are frequently mentioned in virtually every strand of Old Testament literature. They are mentioned in the legal, historical narrative, prophetic, apocalyptic, and wisdom literature. The Psalter and even one of the books (Esther) that reflect a highly propagandic nature mentioned them. I maintain the fact that they would not have been mentioned so frequently had they not held an important place in Israelite life. It is, therefore, only a lack of proper understanding of the entire life of Israel as recorded by the Old Testament, or bias against Africans, that could have made any scholar maintain that the Israelite only knew the Africans as slaves.

Finally, this study on the place of Africa and Africans in the Old Testament and its environment, is very preliminary and therefore not conclusive. The problem of scarcity of written archaeological documents from Africa, south of Egypt tells the need for further research. Other than that of Leakey and his associates in East Africa, very little archaeological work has been done. Such scarcity may be as a result of scholars' concentration of their excavation in the Near East, with almost the exclusion of Africa south of Egypt. This study and this scarcity of materials from Africa south of Egypt, reveal that scholars should not make hasty conclusions, but wait for further archaeological discoveries which might help to further confirm or enlighten scholars about the place of Africa and Africans in the Old Testament and its environment. Such discoveries may also help to reveal the Aflrican cultrual influence on ancient Israel. There is an urgent need for further research in that area.

Selected Bibliography

Books

Aalders, G. Ch. *Genesis*. vol. 1. Translated by William Heynen. Grand Rapids: Zondervan Publishing House, 1981.

Ackroyd, Peter R. *I and II Chronicles*. Cambridge: Cambridge University Press, 1977.

_____ *I and II Chronicles, Ezra, Nehemiah*. London: SCM Press, 1973.

_____ Israel under Babylon and Persia. Oxford: Oxford University Press, 1970.

Ackroyd, P. R., and Leaney, A. R. C., eds. *The Second Book of Samuel*. Cambridge: Cambridge University Press, 1977.

Ackroyd, P. R., Leaney, A. R. C., and Parker, J. W., eds. Joel, *Obadiah, Nahum, Habakkuk, and Zephaniah*. Camridge: Cambridge University Press, 1975.

Adams, W. Y. et. al. *Africa in Antiquity: The Art of Ancient Nubia and the Sudan*. Vol. 1 6 2. New York: Brooklyn Yiuseum Division of Publication and Marketing Services, 1978.

_____ *Nubia: Corridor to Africa*. Princeton: Princetone University Press, 1977.

Aharoni, Yohanan. *The Archaeology of the Land of Israel*. Translated by A. F. Rainey, Philadelphia: Westminster Press, 1978.

The Land of the Bible: *A Historical Geography*. Translated by A. F. Rainey. Philadelphia: Westminster Press, 1967.

Albright, W. F. *Archaeology and the Religion of Israel*. 5th ed. Baltimore: Johns Hopkins Press, 1968.

Alexander, Joseph. *Commentary on the Prophecies of Isaiah*. Grand Rapids: Zondervan Publishing House, 1953.

Ali, Ibn. Japhet. *A Commentary on the Book of Daniel*. Trans- lated by D. S. Margoliouth, Oxford, Clarendon Press, 1889.

Allen, J. Clifton, pen. ed. *The Broadman Bible Commentary*. 12 vole. Nashville: Broadrnan Press, 1969-1971. vole. 1-6.

Alt, Albrecht. *Essays on the Old Testament History and Religion*. Translated by R. A. Wilson. Garden City: Doubleday Anchor Books, 1968.

Anderson, A. A. *The Book of Psalms*. 2 vole. New Century Bible. Edited by Ronald Clement. London: Marshall Morgan and Scott, 1972.

Anderson, G. W. *The History and Religion of Israel*. Oxford: Oxford University Press, 1966.

Arkell, A. J. A History of Sudan: From the Earliest Times to 1821. Rev. ed. London: London University Press, 1961.

Backlay, William and Bruce F. F., eds. Historians of Israel. vol. 1 and 2. London: Lutherworth Press, 1962.

Baldwin, J. D. *Pre-Historic Nations or Inquiries Concerning Some of the Great Peoples and Civilizations of Antinguity and Their Probable Relation to a*

Still Older Civilization of Ethiopians or Cushites of Arab ia. New York: Harper and Brothers, Publishers, n.d.

Barton, John. *Amos's Oracles Against the Nations*. University Press, 1980. Cambridge, Cambridge University Press, 1980.

Baynes, Norman H. *Israel Amongst the Nations: An Outline of Old Testament History*. London: Edinburg Press, 1927.

Beardsley, G. H. *The Negro in Greek and Roman Civilization*. New York: Arno Press, 1979.

Becken, H. G. *Relevant Theology for Africa* Duban: Lutheran Publication House, 1972.

BEwer, J. A. *The Book of Jeremiah II*. New York: Harper and Brothers, 1952.

Sierbrier, M. L. *The Late New Kingdom in Egypt (1300-664 BC):A Geological Investigation*. Warminster: Aris and Philips, 1975.

Binns, Elliot. *The Book of Numbers*. London: Methuen R. Co., 1927.

Blackwood, A. W., Jr. *Ezekiel: Prophecy of Hope*. Grand Rapids: Baker House, 1965.

Blank, S. H. *Jeremiah: The Man and the Prophet*. Cincinnati: Hebrew Union College Press, 1961.

Blumenbach, J. F. *Anthropological Treatise*. Translated by T. Bendyche. London: Anthropological Society, 1865.

Breasted, James H. *Ancient Records of Egypt*. 5 vole. Chicago: University of Chicago Press, 1906.

_____ *A History of Egypt*. New York: Charles Scribner's Sons, 1912.

Briggs, C. A., and Emillie Briggs. *A Critical and Exegetical Commentary on the Book of Psalms*. 2 vols. *International Critical Commentary*. Edited by C. A. Briggs, S. R. Driver and A. Plummer. Edinburgh: T & T. Clark, 1906, 1907.

Bright, John. *A History of Israel*. 3d ed. Philadelphia: Westminster Press, 1972.

_____ *Jeremiah. The Anchor Bible*. Garden City: Doubleday and Co., 1965.

Brockington, L. H., ed. *Ezra, Nehemiah and Esther, The New Century Bible*. Edited by Ronald Clements. London: Marshall Morgan & Scott, 1972.

Brooks, Lester, *Great Civilization of Ancient Africa*. New York: Four Winds Press, 1972.

Brown, F. E., Driver, S. R. and Briggs, C. A. *A Hebrew and English Lexicon of the Old Testament*. Oxford: Clarendon Press, 1907.

Brueggemann, Walter. *Genesis*. John Knox Press, 1982.

Budd, P. J. *Numbers: Word Biblical Conmentary*. vol. 5, eds. David A. Hubbard; J. D. Watts and R. P. Martin. Waco: Word Books Publishers, 1984.

Budge, E. A. Wallis. *A History of Ethiopia, Nubia, and Abyssinia*. 2 vole. London: Methuen and Company, 1928.

_____ *The Queen of Sheba and Her Only Son Menyelek*. London: London University Press, 1932.

Budge, E. A. W. *An Egyptian Hieroglyphic Dictionary*. New York: Dover Publications, reprinted 1978.

_____ *Egyptian Sudan*. vol. 1 & 2. New York: Arno Press, 1976.

Bunbury, E. H. *A History of Ancient Geography*. vol. 2. New York: Dover Publications, 1959.

Burney, C. F. *Notes on the Hebrew Texts of the Books of Kings*. Oxford: Clarendon Press, 1903.

Burton, Harry E. *The Discovery of the Ancient World*. Cambridge: Harvard University Press, 1932.

Buttrick, G. A., gen. ed. *The Interpreter's Bible*. 6 vols. Nashville: Abingdon Press, 1952-1956.

Calkins, R. *Jeremiah the Prophet*. New York: Macmillan Co., 1930.

Carley, Keith. *Ezekiel Among the Prophets: Studies in Biblical Theology*. 2nd series. Naperville: Alee R. Allenson, n.d.

Cassuto, U. *A Commentary on the Book of Genesis*. Part I and Part II. Jerusalem: Magnes Press, 1961.

Cheilik, Michael. *Ancient History*. New York: Barnes and Nobles, 1969.

Childs, B. S. *Introduction to the Old Testament as Scripture*. Philadelphia: Fortress Press, 1979.

_____ *Isaiah and Assyrian Crisis*. Naperville: Alee R. Allenson, 1967.

300 Clark, R. J., ed. *The Cambridge History of Africa*. Cambridge: Cambridge University Press, 1982.

Clements, R. E. *Isaiah 1-39: The New Century Bible*. Grand Rapids: Wm. B. Eerdmans Publishing Col., 1980.

Coats, George. *African Empires and Civilizations*. New York: African Heritage Studies, 1974.

Coats, W. J. *Rebellion in the Wilderness*. Nashville: Abingdon Press, 1968.

Coggins, R. J. *The First and Second Books of Chronicles*. Cambridge: Cambridge University Press, 1976.

Collins, J. *Daniel with an Introduction to Apocalyptic Literature*. Vol. XX. Grand Rapids: Wm. B. Eerdmans Publishing House, 1984.

Collins, R. O., ed. *Problems in African History*. Englewood Cliffs: Prentice-Hall, 1968.

Cooke, C. A. *A Critical Commentary on the Book of Ezekiel: The International Critical Commentary*. Edited by C. Edinburgh: T. and Exegetical A. Briggs, S. R. Driver and A. Plummer. R. T. Clark, 1936.

Coote, Robert B. *Amos Among the Prophets*. Philadelphia: Fortress Press, 1981.

Cornfeld, Gaalyah and Freedman, D. N. *Archaeology of the Bible Book by Book*. New York: Harper and Row, Publishers, 1976.

Crim, Keith, gen. ed. *Interpreter's Dictionary of the Bible*. Supplementary Volume. Nashville: Aingdon Press, 1976.

Cripps, Richard A. *A Critical and Exegetical Commentary on the Book of Amos*. 3rd ed. London: Society for the Promotion of Christian Knowledge, 1955.

Crockett, William Day. *A Harmony of the Books of Samuel, Kings and Chronicles*. Grand Rapids: Baker Book House, 1951.

Cross, F. M. *Canaanite Myth and Hebrew Epic*. Cambridge: Harvard University Press, 1973.

Curtis, E. L. and Madsen, A. A. *Critical and Exegetical Commentary on the Books of Chronicles. The International Critical Commentary*. Edited by S. R. Driver, C. A. Briggs and A. Plummer. edinburgh: T & T Clark, 1911.

Dahood, M. *Psalms II 51-100*. Anchor Bible. Edited by J. W. Rogers and J. W. McKay. Garden City, N.Y.: Double-Day and Co., 1968.

Davidson, Basil. *African Past*. New York: Grosset Dunlap, 1964.

_____ *Lost Cities of Africa*. Boston: Little, Brown and Co., 1959.

Davidson, Robert. *Genesis 1-11*. Cambridge: Cambridge University Press, 1973.

Desanges, Jehan et al. *The Image of the Black in the Western Art*. vole. 1 & 2. New York: William Morrow and Co., 1976.

Diop, Anta Cheikh. *African Origin of Civilization: Myth or Reality?* Translated by Mercer Cook. Westport: Lawrence Hill & Co., 1974.

Drijvers, Pius. *The Psalms: Their Structure and Meaning*, New York: Herder and Herder, 1965.

Driver, S. R. *The Book of Genesis*. New York: Methuen and Co., 1904.

_____ *An Introduction to the Literature of the Old Testament*. Glucester: World Publishing, 1972. reprint of 1897 edition.

_____ *Notes on the Hebrew Text and Topography on the Books of Samuel*. 2d ea., revised and enlarged. Oxford: Clarendon Press, 1913.

_____ *The Prophet Jeremiah*. London: Hodder R. Stoughton, 1906.

Dunston, Alfred G. *The Black Man in the Old Testament and Its World*. Philadelphia: Dorrance R. Co., 1974.

Edwards, L. E. S. et al. *Cambridge Ancient History*. Cambridge: Cambirdge University Press, 1980.

Eichrodt, Walther. *Ezekiel*. Translated by C. Quin. Philadelphia: Westminster Press, 1970.

Eissfeldt, Otto. *The Old Testament: An Introduction*. Translated by Peter R. Ackroyd. New York: Harper R. Row, Publishers, 1965.

Elliot, R. H. *The Message of Genesis*. Nashville: Broadman Press, 1961.

Ellison, H. L. *Ezekiel: The Man and His Message*. Grand Rapids: Wm. B. Eerdmans Publishing Co., 1956.

Emery, W. B. *Egypt in Nubia*. London: Hutchinson and Co., 1965.

Erman, Adolf. *The Literature of Ancient Egyptians*. Translated by A. M. Blackman. London: Methuen and Co., 1927.

Etheridge, J. W. *The Targums of Onkelos and Jonathan Ben Uzziel on the Pentateuch*. New York: KTAV Publication House, 1968.

Fage, J. D., ed. *Africa Discovers Her Past*. Oxford: Oxford University Press, 1970.

Felder, C. H., ed. *Stony the Road we Trod*. Minneapolis: Fortress Press, 1991.
_____ *Troubling Biblical Waters*. Maryknoll: Orbis books, 1989.

Fettke, S. M. *Messages to a Nation in Crisis*. Washington, D. C.: University Press of America, 1982.

Finegan, Jack. *In the Beginning*. New York: Harper and Brothers Publishers, 1962.

Flanders, J. and Cresson, B. *Introduction to the Bible*. New York: Ronald Press, 1973.

Frank, H. T. *Discovering the Biblical World*. New York: Hammond, 1971.

Frankfort, Henri. *The Birth of Civilization in the Near East*. New York: Barnes Noble, 1968.

Freedman, H. *Jeremiah*. London: Soncino Press, 1949.

Gann, L. H. and Duignan, Peter. *Africa and the World*. San Francisco: Chandler Publishing Col., 1972.

Gardiner, Alan. *Egypt of the Paraohs*. Oxford: Oxford University Press, 1961.

Gordon, Cyrus H. *The World of the Old Testament*. Garden City: Doubleday and Co., 1958.

Gottwald, Norman K. *The Hebrew Bible: Introduction*. Philadelphia: A Socio-Literary Fortress Press, 1985.

Gray, G. B. *A Critical and exegetical Commentary on the Book of Numbers. The International Critical Commentary*. Edited by C. A. Briggs, S. R. Driver, and A. Plummer. New York: Charles Scribuer's Sons, 1906.
_____ *Studies in Hebrew Proper Names*. London: Adam and Charles Black, 1896.

Gray, G. B. and Peake, A. S., *A Critical and Exegetical Commentary on the Book of Isaiah*. Latest Impression. Edinburgh: T & T Clark, 1962.

Gray, John. *Archaeology and the Old Testament World*. London: Thomas Nelson and Sons, 1962.
_____ *I and II Kings*. London: SCM Press, 1963.

Greenburg, J. H. *Languages of Africa*. The Hague: Indiana University Press, 1966.

Gunkel, Hermann. *The Legends of Genesis*. New York: Schocken Press, 1964.
_____ *The Psalms*. Translated by Thomas M. Homer. Philadelphai: Fortress Press, 1967.

Haddon, Alfred C. *History of Anthropology*. London: Watts R. Co., 1934.

Hammershaimb, Erling. *The Book of Amos: A Commentary*. Translated by John Sturdy. New York: Schocken Books, 1970.

Hansberry, William Leo. *Africa and Africans as Seen by the Classical Writers.*
    Washington, D.C.: Howard University Press, 1977.
Hapgood, Charles H. *Maps of the Ancient Sea King's.* New York: Chilton Book
    Co., 1966.
Harper, William Rainey. *A Critical and exegetical Commentary on the Books of
    Amos and Hosea.* The International Critical Commentary. Edited by C. A.
    Briggs, S. R. Driver, and A. Plummer. New York: Charles Scriboer's
    Sons, 1915.
Harrelson, Walter. *Jeremiah: Prophet to the Nations.* Philadelphia: Judson Press,
    1959.
Harris, J. E. ed. *Africa and Africans as Seen by Classical Writers.* Washington,
    D.C.: Howard University Press, 1977.
Harris, R. L., Waltke, B. K., and Archer, G. L., eds. *Theological Wordbook of
    the Old Testament.* vols. 1 & 2. Chicago: Moody Press, 1980.
Harrison, R. K. *Introduction to the Old Testament.* Grand Rapids: William
    Eerdmans Publishing Co., 1979.
_____ *Jeremiah and Lamentations.* Downers Grove: Inter-Varsity Press, 1973.
Heaton, E. W. *The Book of Daniel.* London: SCM Press, 1956.
_____ *The Hebrew Kingdoms.* Oxford: Oxford University Press, 1968.
Heeren, A. H. L. *Historical Researches into the Politics, Intercourse and Trade
    of the Carthaginians, Ethiopians, and Egyptians.* New York: Negro
    University Press, 1969.
Heidel, A. *Babylonian Genesis.* Chicago: University of Chicago Press, 1950.
_____ *Gilgamesh Epic and the Near Eastern Parallels.* Chicago: University of
    Chicago Press, 1946.
Herbert, A. S. *The Book of the Prophet Isaiah 1-39, Cambridge Commentary to
    the New English Bible.* Cambridge: Cambridge University Press, 1973.

Herrmann, Siegfried. *A History of Israel in the Old Testament Times.* Translated
    by John Bowden, Philadelphia Fortress Press, 1975.
Hertzberg, Hans Wilhelm. *I and II Samuel.* Philadelphia: Westminster Press,
    1964.
Holladay, William L. *The Architecture of Jeremiah 1-20.* Cranbury, N. J.
    Associated University Presses, 1976.
_____ *Jeremiah.* Philadelphia: United Church Press, 1974.
Honeycutt, Roy L. *Amos and His Yiessage.* Nashville: Broadman Press, 1963.
Howe, R. W. *Black Africa.* vol. 1. New York: Walker and Co., 1966.
Huggins, Willis N. *An Introduction to African Civilizations.* New York: Negro
    University Press, 1909.
Hulst, A. O., *Old Testament Translation.* Leiden: E. J. Brill, 1960.
Hyatt, J. P. Jeremiah, *Prophet of Courage and Hope.* New York: Abingdon
    Press, 1958.

Idowu, E. B. *Olodumare, God in Yoruba Belief.* London: Longmans 1962.

Irwin, William A. *The Problem of Ezekiel.* Chicago: University of Chicago Press, 1943.

Jackson, J. G. *Ethiopia and the Origin of Civilization.* Baltimore: Black Classic Press, 1982.

_____ *Introduction to African Civilizations.* Secaucus: Citadel Press, 1970.

_____ *Man, God and Civilization.* Secaucus, N.J.: Citadel Press, 1972.

Janzen, J. G. *Studies in the Text of Jeremiah.* Cambridge: Harvard University Press, 1973.

Janzen, W. *Mourning Cry and Woe Oracle.* New York/Berlin: BZAW, 1972.

Jastrow, Morris. *The Civilization of Babylon and Assyria.* Philadelphia: J. B. Lippincott Co., 1915.

Jenks, A. W. *The Elohists and North Israelite Traditions.* Missoula: Scholars Press, 1977.

Jensen, I. L. *Numbers.* Chicago: Moody Press, 1964.

Jeremiah, Alfred. *The Old Testament in the Light of the Ancient Near East.* New York: G. P. Putnam's Sons, 1911.

Jirku, Anton. *The World of the Bible.* Translated by Ann E. Keep. Cleverland: World Publishing Co., 1967.

Johnson, H. H. *A History of the Colonization of Africa by Alien Races.* Cambridge: Cambridge University Press, 1913.

_____ *The Openings of Africa.* New York: Henry Holt and Co., n.d. 1975.

July, Robert N. *Precolonial Africa.* New York: Charles Scribner's Sons, 1975.

Kaiser, Otto. *Isaiah 1-17.* Philadelphia: Westminster Press, 1972.

Kapelrud, Arvid S. *Central Ideas in Amos.* Oslo: Oslo University Press, 1961.

_____ *Isaiah 13-19.* Philadelphia: Westminster Press, 1974.

_____ *The Message of the Prophet Zephaniah.* Kregoro: Naper Boktrykkeri, 1975.

Kaufman, Yehezkel. *The Babylonian Captivity and Deutero-Isaiah, History of the Religion of Israel.* vol. 4. New Yark: Union of American Hebrew Congregation, 1970.

Keil, C. F. and Delitzsch, F. *Biblical Commentary on the Books of Samuel.* Translated by James Martin. Grand Rapids: Wm. B. Eerdmans Publishing Co., 1950.

_____ *Biblical Commentary on the Prophecies of Isaiah.* 2 vols. Translated by James Martin. Grand Rapids: Wm. B. Eerdmans Publishing Co., 1954.

_____ *The Book of Chronicles.* Translated by Andrew Harper. Biblical Commentary on the Old Testament. Grand Rapids: Wm. B. Eerdmans Publishing Co., 1950.

_____ *The Books of Kings.* Translated by James Martin, Grand Rapids: Wm. B. Eerdmans Publishing Co., 1950.

Kempin, A. J. *Daniel for Today.* Anderson: Gospel Trumpet Co., 1952.

Kissane, E. J. *The Book of Isaiah.* vol.2. Dublin: Browne and Nolan, 1960.
_____ *The Book of Psalms.* vol. 2. Dublin: Reichview Press, 1954.
Kitchen, R. A. *The Third Intermediate Period in Egypt.* Warminster: Aris & Philips, 1973.
Knight, G. A. F. *Deutero-Isaiah: A Theological Commentary on Isaiah 40-55.* New York: Abingdon Press,1965.
_____ *Nile and Jordan.* London: James Clark and Co., 1921.
Koch, Klaus. *The Prophets, the Babylonian and Persian Period.* Philadelphia: Fortress Press, 1982.
Kraeling, E. G. *The Prophets.* Chicago: Rand McNally R. Co., 1969.
Kramer, Samuel Noah. *The Sumerians: Their History, Culture, and Character.* Chicago: University of Chicago Press, 1963.
Lacocque, Andre. *The Book of Daniel.* Trans. by David Pellaner. Atlanta: John Knox Press, 1974.
Leslie, E. A. *Isaiah.* Nashville: Abingdon Press, 1963.
_____ *Jeremiah.* New York: Abingdon Press, 1954.
_____ *The Psalms.* Nashville: Abingdon Press, n.d.
Long, Burke O. *I Kings with Introduction to Historical Literature.* Grand Rapids: Wm. B. Eerdmans Publishing Co., 1984.
Luckenbill, D. D. *Ancient Records of Assyria and Babylonia.* vols. 1 & 2. New York: Greenwood Press, 1965.
Mbiti, J. S. *Concepts of God in Africa.* London, SPCK, 1975.
McKane, William. *I & II Samuel.* London: SCM Press, 1963
McKeating, Henry. *The Books of Amos, Hosea and Micah The Cambridge Bible Commentaries.* Ed. P. R. Ackroyd, A.R.C. Leaney, J. W. Parker. Cambridge: Cambirdge University Press, 1971.
Mckenzie, J. L. *Dictionary of the Bible.* Milwaukee: Bruce Publishing Co., 1965.
Maier, Walter. *The Book of Nahum.* St. Louis: Concordia Publishing House, 1959.
Maspero, Gaston. *The Dawn of Civilization.* vole. 1 & 2. Translated by M. L. McClure. New York: Frederick Ungar Publication Co., reprinted 1968.
Massey, Gerald. *Book of Beginnings.* vol. 1. Secaucus, N.J.: University Books, 1974.
Mauchline, John. ed. *I and II Samuel: The New Century Bible.* London: Marshall Morgan and Scott, 1971.

Mays, James Luther. *Amos.* Philadelphia: Westminster Press, 1969.
Means, S. K. *Black Egypt and Her Negro Pharaoh.* Baltimore: Black Classical Press, 1949.
Mendelsohn, I. *Slavery in the Ancient Near East.* New York: Oxford University Press, 1949.

Mertz, Barbara. *Red Land, Black Land*. Revised edition. New York: Dodd, Mead and Co., 1978.

Mettinger, T. N. D. *Solomonic State Offcials: A Study of the Civil Government Officials ofthe Israelite Monarchy*. Lund: Cwk Gleerup, 1971.

Mitchell, T. C. *New Bible Dictionary*. Second edition. Wheaton, 111.: Tyndale House Publication, 1982.

Mokhtar, G., gen. ed. *General History of Africa*. vol. 2. New York: UNESCO International Scientific Committee for Drafting a General History of Africa, 1981.

Montet, Pierre. *Egypt and the Bible*. Translated by Leslie R. Keylar. Philadelphia: Fortress Press, 1968

Montgomery, Jame A. *A Critical and Exegetical Commentary on the Book of Daniel: The Critical International Commentary*. Edited by C. A. Briggs. S. R. Driver and A. Plummer. Edinburgh: T. & T Clark, 1959.

Moore, C. A. *Esther, Anchor Bible*. Garden City, N.Y.: Doubleday & Co., 1971.

Morgenstern, Julian. *The Book of Genesis: A Jewish Interpretation*. New York: Schocken Books, 1965.

Moscati, Sabatino, *Ancient Semitic Civilizations*. New York: G. P. Putnam Sons, 1957.

_____ *The Semites in Ancient History*. Cardiff: University of Wales Press, 1959.

Mowinckel, Sigmund. *The Psalms in Israel's Worship*. Translated by Dr. A. D. Thomas. vols. 1-3. Nashville: Abingdon Press, 1962.

Murdock, G. P. *Africa: Its People and Their Culture History New York*: McGraw-Hill Book Co., 1959.

Murphy, E. J. *A History of African Civilization*. New York: Thomas Crowell Co., 1972.

Nida, Eugene, and Taber, C. R. *The Theory and Practice of Translation*. Leiden: United Bible Societies, 1982.

Nielson,E. *Oral Tradition*. Chicago: Alee R. Allenson, 1954.

North, C. R. *Isaiah 40-55*. Oxford: Clarendon Press, 1952.

Noth, Martin. *A History of Israel*. Translated by Peter R. Ackro. Revised English Translation. New York: Harper and Brothers Co., 1960.

_____ *A History of Pentateuchal Traditions*. Englewood Cliffs: Prentice Hall, 1972.

_____ *Numbers*. Philadelphia: Westminster Press, 1968.

Odoyoye, Modupe. *The Sons of Gods and the Daughters of Men: An Afro-Asiatic Interpretation of Genesis 1-11*. Maryknoll, N.Y.: Orbis Books, 1974.

Oesterley, W. O. E., and Robinson, T. H. *A History of Israel*. 2 vols. Oxford: Clarendon Press, 1932.

_____ *The Psalms*. vol.2. London: Macmillan Co., 1939.

Oliver, Roland and Fagan, B. *Africa in the Iron Age*. Cambridge: Cambridge University Press, 1975.

Olmstead, A. T. *History of Palestine and Syria*. New,York: Charles Scribner's Sons, 1930.

Oppenheim, A. L. *Ancient Mesopotamia*. Chicago: University of Chicago Press, 1964.

Pankhurst, Sylvia, *Ethiopia: A Cultural History*. Essex: Lalibela House, 1959.

Paton, L. B. *A Critical and Exegetical Commentary on the Book of Esther: The International Critical Commentary*. New York: Charles Scribner's Sons, 1908.

Peet, T. Eric. *Egypt and the Old Testament*. Liverpool: University of Liverpool Press, 1924.

Perry, W. J. *The Growth of Civilization*. 2nd edition. Hammondsworth: Penguin Books, 1937.

Petrie, Flinders. *The Making of Egypt*. London: Sheldon Press, 1939.

Pfeiffer, Charles F. *The Book of Genesis*. Grand Rapids: Baker House, 1960.

Philbeck, Ben F. *I Samuel—Nehemiah Broadman Bible Commentary*. Edited y. Cliton J. Allen, vol. 3, Broadman Press, 1970.

Plant, W. Gunther. *Numbers: Torah a Modern Commentary*. vol. IV. New York: Union of American Hebrew Congregations, 1979.

Porteous, N. W. *Daniel: A Commentary*. Philadelphia: Westminster Press, 1965.

Pritchard, James, ed. *Ancient Near Eastern Texts Relating to the Old Testament*. 3d ed. with Supplement. Princeton: Princeton University Press, 1969

_____ ed. *The Ancient Near East in Pictures Relating to the Old Testament with Supplements*. 2nd ed. Princeton: Princeton University Press, 1969.

_____ ed. *Solomon and Sheba*. London: Phaidon Press,1974.

Rad, Gerhard von. *Genesis*. Revised edition. Translated by J. H. Marks. Philadelphia: Westminster Press. 1972.

_____ *Old Testament Theology*. vols. 1 & 2. Translated by D. G. Stalker. New York: Harper and Row, 1965.

_____ *The Problem of the Hexateuch and Other Essays*. Edinburgh & London: Oliver & Boyd, 1965.

Rawlinson, George. *History of Ancient Egypt*. vols. 1 & II. Chicago: Clarke & Co., Publishers, n.d.

Redlich, E. B. *The Early Tradition of Genesis*. London: Gerald Duckworth & Co., 1950.

Riggans, Walter. *Numbers*. Philadelphia: Westminster Press 1983.

Ringgren, Helmer. *The Faith of the Psalmists*. Philadelphia: Fortress Press, 1963.

Robinson, H. Wheeler. *Two Hebrew Prophets: Studies in Hoseannd Ezekiel*. London: Lutterworth Press, 1962.

Robinson, J. *First Book of Kings*. Cambridge: Cambridge University Press, 1972.

Rogers, J. A. *The Real Facts About Ethiopia*. Baltimore: Black Classic Press, 1982.

Rowley, Y. H. *Israel's Mission to the World*. London: SCM Press, 1939.

Sabourin, Leopold, S.J. *The Psalms: The Origin and Meanings*. New York: Alba House, 1974.

Schedl, Claus. *History of the Old Testament*. vol. IV. Staten, N.Y.: Alba House, 1971.

Scullion, John. *Isaiah 40-66*. Wilmington, Delaware: Michael Glazier, 1982.

Seignobos, Charles. *History of Ancient Civilization*. London: T. Fisher Unwin, 1910.

Sellin, Ernst and Fohrer, G. *Introduction to the Old Testament*. Translated by David Green. Nashville: Abingdon Press, 1965.

Sertima, Ivan Van, ed. *Egypt Revisited*. New Brunswick: Transaction Periodical Consortium, 1985.

_____ ed. *Nile Valley Civilizations*. New Brunswick Transaction Periodical Consortium, 1985.

Skinner, John. *A Critical and Exegetical Commentary on the Book of Genesis: The International Critical Commentary*. Edited by C. A. Briggs, S. R. Driver end A Plummer. Edinburgh: T R T Clark, 1910.

Smart, J. D. *History and Theology in Second Isaiah*. Philadelphia: Westminster Press, 1965.

Smith, George A. *The Historical Geography of the Holy Land*. 2 vols. 10th ed. New York: A. C. Armstrong and Son, 1903.

Smith, G. A. *Jeremiah*. 4th edition. New York: Harper and Bros., 1929.

Smith, J. M. P. *The Prophets and Their Times*. 2nd ed. Revised by William A. Irwin. Chicago: University of Chicago Press, 1941.

Smith, Morton. *Palestinian Parties and Politics That Shaped the Old Testament*. New York: Columbia University Press, 1971.

Snaith, N. H. *Amos*. 2 volse: Study Notes on the Bible. London: Epworth Press, 1946.

_____ *Amos, Hosea and Micah*. London: Epworth Press, 1956.

_____ ed. *Leviticus and Numbers*. The Century Bible. New Edition. London: Thomas Nelson, 1967.

Snowden, Jr., and Frank, M. *Before Color Prejudice: Ancient View of the Blacks*. Cambridge: Harvard University Press, 1983.

Speiser, E. A. *Genesis, `The Anchor Bible*. 3rd ed. Garden City, N.Y.: Doubleday and Co., 1979.

Spurrell, G. J. *Notes on the Book of Genesis*. Oxford: Clarendon Press, 1895.

Steindorff, George, and Keith Seele. *When Egypt Ruled the East*. Chicago: University of Chicago Press, 1942.

Strabo, *The Geography of Strabo*. Translated by Horace Leonard Jones. Book VII, vol. B. Cambridge: Harvard University Press, 1949.

Stuhlmueller, C. *Psalms*. Wilmington, Delaware: M. Glazier, 1983.

Sturdy, John. *Numbers*. Cambridge: Cambridge University Press, 1976.

Thiele, E. R. *A Chronology of the Hebrew Kings*. Grand Rapids: Zondervan Publishing House, 1977.

Thompson, J. A. *The Book of Jeremiah The New International Commentary on the Old Testament*. Grand Rapids: Wm. B. Eerdmans Publishing Co., 1980.

Torrey, C. C. *Pseudo-Ezekiel and the Original Prophecy*. Yale Oriental Series, Researches, vol. 18, New Haven: Yale University Press, 1930.

_____ *The Second Isaiah: A New Interpretation*. New York: Charles Scribner's Sons, 1928.

Toynbee, A. J. *A Study of History*. vol. I. Oxford: Oxford University Press, 1968.

Trigger, B. C. et al. *Ancient Egypt: A Social History*. Cambridge: Cambridge University Press, 1983.

Ullendorf, Edward. *Ethiopia and the Bible. The Schweich Lectures of British Academy*. Oxford: Oxford University Press, 1968.

_____ *The Ethiopians*. Oxford: Oxford University Press, 1965

Volney, C. F. *The Ruins of Empires*. New York: Peter Eckler, 1890.

Walvoord, J. F. *Daniel: The Key to Prophetic Revelation*. Chicago: Moody Press, 1971.

Ward, James M. *Amos and Isaiah*. Nashville: Abingdon Press, 1969.

Weiser, Artur. *The Psalms: A Commentary*. Translated by Herbert Hartwell. Philadelphia: Westminster Press, 1962.

Westermann, Claus. *The Psalms: Structure, Content and Message*. Translated by R. D. Gehirke. Min-neapolis: Augsburg Publishing House, 1980.

_____ *Genesis 1-11*. Trans. by J. S. Scullion, S. J. Minneapolis: Augsburg Publishing House. 1984.

Wevers, J. W., ed. *Ezekiel: The Century Bible. New Series*. London: Thomas Nelson and Sons, 1969.

Whybray, R. H. *The Succession Narrative: Studies in the Biblical Theology*. London: SCM Press, 1968.

Williams, Chancellor. *The Destruction of African Civilization*. Chicago: Third World Press, 1974.

Williams, J. J. *Hebrewism of West Africa*. New York: Dial Press, 1930.

Wilson, J. A. *The Culture of Ancient Egypt*. Chicago: University of Chicago Press, 1951.

Windsor, R. R. *From Babylon to TimbuLtu: A History of Ancient Black Races Including Black Hebrews*. Smithtown: Exposition Press, 1969.

Winward, Stephen. *A Guide to the Prophets*. Atlanta: John Knox Press, 1968.

Wisemann, D. J. *Chronicles of Chaldean Kings (626-556 B.C) in the British Museum*. London: British Museum, 1956.

Wolff, Walter, *Joel and Amos*. Philadelphia: Fortress Press, 1977.

Wonderly, William L. *Bible Translations for Popular Use*. London: United Bible Societies, 1968.

Woolley, C. L. *The Sumerians*. New York: W. W. Norton and Co., 1965.

Yadin, Y. *The Art of Warfare in Biblical Lands in the Light of Archaeological Study*. New York: McGraw Hill, 1963.

Young, E. *Introduction to the Old Testament*. Grand Rapids: Wm. B. Eerdmans Publishing Co., 1952.

_____ *The Prophecy of Daniel*. Grand Rapids: Wm. B. Eerdmans Publishing House, 1949.

Zimmerli, Walther. *Ezekiel*. Translated by R. Clement. Philadelphia: Fortress Press, 1970.

_____ *The Old Testament and the World*. Translated by J. J. Scallion. Atlanta: John Knox Press, 1976.

Articles

Adams, W. Y. "Post-Pharaonic Nubia in the Light of Archaeology." *Journal of Egyptian Archaeology* 50 (1964):102-20.

Adamo, D. T. "Translating Hebrew Old Testament Book Titles Into Yoruba Language of Nigeria." *The Bible Translator*. Practical paper 35:4 (Oct. 198): 18-2.

Albright, W. F. "A Brief History of Judah from the Day of Josiah to Alexander." *Biblical Archaeologist* 9 (1946):1-16.

_____ "A Catalogue of Early Hebrew Lyric Poems (Psalm Lxviii)." *Hebrew Union College Annual* 23 (1950- 1951):1-39.

_____ "The Chronology of the Divided Monarchy of Israel." *Bulletin of the American Schools of Oriental Research* No. 100 (19 9):16-23.

_____ "Egypt and the Early History of the Negev." *Journal of the Palestine Oriental Society* 4 (1924): 131-61.

_____ "Further Light on Synchronisms Between Egypt and Asia in the Period of 935-687 B.C." *Bulletin of the American Schools of Oriental Research* No. 141 (1956):23-27.

_____ "Ivory and Apes of Ophir." *American Journal of Semitic Languages* 37 (1921):14.

_____ "The Lachish Letters After Five Years." *Bulletin of American Schools of Research* 82 (Apr. 19 1):22.

_____ "New Light from Egypt on the Chronology and History of Israel and Judah." *Bulletin of American School of Oriental Research* 130 (1953):4-11.

Baer, Klaus, "Libyan and Nubian Kings of Egypt: Notes on the Chronology of Dynasties, XXII-XXVI." *Journal of Near Eastern Studies* 32 (1973):4-25.

Ball, E. "The Co-regency of David and Solomon (I Kings 1)." *Vetus Testamentum* 27 (1977):268-79.

Bennett, Jr. Robert A. "Africa and the Biblical Period." *Harvard Theological Review* 64 (1971):501-524.

Berry, G. R. "Was Ezekiel in Exile?" *Journal of Biblical Literature* XLIX (1930):83-93.

Broshi, Magen. "The Expansion of Jerusalem in the Reigns of Hezekiah and Manasseh." *Israel Exploration Journal* 24 (1974):21-26.

Cathacart, K. J. "The Treaty Curses and the Book of Nahum." *Catholic Theological Quarterly* 4 (1963):433-39.

Copher, C. B. "The Black Man in the Biblical World." *The Journal of Interdenominantional Theological Center*, vol. 1 No. 2, 1974.

Cross, F. M. and Freedman, D. N. "Josiah's-Revolt Against Assyria." *Journal of Near Eastern Studies* 10 (1953):56-58.

Cross, F.M., and Wright, G. E. "The Boundary and Province Lists of the Kingdom of Judah." *Journal of Biblical Lierature* 75 (1956):202-226.

Dickson, K. "The Old Testament and African Theology." *Ghana Bulletin of Theology*, vol. 4 No. 4 (June 1973): 4 0-1.

Dixon, D. M. "The Origin of the Kingdom of Kush (Napata-Meroe)." *Journal of Egyptian Archaeology* 50 (1904):121-32.

Driver, G. Rolles. "Ezekiel, Linguistic and Textual Problems" *Biblica* 35 (1959):145-59, 299-312.

Dunham, Dows, and MacAdam, M. F. L. "Names and Relationship of the Royal Family of Napata." *Journal of Egyptian Archaeology* 35 (1949):139-49.

_____ "Notes on the History of Kush 850 B.C.-350 A.D." *American Journal of Archaeology* 50 (1946):378-88.

Frost, Stanley Brice. "The Death of Josiah: A Conspiracy of Silence." *Journal of Biblical Literature* 87 (1968) 369-82.

Gardiner, A. H. "Piankhi's Instructions to His Army." *Journal of Egyptian Archaeology* 21 (1939):219-23.

Giveon, Raphael. "An Egyptian Official at Gezer?" *Israel Exploration Journal* 22 (1972): 143-44.

Gording, T. C. "A New Date for Jeremiah." *Expository Times* XLIV (1932-33):26265.

Halas, R. "The Universalism of Isaiah." *Catholic Biblical Quarterly* 12 (1950):162-70.

Hallo, William W. "From Qarqar to Carchemish: Assyria and Israel in the Light of New Discoveries." *Biblical Archaeologist* 23 (1960):34-61.

Harran, M. "The Literary Structure and Chronological Framework of the Prophecies in Isaiah XL-XLVIII." *Vetus Testamentum Supplement*, IX (1963):127-55.

Haupt, P. "The Book of Nahum." *Journal of Biblical Literature* 26 (1907):1-53.

Hollenberg, D. E. "Nationalism and the Nations in Isaiah XL-LV." *Vetus Testamentum* 19 (1969):23-36.

Hommel, Fritz. "Zerah, the Cushite." *Expository Times* 8, (1896-1897):376-79.

Horn, Siegfried. "Who was Solomon's Father-in-Law?" *Biblical Research* 12 (1967):3-17.

Isaacs, E. "Relations Between the Hebrew Bible and Africa." *Jewish Social Studies*, vol 26 No. 2, (April, 1964): 89-98.

Jenkins, A. K. "Hezekiah's Fourteenth Year: A Reinterpre-tation of 2 Kings XVIII:13-XIX:37." *Vetus Testamentum* 26 (1976):284-98.

Junker, Hermann. "The First Appearance of the Negroes in History." *Egyptian Archaeology* 7, (1921):121-32.

Katzenstein, H. Jacob. "The Royal Steward." *Israel Exploration Journal* 10 (1960):149-53.

Kitchen, K. A. "Late-Egyptian Chronology and the Hebrew Monarch: Critical studies in Old Testament Mythology." *Journal of the Near Eastern Society of Columbia University* 10 (1973):225-33.

Leene, H. "Universalism or Nationalism: Isaiah XLV:9-13 and Its Context?" *Bijdragen* 35 (1974):309-34.

Lind, M. C. "The Concept of Political Power in Ancient Israel." *Annual of the Swedish Theological Institute* 7 (1970):4-2.

Long, B. L. "The Stylistic Components of Jeremiah 3:1-5." *Zeitschrift für die Alttestamentliche Wissen-schaft* 88 (1970):386-90.

McKenzie, J. L. "The Literary Characteristic of Genesis 2-3." *Theological studies* 15 (1954):541-72

Malamat, Abraham. "Aspect of the Foreign Policies of David and Solomon." *Journal of Near Eastern Studies* 22 (1963):1-17.

_____ "The Historical Background of the Assassination of Amon, King of Judah." *Israel Exploration Journal* III (1953):26-29.

_____ "The Historical Setting on Two Biblical Prophecies of the Nations." *Israel Exploration Journal* 1 (1950):147-59.

May, H. G. "The Chronology of Jeremiah's Oracles." *Eastern Studies* 4 (1949):217-27.

_____ "Theological Universalism in the Old Testament." *Journal of Bible and Religion* 17 (1948):100-107.

Mazar, B. "The Campaign of Pharoah Shishak to Palestine." *Vetus Testamentum Supplement* IV (1957):57-66.

_____ "The Military Elite of King David." *Vetus Testamentum* 13 (1963):310-20.

Morgenstern, Julian. "Deutero-Isaiah's Terminology for `Universal God'." *Journal of Biblical Literature* 63 (1943):269-180.

_____ "The Message of Deutero-Isaiah in Its Sequential Unfolding." *Hebrew Union College Annual* XXIX.

_____ "Two Prophecies from 520-516 B.C." *Hebrew Union College Annual* XXII (1949):365-431.

Moriarty, Frederick L. "The Chronicler's Account of Hezekiah's Reforms." *Catholic Bible Quarterly* 27 (1965):399-406.

Orlinsky, H. M. "Nationalism-Universalism and Interactionism in Ancient Israel." *In Translating and Understanding the Old Testament*, Festschriff, H. G.; May ed. H. T. Frank and W. L. Reed (Nashville: Abingdon Press, 1970), 206-36.

Patai, Raphael. "Hebrew Installation Rites, a Contribution to the Study of Ancient Near-Eastern African Culture Contact." *Hebrew Union Annual* 20 (1947):143-225.

_____ "Ritual Approach to the Hebrew-African Culture Contact." *Jewish Social Studies* 24 (Apr. 1962):86-96.

Rainey, Anson F. "The Fate of Lachish During the Campaign of Sennacherib and Nebuchadnezzar." *Investigation at Lachish. The Sanctuary and Risidency* (Lachish V); ed. by Y. Aharoni, 47-60. Tel Aviv: Gateway Publishers, 1975.

_____ "Taharqa and Syntax." *Tel Aviv* 3 (1976):38-40.

Redford, Donald B. "Studies in Relations Between Palestine and Egypt During the First Millenium B.C 1: The Taxation System of Solomon." *Studies on the Ancient Palestinian World: Essays Presented to F. W. Winnett*; ed. 3iy J. W. Wevers and D. B. Redford, 141-56. University of Toronto Press, 1972.

_____ "Studies in Relations Between Palestine and Egypt During the First Millenium B.C. 11: The Twenty-Second Dynasty." *Journal of American Schools of Oriental Society* 93 (1973):3-17.

Reider, Joseph. "Etymological Studies in Biblical Hebrew." *Vetus Testamentum* 4 (1954):276-95.

Reisner, G. A. "The Viceroys of Ethiopia." *Journal of Egyptian Archaeology* 6 (1920):28-5585.

Rice, Gene. "African Roots of the Prophet Zephaniah." *Journal of Religious Thought* 36 (1979):21-31.

_____ "Two Contemporaries of Jeremiah." *Journal of Religious Thought* XXXII (Spring-Summer 1975):95-109.

Rowley, H. H. "Hezekiah's Reform and Rebellion." *Bulletin of John Rylands Library* 44 (1961):395-431.

Runnalls, Donna. "Moses' Ethiopian Campaign." *Journal for the Study of Judaism in the Persian, Hellenistic and Roman Period* vol. XIV, 140. 2, 1983.

Save-Soderbergh, T. "The Nubian Kingdom of the Second Intermediate Period." *Journal of Sudan Antiquities Service, Kush* 4 (1956):5-61.

Schulman, Alan R. "Diplomatic Marriage in the Egyptian New Kingdom." *Journal of Near Eastern Studies* 38 (1979):177-193.

Shea, William H. "Nebuchadnezzar's Chronicle and the Date of Destruction of Lachish III." Palestinian *Exploration Quarterly* III (1979):113-16.

Simons, J. "The Table of Nations (Gen. X); Its General Structure and Meaning." *Oudtestamentliche Studien* X, ed. Pieter de Boer. Leiden: E. J. Brill, 1952.

Spalinger, Anthony. "Ashurbanipal and Egypt." An Analysis of the First Invasion of Egypt, *Orientala* 43 (1974):295-326.

_____ "The Year 712 and Its Implications for Egyptian History." *Journal of the American Research Center in Egypt* 10 (1973):95-101.

Speigel, S. "Ezekiel or Pseudo-Ezekiel?" *Harvard Theological Review* XXIV (1931):245-321.

Stieglitz, R. R. "Long Distance Sea-Faring in the Ancient Near East." *Biblical Archaeologist* vol. 47, No. 3 (Sept.1984): 13-2.

Tadmor, H. "The Campaign of Sargon II of Ashur: A Chronological Historical study." *Journal of Cuneiform Studies* XII (1958):78-84.

Thompson, P. E. S. "The Approach to the Old Testament in an African Setting." *Ghana Bulletin of Theology* vol. 2, No. 2 (Dec. 1962):1-11.

Torrey, C. C. "Certainly Pseudo-Ezekiel." *Journal of Biblical Literature* 53 (1934):291-320.

_____ "Notes on Ezekiel." *Journal of Biblical Literature* 58 (1939):68-86.

Ullendorff, Edward. "The Queen of Sheba." *Bulletin of John Rylands Library*, March 1963.

_____ "The Semitic Language of Ethiopia and Their Contribution to General Semitic Studies." *Africa*, April 1955.

Weir, Mull. "Aspects of the Book of Ezekiel." *Vetus Testamentum* 2 (1952):97

Whitley, C. F. "The Date of Jeremiah's Call." *Vetus Testamentum* XIV (1964):467

Williams, D. L. "The Date of Zephaniah." *Journal of Biblical Literature* LXXXII (1963):77-88.

Williams, Ronald J. "A People Come Out of Egypt." *Supplement of Vetus Testamentum* XXVIII, 231-52. Leiden: E. J. Brill, 1975.

Wright, George Ernest. "Iron in Israel." *Biblical Archaeologist* 1 (1938):5-8.

Yeivin, S. "Did the Kingdom of Israel Have a Maritime Policy?" *Jewish Quarterly Review* V (1959-60):207-15.

_____ "Topographic and Ethnic Notes." *Journal of Egyptian Archaeology* 48 (1926):75-80.

Dissertations

Grau, James, Jr. "Gentiles in Genesis: Israel and the Nations in the Primeval and Patriarchal Histories." Unpublished Ph.D. Dissertation, Southern Methodist University, Dallas, 1980.

Hamkin, E. J. "The Nations in Second-Isaiah." Unpublished Ph.D. Dissertation Union Theological Seminary, New York, 1960.

Hay, Lawrence Cord. "The Oracles Against the Foreign Nations in Jeremiah 46-51." Unpublished Ph.D. Dissertation, Vanderbilt University, 1960.

Index

Made in the USA
Columbia, SC
25 August 2020